SECRETS

from the

WHITE
HOUSE
KITCHENS

SECRETS

from the

WHITE
HOUSE
KITCHENS

JOHN R HANNY

LaMarque
PUBLICATIONS

Published by LaMarque Publications, LLC
P.O. Box 528, Gordonsville, VA 22942

Manufactured in the United States of America

Photographs of all recipes by Steven Hash

Cover design by Alycia Worthington – www.aworthydesign.com
Inside design by Ronnie Whitson – www.whitsongroup.com

Blue Room, 1999, Clinton Administration by Bruce White - White House Historical Association © WHHA

China Room - WHGB, 21st ed., p.22-23 ©WHHA

East Room of the White House - WHGB, 20th ed., p.34-35 ©WHHA

In the White House Kitchen, photo by Mel Curtis, 1996 - White House Historical Association © WHHA

Red Room, photo by Erik Kvalsik, Dec. 2000 - White House Historical Association © WHHA

State Dining Room, 1999 - WHGB, 21st ed. ©WHHA

Cataloging in Publication Data
Hanny, John R.
        Secrets from the White House Kitchens

ISBN: 978-0-9829293-0-8

1. Cookbook. 2. History — United States Presidents — White House.

  2 3 4 5 6 7 8 9 10 — 16 15 14 13 12 11

Special Dedication

To my dear friend, Bonnie Anne Powell

Ah! The days of our youth—the likes of Moose Hirsch—Etta and Eddie Beiter, the Thistley Hill Chowder and Marching Society. Whispering Smith AKA the South Wind and Count Ciro J. Fergosi and, also, the Kiener brothers, Ron and Ken. The laughs and grand times are unsurpassable.

Oh! For just one more time of Kemp for Congress and Kemp for Vice President. Let's have more of those heady days of working our brains overtime for something very real that we could touch—high ideals.

Even though we are both in the "Cocktail Hour of Life," I believe that the idealistic fire still burns in our souls. Only, now it takes bellows to keep the coals alive.

Be well, my friend.
Jack

Contents

AUTHOR WITH HIS GOOD FRIEND, CHEF GÉRARD GASPARINI, A MASTER CHEF OF FRANCE
AND OWNER/CHEF OF RESTAURANT POMME IN GORDONSVILLE, VA

ERICA HALL USING PRESIDENTIAL CHINA TO DISPLAY HER PRIDE.
PASTRY CHEF ERICA IS THE OWNER OF "FROM SCRATCH BAKERY" IN CHARLOTTESVILLE, VA

Acknowledgements

To write a book not only takes the author but requires a special talented team to support him. It's not simply writing eighty or ninety thousand words and sending it off to a publisher.

First of all I would like to thank my wife Debbie for putting up with my temperament during this project, and for her ability to keep me going.

Thanks too to my brother Bud for relieving me of the responsibilities of running our family business, giving me the time I needed to research and write. Also to my very capable niece, Tricia Hanny-Browne, who assists her father as the General Manager of our *Eagle House Restaurant* in Buffalo, New York.

Steve Hash is an amazingly talented photographer. All you need to do is look at the photographs in this book and you'll agree. Thank you Steve for all your efforts and friendship.

My dear friend Paul Manning for his marketing expertise and support in this project.

There are two chefs who must be mentioned who contributed more than you'll ever know. First is Master Chef of France, Gérard Gasparini, owner of the *Pomme Restaurant* in Gordonsville, Virginia. Chef Gerard is a true culinary genius who was responsible for putting together the food we photographed—a monumental job. The second person is Pastry Chef Erica Hall who owns *From Scratch Bakery* in Charlottesville, Virginia. Erica was responsible for all the pastries that jump off the pages, begging to be eaten. I am proud to know these two talented chefs.

Also thank you to Ronnie Whitson, my editor who is also responsible for the interior design of this beautiful book, a challenge which she tackled with no complaints.

The cover design is a big thank you to Alycia Worthington for her hard work and friendship.

Then there is my dear friend, Ivor Whitson, an invaluable member of the team, whose publishing expertise guided this project to completion. Thank you Ivor.

And finally to the White House Historical Association staff for their assistance. A great team works out of that office and I thank them all for being there.

AUTHOR JOHN R. HANNY IN THE WHITE HOUSE KITCHEN

Foreword

All my life I wanted to follow the two hundred year old Hanny tradition by becoming part of it. I wanted my name indelibly stamped on our restaurant and its fine reputation.

My family owned restaurants in the Buffalo area for that many years and being the eldest I was expected to follow those before me. My Father and Grandfather both agreed if I were to succeed I must become a Chef. And become one I did. Many years of training, starting at 14, hopping a bus after school to Dad's La Marque Restaurant on Delaware Avenue—then the garden district of the city— to work with some of the finest chefs in the country.

My apprenticeship started with my father's Executive Chef, Jean Citheral, and his Sous Chef Klaiber Prequoxe. When finished for the night I would quietly climb the back stairs to the office and do my homework, then Dad would drive me home. This lasted for years and years until finally I earned the privilege of the title of Master Chef. I was twenty years old. When I add up the years it had taken I could have acquired a medical degree quicker. The difference being I wanted to be a chef and a restaurateur.

Back in '62 at the age of twenty three I was invited to the White house by the Canadian Food Journal to interview President and Mrs. Kennedy and their Chef Rene Verdon. I raced to Toronto for a meeting with the editor at the time, a Mr. George Rogers, who was interested in me as a contributing journalist. He had heard about my hobby—collecting the likes and dislikes of foods of different heads of state, kings and queens, plus a few dictators thrown into the mix—and felt it would make for an interesting story. So off I went to see the President and I never wanted to come back, but had to because of responsibilities back home with my family's business. I therefore settled to becoming a visiting Chef at the White House for several years, mostly with Presidents Kennedy and Johnson.

A visiting Chef is someone who is called when needed, or someone who knows the likes, dislikes and possible strange eating habits of the honored guest. I helped with both. I would fly back and forth when requested, and enjoyed the best years of my life.

My interest in the White House, the Presidents and their history has never waned. As a matter of fact I love it "more today than yesterday, but not as much as tomorrow." I will never get enough of the protocol, the pomp and circumstance, and the priceless reward—the great feeling that I always enjoy at the end of the day.

My other interest is in writing. Hence "SECRETS FROM THE WHITE HOUSE KITCHENS", "ASLEEP AT THE WHEEL", and soon to be released, "THE THIRD OPTION", and "LUCIFER'S TROPHY".

"SECRETS" however is my first book and my first love. It was awarded the National Press Club's book selection of the year. This revision is even better than the first thanks to some real pros who have added exquisite color photos and additional information for your enjoyment. Working with these talented people was a real honor and I will not forget them. Please enjoy the recipes and food and, as importantly, the Presidents I served—Kennedy, Johnson, Nixon, Ford, Reagan and Clinton. Enjoy too stories about, and the food served to, those Presidents I met through the pages of history books, newspapers, magazines and television.

Bon Apetit!
John R. Hanny

THE WHITE HOUSE KITCHEN AND STAFF PREPARING A STATE DINNER FOR PRESIDENT SARKOZY OF FRANCE

Franklin Delano Roosevelt
Anna Eleanor Roosevelt

"I am certain that my fellow Americans expect that on my induction into the Presidency I will address them with a candor and a decision which the present situation of our people impel. This is preeminently the time to speak the truth, the whole truth, frankly and boldly. Nor need we shrink from honestly facing conditions in our country today. This great Nation will endure as it has endured, will revive and will prosper. So, first of all, let me assert my firm belief that the only thing we have to fear is fear itself—nameless, unreasoning, unjustified terror which paralyzes needed efforts to convert retreat into advance. In every dark hour of our national life a leadership of frankness and vigor has met with that understanding and support of the people themselves which is essential to victory. I am convinced that you will again give that support to leadership in these critical days."

FRANKLIN D. ROOSEVELT INAUGURAL ADDRESS, MARCH 4, 1933

FDR BY SALISBURY © WHHA (WHITE HOUSE COLLECTION)

*J*ust before the Roosevelts moved into the White House in 1933, Mrs. Roosevelt met with Ike Hoover, the chief usher, to be shown around the mansion, decide how the several rooms of the house were to be used, and to plan out the many arrangements for Inauguration Day.

With the Depression at hand, Inauguration Day was not a lighthearted occasion. Most of the ceremonies were canceled, and only a buffet lunch for the family and a few friends and a reception in the early evening was held. The president did not even attend the Inaugural Ball, but was represented by Mrs. Roosevelt and her children.

There were many things about living in the White House that proved to be nuisances to this First Family, not the least of which was FDR's children's habit of raiding the icebox when they were hungry. They were upset to discover that it was locked every night.

Mrs. Roosevelt was more concerned with the social welfare of the nation than with the daily intricacies and protocols of the White House. Her personal secretary, Edith Helm, also served as her social secretary and had a vast knowledge of the White House procedures. Mrs. Roosevelt never shirked her duties and met with the bookkeeper, chief usher, and Mrs. Helm every day she was in residence. The housekeeper, Mrs. Henry Nesbitt, made out the menus, bought the food, and gave the daily orders to the house staff. FDR was not difficult to please about food, but grew tired of meals prepared by the same cook. Mrs. Nesbitt believed in plain food, plainly cooked, and was very difficult to get along with. Mrs. Roosevelt followed her lead, but FDR quickly tired of the simple fare, "My stomach positively rebels and this does not help my relations with foreign powers," he said. "I bit two of them yesterday!" He went on to say he wanted to run for a fourth term so he could fire Mrs. Nesbitt!

Due to his disability, FDR seldom dined out. Because of this, his personal cook was soon brought from Hyde Park and installed in a small kitchen on the third floor, where she cooked him two meals a day, for variety.

Although Mrs. Roosevelt thought her husband was not that interested in food, some considered him a connoisseur. Actually, it was Mrs. Roosevelt who didn't care about food. Take the official State Luncheon she hosted for the king and queen of England, for example. Mrs. Roosevelt was not interested in American food, only its history, and thought it would be nice to have a picnic for the royal highnesses at Hyde Park. The now-famous menu consisted of hot dogs, smoked turkey, baked beans, cured hams, potato salad, and strawberry shortcake for dessert. This sounds pretty good to us colonials, but the picture of Queen Elizabeth and King George eating hot dogs and baked beans, dripping mustard on themselves, and asking for a Beano® after dinner, is priceless. This simplicity, nevertheless, never made it to the state dining room. During FDR's administration, the table was set formally with special plates, napkins and wine glasses for each course, all the silverware, except for dessert and water glasses, the colonial saltcellars of art glass and diamond design, and never a pepper shaker. All the official affairs used a decorative gold china. The centerpieces were bowls of cut flowers, usually yellow roses, as they were Mrs. Roosevelt's favorite.

A big silver ship in full sail was used for high tea, usually served in the family's private quarters around 4 o'clock p.m. This gave guests of honor the opportunity to meet privately and informally with the president and his wife, to get to know one another. Today, this is accomplished over cocktails and hors d'oeuvres.

During wartime, entertaining at the White House was greatly reduced. In spite of this, FDR invited the Right Honorable Winston Churchill to spend Christmas with him and his family in 1941. The prime minister ended up staying for twenty-four days, which proved to be very, very important as the overall strategy of the Allies in World War II was planned during the visit. In addition to our generals coming and going, and Churchill's wartime military counselors, security was at its height and no one, according to the Secret Service, was welcome unless it was business of the utmost importance.

The war meant that the White House was put on an austerity plan just like the rest of America. Part of the defense effort involved cutting down on food provided for the staff. According to Mrs. Roosevelt, an order of one egg instead of two, one slice of bacon, toast, and coffee for breakfast was plenty. The midday meal consisted of whatever was available at the market, and all servants were asked to bring their own sugar.

At a private dinner before FDR's third inauguration, Chief Justice Charles Evans Hughes and Roosevelt discussed arrangements for the administration of the Oath of Office.

"Mr. President," said Hughes, "after I have read the oath and you have repeated it, how would it be for me to lean forward and whisper to you, 'Don't you think this is getting a little bit monotonous for the both of us?'"

President Roosevelt was a great joker, but the job was so serious and demanding, especially during a world war, that it took a great toll on him. In January 1945, Roosevelt arranged to bring his son, James, home from the Pacific so he could be present for the fourth inauguration. Although the Americans were winning the war in the Pacific, they still had a lot of fighting to do and knew that an invasion of Japan would be very bloody. James told his father he was not sure he would ever return to see his father again.

"James," said Roosevelt softly, "There will be no invasion of Japan. We have something that will end the war before any invasion takes place." As to what it was, James was told, "I cannot tell you, only those who need to know about it. It is something we can use and will use if we have to. Something we will use before you or any of our sons die on Japanese soil." He then smiled and said, "So you can come back home to me, son."

"Meeting Franklin Roosevelt was like uncorking your first bottle of champagne."

WINSTON CHURCHILL, PRIME MINISTER OF GREAT BRITAIN, 1946

MARTHA WASHINGTON'S CRAB SOUP

1-1/2	pounds Chesapeake crab meat (cut in chunks)
1	quart milk or light cream
2	tablespoons butter
2	hard-cooked eggs (mashed)
1	tablespoon flour
	grated lemon peel or lemon zest
1	tablespoon Worcestershire sauce
1/2	cup sherry
	salt and pepper to taste
	paprika for garnish

In the top of a double boiler, blend the butter and flour, and add the eggs and the lemon peel or lemon zest. Gradually add the milk or light cream (I prefer the light cream). Stir until it thickens. Add the crab meat and let it simmer for 5 minutes Then add the seasonings. Just before serving, stir in the sherry and bring the temperature back up. DO NOT allow the soup to boil. Sprinkle the top with paprika, preferably Hungarian paprika.

Author's note: This is a White House favorite with most First Families and their guests.

SCOTCH BROTH

2	cups diced lamb
	bone from lamb roast
3	leeks, thinly sliced
1/2	cup butter
4	chicken bouillon cubes
1/2	cup pearl barley
1	cup diced carrots
1	cup chopped celery
1/2	cup chopped parsley
	freshly ground black pepper

Crack bone. Sauté lamb, leeks and bone in butter for 10 minutes, stirring frequently. Add 3 quarts of water, bouillon cubes and pepper. Bring to a boil, reduce heat, cover and simmer for 1 hour. Add barley and simmer for another hour. Add carrots, celery and parsley and simmer uncovered for 30 minutes.

Serves 6

SCOTCH WOODCOCK

12	eggs lightly beaten
2	tablespoons butter
1/3	cup dry sherry
	freshly ground black pepper
6	slices toast
	anchovy paste

Beat eggs with salt and pepper until foamy. Cook in butter over low heat until the eggs begin to set, stirring gently. Stir in sherry and continue cooking until eggs are done. Meanwhile, spread lightly on toast with anchovy paste. Serve eggs on top of toast.

Serves 6

Author's note: Surprisingly a great breakfast

BOILED SALMON WITH EGG SAUCE

  3–4 pounds fresh salmon
    1 cup vinegar
    2 tablespoons salt
       hard-cooked eggs (partially for garnish)

To cook the salmon, place the fish in boiling water to cover. Salmon may be wrapped in muslin first. Add the vinegar and the salt. Cook the salmon until tender, which is about 25–35 minutes. Do not allow the water to boil too vigorously or the fish will break apart.

Egg Sauce

    2 cups milk or cream
    2 tablespoons butter
    2 tablespoons flour
  1/2 teaspoon salt
  1/8 teaspoon pepper
    2 hard cooked eggs

Melt the butter and stir in the flour and seasoning. Remove from heat. Gradually pour in the milk or cream, which has first been warmed by stirring constantly, and cooking over low heat until thickened. Mash the hard-cooked eggs with a fork and add to the sauce. Pour the sauce over the fish. Decorate with hard-cooked eggs, cut in half. Garnish with parsley.

Author's note: Instead of using boiling water to boil the salmon, I would suggest using a fish stock in which to poach. A favorite dish of the Roosevelt family at their quarters in the President's Mansion.

KEDGEREE

1	cup boiled flaked white fish
1	cup boiled rice
2 or 3	hard-boiled eggs (minced)
2	tablespoons butter
1/2	teaspoon salt & pepper (to taste)
1/4	cup cream (heavy cream is best)
1	teaspoon grated onions (optional)
	parsley for garnish

Mix the fish, rice, and onions. Moisten with the cream, or if you like you can add a little bit of the fish stock. Sauté lightly in melted butter. It must be fluffy! Add salt, pepper, and minced hard-boiled eggs and heat everything in a double boiler. Serve hot, trimmed with parsley sprigs.

Author's note: You can also add 1 teaspoon grated Parmesan cheese to the mixture. This is an old—very old—recipe brought over the Pond by the Scots and Irish.

BAKED FISH AND CREAM

    1/2 cup cooked flaked fish
    1/4 cup light cream
         butter
         salt
         freshly ground black pepper

Place fish and cream in shallow individual baking dish. Dot with butter. Sprinkle with salt and pepper. Bake in a hot oven (400° F) for 10 minutes.

Makes one serving

Author's note: Try cod, haddock or salmon for best results. For a nice touch, sprinkle with grated Parmesan cheese.

SCALLOPS EN BROCHETTE: WHITE HOUSE

2 pounds sea scallops
  bacon slices
  oil
  dried bread crumbs (preferably Italian)
  salt
  tartar sauce

Cut each bacon slice into 4 squares. Brush scallops with oil. Dust with bread crumbs. Sprinkle with salt. Thread scallops on skewers alternating with bacon squares. Broil under high heat for about 10 minutes or until bacon is crisp. Serve with tartar sauce.

Serves 6

OPPOSITE: PERSONAL CHINA OF THE AUTHOR.

SHRIMP NEWBURG

    2   pounds shrimp, shelled
    6   tablespoons butter
  1/2   cup sherry
    3   egg yolks, beaten
  3/4   cup heavy cream
  1/8   teaspoon freshly grated nutmeg
        paprika
        cayenne pepper
        salt to taste
        toast

Sauté shrimp in butter in the top pan of a chafing dish for 5 minutes, stirring constantly. Stir in sherry. Remove from heat. Put the bottom pan of the chafing dish on the stand and fill it with boiling water. Set the top pan over the boiling water. Beat egg yolks with cream until thick and foamy. Stir the egg yolks and cream into shrimp mixture. Add a dash of nutmeg and paprika, a few grains of cayenne pepper and a little salt. Cook for 5 minutes or until the sauce thickens, stirring constantly. Serve on toast.

Serves 6

Author's note: Cooked scallops, oysters, or cooked and cut up lobster or crab meat may be used instead of shrimp.

OYSTER-STUFFED CHICKEN: WHITE HOUSE

        3 broiler chickens, split in half
        3 tablespoons chopped green pepper
        3 tablespoons chopped parsley
        1 teaspoon salt
           freshly ground black pepper
           bread crumbs
     1/4 teaspoon cayenne pepper
        1 pint oysters
        2 tablespoons chopped celery
        2 tablespoons chopped onion
        1 clove garlic, crushed
           butter
           cranberry or lingonberry preserves

Drain and chop oysters and save their liquor. Sauté oysters and vegetables with seasonings in 4 tablespoons butter for 10 minutes. Add 1 cup bread crumbs and 1/2 cup oyster liquor. Meanwhile, place chickens in shallow baking pan, skin side up and dot with butter. Add 1/2 cup of water to pan. Bake in a moderate oven (375° F) for 30 minutes or until brown. Remove chicken from oven. Turn chicken skin side down and fill each cavity with oyster stuffing. Sprinkle stuffing with bread crumbs and melted butter. Bake 20 minutes or until crumbs are golden brown. Serve with cranberry or lingonberry preserve.

Serves 6

MAIDEN'S PRAYER

1/2	pound chicken breasts, boned and diced
1/8	teaspoon ground ginger
1	teaspoon soy sauce
3	cups snow peas
1/2	cup thickly sliced canned bamboo shoots
1/2	cup thinly sliced scallions
1/2	cup canned button mushrooms, drained
1/2	teaspoon salt
	freshly ground black pepper
2	tablespoons dry sherry
1/4	cup peanut oil
1/2	cup thinly sliced celery

Season chicken with ginger, sherry, soy sauce, salt and pepper. Cook in 2 tablespoons oil in large skillet over high heat for 5 minutes, stirring constantly. Remove chicken and keep hot. Put 2 tablespoons oil in skillet and add remaining ingredients. Cook over high heat for 5 minutes, stirring constantly. Remove from heat. Put chicken on top of vegetables and allow juices from chicken to soak into vegetables for 5 minutes. Return skillet to high heat and cook for 5 minutes, stirring constantly.

Serves 6

NEW BRUNSWICK STEW

1	3-pound chicken, cut up
2	medium onions, sliced
1	cup chopped celery with leaves
1/4	teaspoon marjoram
1/4	teaspoon thyme
1/4	teaspoon basil
1/4	teaspoon Tabasco® sauce
	freshly ground black pepper
4	tablespoons butter
5	cups canned tomatoes
1	package frozen cut corn
1	package frozen lima beans
1	tablespoon cornstarch
1	tablespoon salt

Season chicken with salt and pepper. Sauté in butter in deep saucepan for 10 minutes or until brown. Remove and keep hot. Sauté onion in the butter remaining in the saucepan for 10 minutes or until lightly browned. Return chicken to pan, add tomatoes, celery, herbs, Tabasco® and 1 cup of water. Bring to a boil, reduce heat, cover and simmer for 45 minutes. Add corn and lima beans and simmer for 20 minutes, stirring occasionally. Combine cornstarch with 1/4 cup cold water, add a small amount of hot liquid from stew and stir until smooth. Stir into stew and simmer for 5 minutes, stirring constantly.

Serves 6

Author's note: FDR's favorite. I've personally served this at family gatherings and vouch for its success.

TURKEY HASH

3	cups diced cooked turkey
4	tablespoons butter
2	tablespoons flour
1/2	cup heavy cream
1/2	cup soft bread crumbs
1/2	cup chopped green pepper
1/2	cup chopped onion
2	tablespoons chopped parsley
1/2	teaspoon ground sage
1/2	teaspoon salt
	freshly ground black pepper

Melt 2 tablespoons of the butter in saucepan, blend in flour and cream and stir until thickened. Add turkey and all the other ingredients except the remaining butter. Melt 2 tablespoons butter in a large skillet and add the turkey mixture. Sauté uncovered for 25 minutes. If desired, brown the top of the hash under the broiler before serving.

Serves 6

Author's note: Good recipe for Thanksgiving leftovers

SCRABBLE

(Some regions of the country call this Scrapple.)

1-1/2	pounds pork shoulder
1/4	pound pork liver (optional)
1	cup yellow cornmeal
1/4	cup finely chopped onion
1/8	teaspoon ground cloves
1/4	teaspoon ground thyme
1	teaspoon ground sage
1	teaspoon ground marjoram
2	teaspoons salt
	freshly ground black pepper

Simmer meats in saucepan with 4 cups of water for 1 hour. Drain and save broth. Bone pork shoulder and chop shoulder and liver. Combine cornmeal, salt, 1 cup cold water, and 2 cups broth in saucepan. Cook, stirring until thickened. Add meat, onion, and spices. Cover and simmer for 1 hour. Pour scrabble into loaf pan (9 x 5 x 3). Chill for 4 hours. To serve, slice, dip in flour and fry.

STEAK AND KIDNEY PIE: WHITE HOUSE

1-1/2	pounds stewing beef, diced
6	ounces kidney, sliced
1/2	pound mushrooms, sliced
1	cup chopped onion
1/4	cup parsley
1/2	bay leaf
1	cup butter
3	cups sifted self-rising flour
1	cup milk
1	teaspoon salt

Put beef, kidneys, mushrooms, onion, parsley, bay leaf, and salt in baking dish with 2 cups of water. Cut butter into flour until it resembles coarse meal. Add milk and mix lightly to form soft dough. Turn out on floured board and roll to 1/8-inch thick. Place on top of baking dish. Cut slits in dough to let steam escape. Bake in a slow oven (325° F) for 1 hour and 45 minutes.

Serves 6

Author's note: Official dish prepared for Sir Winston Churchill during his long visits with FDR during WWII

CAULIFLOWER WITH CHEESE AND OLIVE SAUCE

    1   medium head cauliflower
1/4   cup butter (1/2 stick)
1/4   cup flour
3/4   teaspoon salt
    2   cups milk
    1   cup shredded sharp American cheese (1/4 pound)
1/2   cup sliced stuffed green olives

Remove outer leaves from cauliflower, wash in cold water and drain. Cook, head down, in boiling salted water until crispy tender, 20–25 minutes. Drain thoroughly. Meanwhile, melt butter in a saucepan over low heat, blend in flour and salt. Add milk, stirring constantly and cook until smooth and thickened. Add cheese and stir over low heat until melted. Fold in olive slices and pour over hot drained cauliflower.

Serves 6

DEVILED CARROTS

6	large carrots, quartered lengthwise
1/2	cup butter
2	tablespoons brown sugar
2	teaspoons dry mustard
	Tabasco® sauce
1/2	teaspoon salt
	Freshly ground black pepper

Sauté carrots in butter for 5 minutes. Add brown sugar, mustard, 2 drops of Tabasco® sauce, salt and pepper, and cook for 10 minutes, or until tender.

Serves 6

Author's note: This is so simple and a big hit. Very different. Lasted through almost all the administrations.

PERSONAL CHINA OF THE AUTHOR.

CINNAMON BUNS

2	envelopes granular yeast
1	cup milk
6	tablespoons sugar
2	eggs
6	tablespoons butter
4 to 4 1/2	cups sifted flour
2	teaspoons ground cinnamon
1/2	cup raisins
2	teaspoons salt

Soften yeast in 1/2 cup lukewarm water. Scald milk. Add 2 tablespoons sugar and the salt. Cool to lukewarm and add yeast. Stir well. Beat in eggs and 4 tablespoons butter. Add flour, stirring until a moderately firm dough is formed. Turn dough out on a lightly floured board and knead until the dough is smooth and not sticky. Roll the dough out into an oblong about 1/4 inch thick. Spread with the remaining 2 tablespoons butter and sprinkle with the 4 tablespoons sugar combined with cinnamon. Sprinkle with raisins. Roll up and cut into slices. Put the buns on a buttered baking sheet, cover and let rise for about 30 minutes or until double in bulk. Bake in a hot oven (400° F) for 20 minutes or until brown.

Makes about 24

PECAN PIE

Crust

1-1/2 cups flour
1/2 cup shortening
1/2 teaspoon salt
1 teaspoon baking powder
1/4 cup ice water

Measure 1-1/2 cups flour. Sift with salt and baking powder. Divide shortening into two equal parts. Cut half of shortening into the flour mixture until it looks like cornmeal. Cut the remaining half of the shortening coarsely until it's the size of large green peas. Sprinkle 3 tablespoons ice water over the mixture and blend lightly. If the dough holds together, add no more liquid. If not, add additional water. Line your 10-inch pie pan with the pie crust.

Filling

3 or 4 eggs
1 cup brown sugar
1/3 cup butter
1 cup light corn syrup
1 teaspoon vanilla
1 cup chopped pecans
1/4 teaspoon salt
whole pecans for garnish
1 pint whipped heavy cream for garnish

Cream 1/3 cup butter with 1 cup brown sugar. Beat in 1 egg at a time. Stir in 1 cup light corn syrup, 1 cup coarsely chopped pecans, 1 teaspoon vanilla, and 1/4 teaspoon salt. Fill the pie shell with the mixture. Preheat the oven to 375 F and bake for about 35–40 minutes. When the pie is set and cooled, decorate the top with pecan halves and garnish with whipped cream around the entire edge. The whipped cream may be further trimmed with tiny leaves cut from small pieces of leftover pie dough and baked.

RUM AND BUTTERSCOTCH PIE

1	tablespoon rum
1	package butterscotch flavor instant pudding
18	gingersnaps
2	tablespoons sugar
2	tablespoons melted butter
	light cream

Crush 12 gingersnaps and mix with sugar, butter, and 1 tablespoon of water. Spread over bottom of 8-inch pie plate. Cut 6 gingersnaps in half, arrange around edge of pie plate. Prepare pudding according to package directions, using combined rum and cream instead of milk. Pour pudding into gingersnap shell. Chill for at least 2 hours.

Serves 6

ALMOND BUTTER CRUNCH

1	cup unsalted almonds, chopped
1-1/2	cups butter
2	cups sugar
1/4	pound semisweet chocolate bits
1	cup grated nuts

Combine butter and sugar in a heavy pan. Set candy thermometer in pan. Cook over low heat until sugar dissolves, stirring constantly. Continue cooking until thermometer reads 260° F. Add the almonds and cook until thermometer reads 300° F. Pour into a shallow, buttered pan. Let stand until cold. Remove the block of candy from the pan. Melt the chocolate over hot water. Pour half the melted chocolate over the candy block and sprinkle with half the grated nuts. When the chocolate is cold turn the candy over and pour remaining chocolate over it. Sprinkle with the rest of the grated nuts. When second coating of chocolate is cold, break the candy into pieces.

Makes about 2 pounds

Harry S. Truman
Elizabeth Virginia Wallace Truman

"Each period of our national history has had its special challenges. Those that confront us now are as momentous as any in the past. Today marks the beginning not only of a new administration, but of a period that will be eventful, perhaps decisive, for us and for the world.

It may be our lot to experience, and in a large measure bring about, a major turning point in the long history of the human race. The first half of this century has been marked by unprecedented and brutal attacks on the rights of man, and by the two most frightful wars in history. The supreme need of our time is for men to learn to live together in peace and harmony."

HARRY S TRUMAN INAUGURAL ADDRESS, JANUARY 20, 1949

HARRY TRUMAN BY MARTHA KEMPTON © WHHA (WHITE HOUSE COLLECTION)

"*T*ell them to go to hell and tell him the vice presidency is as useful as a cow's fifth teat." This was Harry Truman's initial response when he heard FDR wanted to tap him as his running mate.

As Truman said, "The room was crowded and every damn politician who was a boss was there plus a half dozen governors. They all said 'Harry, we want you to be vice president.' And I said, 'I'm not going to do it.' Well, Bob Hanagan had put in a call to Roosevelt who was down at San Diego. "They finally got him on the phone, and with Roosevelt you didn't need a phone, all you had to do was raise the window and you could hear him."

"I was sitting on one twin bed and Bob was sitting on the other in this room and Roosevelt said, [here Harry Truman gave a near-perfect imitation of FDR, the Haa-vaard accent and all] 'Bob, have you got that guy lined up for the vice presidency?' And Bob said, 'No, he's the contrariest goddamned mule from Missouri I ever saw.' 'Well,' Roosevelt said, 'You tell him if he wants to break up the Democratic party in the middle of a war and maybe lose the war, that's up to him.'"

Luckily, fate dealt America a great hand. Harry Truman did become FDR's vice president, and only three months later he became president.

FDR's death caught Truman by surprise. At 5:10 p.m., Vice President Truman strolled over to Speaker Sam Rayburn's office. Everyone called his hideaway office "The Board of Education Room." Located at the House end of the Capitol, it was where the speaker's friends usually gathered at the end of the day for some camaraderie and libation. They called it "striking a blow for liberty." Rayburn gave Truman the message to call the White House immediately. "Please come over," he was told, "and come in through the main Pennsylvania Avenue entrance." Harry's face turned white. "Holy General Jackson," he said, and raced to the White House, making it there by 5:25. In Mrs. Roosevelt's study, she gave him the grim news. "Harry," she said "the president is dead."

Truman, stunned into silence, finally managed to choke out, "Is there anything I can do for you?" To which Eleanor replied, "No, Harry. But is there anything we can do for you? For you are the one in trouble now." The next day, Truman's first full day as President, was Friday the 13th of April.

Harry Truman had been content as Senator Truman, the gentleman from Missouri. He knew that as vice president he was only a heartbeat away from the presidency and now that fear had become a reality. But, Truman, who always thought himself unworthy of such an awesome responsibility, tackled the job with his usual gusto. And, luckily for America, he was in the right place at the right time.

FDR is still considered one of the greatest Presidents by present-day historians, and in 1945 he was certainly a tough act to follow. But Harry Truman took the reins of government like no one believed he would. Regarded as a political hack by Washington power brokers, Truman soon proved his outstanding ability to lead.

One of Truman's first statements to the press: "Boys, if you ever pray, pray for me now. I don't know whether you've ever had a load of hay fall on you, but I feel like the stars, the moon, and all the planets have fallen on me."

"Good luck, Mr. President," one of the reporters called out.

Harry Truman responded with a heavy sigh, "Wish you hadn't called me that."

The man from Independence, Missouri, was very different from the patrician Roosevelt. He believed in telling it like it is and was often reprimanded by Mrs. Truman for his peppery language. Harry called his wife the boss and valued her advice. Even Truman's mom knew him as a contrary mule. When he called her one day, she warned him, "Now you behave yourself up there, Harry."

But Truman had a mind of his own and he tolerated no nonsense. During a phone call with former Secretary of Commerce Jessie Jones, the President said, "I've sent John Snyder's name into the Senate for confirmation as federal loan administrator."

"Did the President make that appointment before he died?" Jones asked.

"No," replied Truman with emphasis, "he made it just now."

It was no accident that Harry Truman adopted "The Buck Stops Here" as his own motto. The responsibility of the presidency was his and his alone, and he showed the world what he could do. Truman impressed the nation and foreign dignitaries as a simple, unpretentious, down-to-earth man with no expectation of entering the history books as a great president. Truman was, however, a decisive leader. When he made up his mind, he followed through no matter the consequences. His decision to fire General Douglas MacArthur, though controversial, is an example of something Truman felt he had to do. Asked how he felt after reaching the decision to fire the World War II hero, he replied, "I fixed a sandwich, had a glass of warm milk, and got a good night's sleep." He added, "I fired General MacArthur because he wouldn't respect the authority of the President. I didn't fire him because he was a dumb son-of-a-bitch, although he was, but that's not against the law for generals."

"The American people can always see through a counterfeit. It sometimes takes a little time, but eventually they can always spot one," he said. Truman fiercely believed in the Constitution as the law of the land and he feared that America would lose its innocence if he allowed his generals to run all over him. When he fired MacArthur, he learned he needn't fear that. Truman thought highly of General George C. Marshal and General Omar Bradley, but the rest didn't impress him. And he found it very difficult to say anything good about Dwight D. Eisenhower. He felt that Bradley and Marshal were great men, and would be great men no matter what they did. President Truman considered Ike rude and obnoxious. He said Eisenhower had a reputation for being an easygoing fellow, but he wasn't. "He is one of the most difficult people I have ever encountered in my lifetime. I am told that once he was in the White House he treated his staff worse than a bunch of enlisted men."

At Ike's inaugural, he wanted to treat the President the way MacArthur did at Wake Island. But Truman was president until the swearing in and wouldn't stand for it. Ike had wanted the President to pick him up at the Statler Hotel and take him to the inauguration. Truman said, "A thing like that had never happened before in American history and it indicated to me that not only didn't he know about American history, but he didn't have anyone around who did either." Ike finally arrived at the White House to pick up Truman, but he wouldn't get out of the car. Truman was forced to meet him in the vehicle. "It was shameful and there wasn't much conversation on the way to the Capitol," said Truman.

The ride was described in Truman's book Mr. Citizen: "The journey in the parade down Pennsylvania Avenue was quite restrained as far as the occupants of the car were concerned. We began our trip in silence, then Ike volunteered to inform me, 'I did not attend your inauguration in 1948 out of consideration for you, because if I had been present, I would have drawn attention away from you.'" Truman ended the discussion by pointing out that if he had sent for him, Ike would have been there.

The rest of the journey continued in silence. Later that day, just before the swearing-in ceremony, Ike and Truman were sitting in the Sergeant-of-Arms's office in the Capitol waiting to be escorted to the inauguration platform. Suddenly, General Eisenhower turned to Truman and said, "I wonder who is responsible for my son, John, being ordered to Washington from Korea. I wonder who is trying to embarrass me." Truman answered, "The President of the United States ordered your son to attend your inauguration. The President of the United States thought it was right and proper for your son to witness the swearing in of his father as President, and if you think somebody was trying to embarrass you with this order, then the President assumes full responsibility." The president later confided to friends, "I don't see how a country can produce such men as Robert E. Lee, John Pershing, George C. Marshal and Omar Bradley and, at the same time, produce Custers, Pattons, MacArthurs and Eisenhowers."

Harry Truman was a loyal man, sometimes to a fault. And no one who had anything derogatory to say about his family escaped his ire. When Paul Hume of The Washington Post criticized first daughter, Margaret, on her debut as a professional singer, the president wrote him a letter that has since become a famous example of the president's colorful tongue. "The next time that we meet, Mr. Hume," Truman wrote, "you will need a new nose, a beefsteak for your eye and supporter below." Truman loved using the word "manure" where ever he could slide it in. Once asked why she allowed him to use such language, Mrs. Truman replied that it took her twenty years just to get him to use that word.

Second only to Eisenhower in Harry Truman's low regard was Congressman Richard Nixon. Truman loathed Nixon because Nixon was responsible for a McCarthy communist witch-hunt being mounted against him. The President's response to the allegations was simple and to the point. "If I am a traitor, the United States in in a hellova shape." About his accuser he said, "Nixon was a two-faced, goddamn liar." Several years later, former President Harry Truman was invited to speak at a small college in my hometown. After his talk, Vince Gaughan, my political mentor, and I went to a very small private reception in Truman's honor. I was able to ask him if he still felt the same way about Nixon. He smiled and said, "Son, always remember what a three-time loser is."

"What's that, Mr. President?" I asked.

"That's a pregnant prostitute, driving down the street in an Edsel wearing a Nixon button." Interestingly enough, this happened well before the Watergate scandal captured the headlines. I have never forgotten that day and I never will.

Harry Truman was often heard to say, "With Bess at my side, I can do anything." Mrs. Truman was a grand lady in her own right, who took great delight in her husband and family. She once related a story about the couple taking a steamship vacation to Hawaii after Eisenhower's inauguration. They were to have dinner with George Killian, the head of the steamship company. They arrived in the right San Francisco neighborhood, but the wrong address. Mrs. Truman recounted, "Harry rang the bell and a man answered who looked very Republican. 'Does Mr. Killian live here?' Harry asked. 'No,' said the man, then gave my husband a closer look and said, 'By the way, I hope your feelings won't be hurt, but you look exactly like Harry Truman.' Harry responded, 'I hope your feelings won't be hurt either, because I am Harry Truman.'"

Mrs. Truman never let her extensive calendar of public activities interfere with her devotion to Harry and their only daughter, Margaret. Both parents doted on their child and she returned their affection wholeheartedly. The closeness of the family prompted the White House staff to nickname them "The Three Musketeers."

Bess Wallace Truman had no love for the position of First Lady or the publicity that necessarily surrounded it. She was a reserved woman, very shy and very much the product of her small-town southern background. She was a very formal lady, which sometimes made her seem cold and forbidding. By Victorian tradition, the names of women like Bess were only permitted to appear in the newspaper three times in their lives: to announce her birth, to announce her marriage, and to announce her death. Despite this intense dislike of the spotlight, Bess Truman carried out her duties as First Lady with a dignity that soon garnered the public's respect. She personally greeted visitors to the White House, christened ships and planes, opened bazaars, attended luncheons and hosted receptions and state dinners. She shook so many hands that she required physical therapy after social functions.

Mrs. Truman was the first First Lady to take on the job of bookkeeping for the White House. She tried to run the White House like a business and began by cutting out the daily breakfast for the "sleep out" employees. Mrs. Truman paid careful attention to the menus and made sure that food was carefully prepared. She believed that the refreshments for all social functions should be prepared in the White House; even the teas that were attended by thousands of people.

In the midst of one formal reception for officials of the federal government, the President heard a chandelier above his head in the blue room make an unnatural tinkling. An investigation soon showed that the floor of the second-floor oval study was in bad condition. Structurally, the White House was about to collapse. The only part of the original mansion found to be solid was the old outer wall. The President and his family moved into Blair House, the nation's guest house for foreign dignitaries across the street from the White House. The job of restoring the White House and making it safe for future presidents required five million dollars and three years to complete.

The move to Blair House meant that social activities during the President's second term in office would have to be curtailed. The obligatory state dinners were held in one of Washington's hotels, usually the Mayflower. A whole series of parties were often necessary where one would have sufficed. But the Trumans handled the problem with grace, even inaugurating a series of parties for the wounded war veterans still being treated at military hospitals around Washington. The social highlight of the second Truman administration was the 1951 visit of Princess Elizabeth, then heir to the throne of Great Britain, and her husband Prince Philip. It was not easy to accommodate royalty in the temporary White House. Mrs. Truman and her staff managed it beautifully, right down to a full state dinner.

The Trumans brought both simplicity and panache to the White House. While Harry Truman will certainly be considered one of the great American presidents, Bess was an integral part of that success. Truman wrote after his retirement, "I hope someday someone will take the time to evaluate the true role of the wife of a President and to assess the many burdens she has to bear and contributions she makes."

MACARONI AND CHEESE

- 8 ounces elbow macaroni, boiled & drained
- 1 cup diced mozzarella cheese
- 4 tablespoons butter
- 3 cups milk
- 1 tablespoon A-1® sauce
- 4 medium tomatoes, peeled and sliced
- 1 teaspoon salt
- 1/2 cup grated Parmesan or cheddar cheese
- 2 tablespoons flour
- 1 teaspoon grated onion
  freshly ground black pepper

Melt butter. Add flour and blend until smooth. Add milk and cook until thickened, stirring constantly. Add cheeses, onion, A-1® sauce, salt and pepper. Cook until cheese melts, stirring constantly. Remove from heat and combine with macaroni. Put half of this mixture into a greased casserole and arrange half of the tomato slices on top. Repeat. Bake in oven (350° F) for 20 minutes. Broil under medium heat for about 10 minutes or until cheese sauce bubbles and begins to brown.

Serves 6

TUNA AND NOODLE CASSEROLE

      1   7 ounce can tuna fish (drained)
    1/2   package egg noodles
          boiling salted water
          dabs of butter
          hard-boiled eggs
          parsley for garnish

White Cheese Sauce

      2   tablespoons butter
    1-1/2 cups milk or light cream
    1/4   teaspoon salt
    1-1/2 tablespoons flour
    1/8   teaspoon pepper
    1/4   pound sharp cheddar cheese (grated)

Boil the noodles in salted water for 12 minutes, or until tender. Drain well and rinse. Flake the tuna with a fork.

Make the cheese sauce as follows: Over low heat, melt the butter and blend in the flour, stirring constantly until smooth. Gradually add the milk, continuing to stir constantly until the boiling point is reached. Add the grated cheddar cheese and the seasonings to taste. Reduce the heat and cook for 3 minutes longer, stirring all the while. In a well-buttered casserole, put alternate layers of the boiled noodles and tuna, covering it all with the cheese sauce. Top generously with dabs of butter and bake in a moderate oven (375° F) for 30 minutes. Garnish with sliced hard-boiled egg and sprigs of parsley.

CUCUMBER AND SALMON

    2   medium cucumbers
  1/4   pound smoked salmon, sliced
        freshly ground black pepper
        lemon wedges

Score cucumber skin with a fork. Cut cucumbers into 1/4-inch slices. Put a piece of sliced salmon on each cucumber. Serve with pepper and lemon wedges.

BAKED RED FISH A LA WHITE HOUSE

1	5-pound red fish (channel bass)
1/2	cup chopped celery
1/2	cup olive oil
2	cups canned tomato sauce
	salt to taste
	freshly ground black pepper to taste
	chopped parsley
1/2	cup chopped onion
1	clove garlic, minced
2-1/2	cups canned tomatoes
	cayenne pepper to taste
	chopped scallion tops
1	lemon, sliced thin

Sauté the onion, celery, and garlic in oil in a heavy pot for 10 minutes. Add tomatoes and tomato sauce. Cook uncovered over medium heat for 40 minutes, stirring occasionally. Add 1 cup cold water. Cook for 20 minutes.

Meanwhile, season the fish with the salt, black pepper, and a few grains cayenne pepper. Put in baking dish. Pour tomato mixture over the fish. Bake in slow oven (325° F) for 30 minutes, basting several times with the sauce. Garnish with scallion, parsley, and lemon slices.

Serves 6

QUENELLES DE BROCHET: WHITE HOUSE

1   pound boned pike or cod
     ground nutmeg
2   egg whites
3   cups heavy cream
     cayenne pepper
     salt
     freshly ground black pepper
     lobster sauce

Pound boned pike, adding a dash of nutmeg, a few grains of cayenne, salt and black pepper. Add egg whites gradually. Rub through a fine sieve and place in a saucepan set on ice. Beat with a wooden spoon and gradually work in cream. To form quenelles, heap a tablespoon with mixture and round off the top with the inside of another tablespoon. Carefully scoop quenelle out of first spoon with a spoon that has been dipped in warm water. Invert spoon and slip quenelle into a buttered pan. Form all quenelles this way. Pour a little salted water in pan. Bring water to a boil and poach quenelles over low heat for 10 minutes. Serve with lobster sauce.

Serves 6

Author's note: As you can see from the picture, this is an exciting dish.

VEAL AND CHICKEN SALAD

1	cup cooked veal strips
1	cup cooked chicken strips
1/2	cup sliced celery
2	medium apples, cubed
6	stuffed olives, sliced
1	teaspoon minced chives
	pistachio nuts
	mixed greens
	salad dressing (preferably a vidalia onion cream)

Arrange veal, chicken, celery, apples and olives on a bed of mixed greens. Garnish with chives and a few pistachio nuts. To serve, toss with classic French or sweet and sour dressing.

Serves 6

Author's note: Any leftover meat or fowl may be substituted for veal and chicken.

CHICKEN PAPRIKAS

         3   2 1/2 pound chickens
         2   large onions (about 1 pound), chopped
         2   green peppers, chopped
         6   ounces vegetable shortening
         1   tablespoon salt
         2   tablespoons Hungarian sweet paprika
       1/2   pint sour cream
             spaetzle or toasted egg barley

Wash, dry, and disjoint chickens. Sauté onions and peppers until onions are soft (not yellow). Add chicken breasts and legs, reserving the bony pieces for other use. Add salt to paprika and sprinkle over chicken. Pull from the fire and stir thoroughly. Return to fire, cover and simmer until tender (about an hour). Turn chicken frequently. Note: Water is not necessary as the natural juices of the chicken are adequate. Remove from the fire and just before serving, slowly blend in the sour cream. Return to the fire and bring to the boiling point, but do not boil. Serve with spaetzle or barley.

Serves 6

SWEET AND SOUR TURKEY

1	wild turkey, cut up (breast and thighs only)
2	onions, cut up
1	clove garlic
1	bay leaf
2	whole cloves
1/2	teaspoon mustard seed
2	tablespoons cornstarch
1/4	cup sugar
1/2	cup vinegar
2	teaspoons salt
10	peppercorns

Place turkey in pot with 4 cups of water. Add onion, garlic, bay leaf, cloves, mustard, salt, and peppercorns. Bring to a boil, reduce heat, cover and simmer for 2 hours. Remove turkey and strain broth. Return broth to pot, add cornstarch combined with sugar and vinegar. Cook, stirring constantly, until the sauce thickens. Add turkey and simmer for 15 minutes.

Serves 6

VEAL AL PROSCIUTTO

24 veal scallops about 3 x 4 inches each
24 very thin slices of prosciutto
    flour
    sweet butter
    Marsala wine
    lemon juice
    chopped parsley
    salt
    freshly ground black pepper

Dip the veal scallops in flour and sauté them in butter over high heat, allowing a scant 2 minutes for each side. Add a generous splash of Marsala, enough to deglaze the pan thoroughly. Cover each veal scallop with a slice of prosciutto and season with salt and pepper. Sprinkle with lemon juice and parsley. Pour in 3/4 cup of Marsala and simmer uncovered for 10 minutes, or until tender. Just before serving, sprinkle the veal and prosciutto very lightly with more of the wine and serve immediately on very hot plates.

Serves 6

PORK CROWN ROAST WITH CRANBERRIES

1	7 pound crown roast of pork
1-1/2	cups raw cranberries
4	cups bread cubes
2	tablespoons grated onion
1	clove garlic, minced
1/2	cup butter
1/2	cup dry white wine
1/2	teaspoon marjoram
1/4	cup sugar
1/4	teaspoon thyme
1	teaspoon salt
	freshly ground black pepper

Chop cranberries. Sauté bread cubes, onion, and garlic in butter for 10 minutes. Add cranberries and remaining ingredients. Fill center of roast with this mixture. Roast in slow oven (325° F) for 3 1/2 hours or until meat thermometer registers 185° F.

Serves 6

Author's note: Perfect for a few hungry friends.

MEAT LOAF

        2   pounds ground beef
        2   egg yolks
        4   tablespoons parsley (minced very fine)
        2   tablespoons butter
      1/4   cup bread crumbs
        2   tablespoons chili sauce
        2   teaspoons salt
      1/2   teaspoon pepper
        1   teaspoon onion juice

For basting:

      1/2   cup melted butter and 1/2 cup boiling water
            tomato sauce (which can be bought in cans)
        1   box frozen peas butter

For garnish:

            parsley & radish roses

Combine the first nine ingredients and shape into a loaf. Butter a loaf pan and place the meat in the pan. Bake in a moderate oven (350° F) for 1 hour, basting frequently with the butter and water combination. Remove meat loaf from the pan onto a heated platter. Garnish with sprigs of parsley and radish roses. Serve with the tomato sauce and green peas, to which a dab of butter is added when served.

BEEHIVE HONEY CAKE: WHITE HOUSE

1/2	cup milk
1/2	cup sugar
1	teaspoon salt
2	envelopes granular yeast
2	eggs
1/2	cup soft shortening
4 1/2	cups sifted flour
3	tablespoons honey
6	tablespoons sugar
6	tablespoons cream
6	tablespoons chopped cashews
6	tablespoons chopped pine nuts
6	tablespoons butter

Scald milk, add sugar and salt, and stir until sugar is dissolved. Cool to lukewarm. Soften yeast in 1/2 cup lukewarm water for 5 minutes. Add to milk mixture and stir until yeast is dissolved. Stir in eggs and shortening. Add half the flour and beat well. Add remaining flour and mix thoroughly. Turn out onto floured board and knead until dough is smooth and elastic. Place in greased bowl, turning once to bring greased side up. Cover with damp cloth and let rise in warm place until double in bulk (about 1-1/2 hours).

Punch dough down, cover and let rise again until almost double in bulk. Meanwhile combine butter, honey, sugar, and cream and bring to a boil, stirring constantly. Boil gently for 10 minutes, stirring constantly. Remove from heat, stir in nuts. Form dough into ball, flatten and fit into greased 10-inch baking pan. Spread honey and nut mixture over dough and let rise 1 inch. Bake in a moderate oven (375° F) for 30 minutes.

Serves 6

OZARK PUDDING

1	egg
3/4	cup sugar
1	tablespoon flour
1	teaspoon baking powder
1/8	teaspoon salt
5	small raw apples (peeled, cored & diced)
1	teaspoon vanilla extract
1/2	cup chopped walnuts (for garnish)
1	pint heavy cream

Beat the egg and sugar until very smooth and light. Mix the flour, baking powder, and salt, and stir into sugar and egg mixture. Add the apples, nuts and vanilla. Bake in a buttered, covered dish in a 350° F oven for 35 minutes or until the apples are very tender. Remove the cover to brown the top. Serve the pudding cold with whipped cream and garnish with chopped walnuts.

Author's note: This dessert is one of the best and easiest to make. It was enjoyed often by Harry and Mrs. Truman in the Family Quarters

RAISIN-STUFFED BAKED APPLES

    4 baking apples
1/2 cup seedless raisins
1/4 cup honey
    2 teaspoons melted butter
1/4 teaspoon ground cinnamon
1/4 teaspoon ground nutmeg
      red food coloring

Core each apple and peel the top half. Arrange the apples in a baking pan. Combine the raisins, honey, butter, cinnamon and nutmeg and fill the apples with the raisin mixture. Pour 2 cups of hot water into the pan around the apples. Add a few drops of red food coloring to the water. Bake in a moderate oven (375° F) for about 45 minutes or until the apples are tender, basting them frequently with the colored water.

Serve hot or cold.

CORN BREAD

    3/4   cup yellow cornmeal
1 2/3 cups sifted flour
     1 tablespoon baking powder
     1 egg, well beaten
     1 cup milk
     4 tablespoons melted butter
   1/2 teaspoon salt

Combine dry ingredients. Mix egg, milk, and butter. Stir together until lightly mixed. Bake in greased pan (8″ x 8″ x 2″) in hot oven (425° F) for 30 minutes.

Serves 6

OPPOSITE: CHINA LEFT TO RIGHT: PLATES JAMES K. POLK; THOMAS JEFFERSON
CUPS AND SAUCERS MARTHA JEFFERSON RANDOLPH; ABRAHAM LINCOLN

CHOCOLATE CHIP COOKIES

- 1/2 cup butter
- 1/4 cup sugar
- 1/2 cup brown sugar
- 1 egg
- 1 cup sifted flour
- 1/2 teaspoon baking soda
- 1/2 cup chopped nuts
- 1/2 teaspoon vanilla extract
- 1/2 teaspoon salt
- 1 cup chocolate chips

Cream butter until soft. Add both sugars gradually and cream until light and fluffy. Stir in egg. Sift flour with baking soda and salt and add it. Stir in chocolate chips, nuts, and vanilla. Mix thoroughly. Drop teaspoonfuls of batter onto greased cookie sheet about 2 inches apart. Bake in a moderate oven (375° F) for 10 minutes or until lightly browned.

Makes about 4 dozen

DEEP DISH APPLE PIE

  6 cups peeled apple slices
1/2 cup brown sugar
1/2 teaspoon ground cinnamon
1/4 teaspoon ground nutmeg
  2 tablespoons butter
1/2 pie crust recipe
  2 tablespoons heavy cream

Combine apples, sugar, cinnamon, and nutmeg in deep baking dish. Dot with butter. Top with pie crust rolled 1/8 inch thick. Brush crust with cream and bake in a hot oven (425° F) for 40 minutes.

Serves 6

GRAPE AND LEMON JELL-O® MOLD

1	envelope unflavored gelatin
1/4	cup cold water
1/2	cup boiling water
1/4	cup sugar
1	cup grape juice
2	tablespoons lemon juice
1/4	teaspoon salt
1/2	cup finely chopped celery
1	cup diced red-skinned apples

Soften gelatin in cold water and dissolve in boiling water. Add sugar, grape juice, lemon juice, and salt. Stir until sugar is dissolved. Chill. When mixture begins to thicken, fold in celery and apple. Turn into 3 oiled mold cups and chill until firm. Unmold on lettuce and serve with salad dressing.

STATE DINING ROOM, 1999 - WHGB, 21ST ED. ©WHHA

Dwight David Eisenhower
Mamie Geneva Dowd Eisenhower

"... So we voice our hope and our belief that we can help to heal this divided world. Thus may the nations cease to live in trembling before the menace of force. Thus may the weight of fear and the weight of arms be taken from the burdened shoulders of mankind.

This, nothing less, is the labor to which we are called and our strength dedicated.

And so the prayer of our people carries far beyond our own frontiers, to the wide world of our duty and our destiny.

May the light of freedom, coming to all darkened lands, flame brightly—until at last the darkness is no more."

DWIGHT D. EISENHOWER SECOND INAUGURAL ADDRESS, MONDAY, JANUARY 21, 1957

Dwight Eisenhower by Wills © WHHA (White House Collection)

*O*nce the inaugural festivities had passed and Harry Truman turned over the reins of government to President Eisenhower, the Eisenhowers quickly settled into a routine with the new First Lady taking managerial control of the President's house. The President and First Lady brought with them their own personal servants plus Mrs. Eisenhower's social secretary, Mary Jane McCaffree.

Mamie Eisenhower concentrated on the second-floor family quarters where she could create the pleasant surroundings that made the General and her family comfortable. Her new home was in fine condition after the Trumans' renovations and she was happy, but she soon realized that managing the White House was double duty. Not only did she have to run the private quarters, which included her family and personal guests, but also the state establishment for official entertaining. The new First Lady and Mrs. Mabel Walker, the housekeeper, discussed all details of the house and Mrs. Eisenhower prepared all the menus personally. This included everything from dinners for two to the complicated state dinners for one hundred or more.

At all the state dinners, Ike and Mamie sat next to one another in high-backed carved chairs at an E-shaped table in the state dining room. A typical menu could be quite elaborate, as was the protocol. Both she and Ike were used to these functions. During the war, they dined with virtually every king, queen, and prime minister of every Allied country in Europe.

A typical menu for a state function consisted of a first course of blue point oysters on the half shell, a second course of consommé with balls of beef marrow au sherry, and a third course of lobster thermador. The elaborate meal often stretched on with a fourth course of roast breast of Long Island duckling, applesauce, wild rice, French style string beans, and buttered beets with a special a l'orange sauce. The guests sipped a fine Burgundy with this course. The fifth course, an orange salad with roquefort cheese and wafers, was usually served with champagne. The sixth course, Spanish cream with caramel sauce, petit fours, nuts, and candies was accompanied by a demitasse.

When Ike and his wife dined alone or with close friends, they preferred TV trays so they could watch television or play bridge. Sometimes they all ended up singing while Mamie played the electric organ. Ike often cooked and painted to help relieve stress and he soon became an accomplished chef. As far as his art is concerned, Ike directed a member of his staff to do the drawing and Ike would paint inside the lines, hence a new industry was created—paint-by-numbers.

In addition to her role as wife and mother, Mamie Eisenhower was always at the beck and call of the public, whether for a tea, a reception or visits to a hospital. It is estimated she shook 16,000 hands during the first social season in 1953. In just a short six months she must have broken a few records.

After the President's heart attack, the First Family's social calendar was scaled back to ensure that Ike had plenty of rest. All large receptions were virtually eliminated and, whenever possible, state dinners became luncheons.

During the first three years of the Eisenhower administration, Mrs. Eisenhower employed François Rysarvy, one of the most famous chefs and pastry men of his time. Few chefs conquer both the art of the culinary and the bakery, and Chef Rysarvy was very much in demand. But after only three years, he grew bored with the pomp and circumstance of the White House and returned to Hollywood to feed the (to him) more interesting appetites of the stars.

During their years in the White House, the Eisenhowers enjoyed the pleasure of owning their own home for the first time. In 1950, before Ike was elected president, they purchased a farm in Gettysburg, Pennsylvania. Early on, they remodeled the 200-year-old farm house and it became a retreat for the whole Eisenhower family.

General Montgomery, who served under Eisenhower during World War II, once visited Ike at the farm. Monty was known for his ego and always thought he should have been supreme commander during the war instead of Ike. With this in mind, Monty was not kind to Ike in his memoirs. Ike proved that payback can be great fun if you are the President of the United States. Ike never greeted Monty officially at the airport, never supplied him with an official escort to the farm, but went golfing instead. The general was not put up at the main house but at a tiny guest house in the rear of the farm. General Montgomery never paid the Eisenhowers a visit again, much to the President's pleasure.

Although Ike was a West Pointer, a five-star general, and President of the United States for two terms, he seemed to be a very down-to-earth man. He was often exasperated by the antics of the "glory hoppers," during the war and later in his political life. He once told a group of reporters, "I hope I never get pontifical or stuffed shirty with you fellas."

In the late 1930s, Ike served on the staff of General Douglas MacArthur in the Philippines. Eisenhower had a lot of respect for the General but was amused by his grandiosity.

"He acts like an aristocrat," Ike once said, "but I'm just plain folks. I come from very ordinary people."

Winston Churchill was overheard telling him, "The reason I like you so much is because you ain't no glory hopper."

The Eisenhower administrations were political and social successes. When his presidency finally came to an end, the Eisenhowers retired to their much-loved farm. There they tended to their grandchildren and friends, and jealously guarded their privacy from any interference from the press. Free to spend their time in whatever way they wanted, they enjoyed a well-deserved retirement.

WINTER MELON BROTH

        1   10 pound watermelon
        1   squab
      1/4   pound canned abalone, diced
      1/2   cup chopped mushrooms
      1/2   cup chopped canned water chestnuts
      1/2   cup chopped canned bamboo shoots
        2   tablespoons dry sherry
        1   teaspoon soy sauce
            chicken bouillon
        1   teaspoon salt
            freshly ground black pepper
        1   cup cooked peas
        2   tablespoons finely chopped lean Smithfield ham

Wash melon and cut off the top, using a zigzag pattern. Remove melon seeds. Put whole squab, abalone, mushrooms, chestnuts, bamboo shoots, sherry, soy sauce, salt, and pepper in melon. Add bouillon until it comes to within 1/2 inch of top of melon. Set melon on a rack in a deep kettle over 1 inch of boiling water.

Cover and steam over medium heat for 8 hours, adding more water when necessary to keep it at the 1-inch level. Remove melon. Skim fat from soup. Before serving, sprinkle soup with peas and ham.

Serves 6

FLOUNDER WITH CHABLIS SAUCE

6	flounder fillets
1/2	cup Chablis wine
6	small onion rings
2	tablespoons lemon juice
1/2	bay leaf
1	tablespoon butter
1	tablespoon flour
2	egg yolks
1/4	teaspoon salt
6	peppercorns

Place flounder fillets on onion rings in greased shallow baking dish. Add Chablis, lemon juice, bay leaf, salt, and peppercorns. Cover with a sheet of buttered waxed paper. Bake in a moderate oven (350° F) for 15 minutes. Remove fillets from baking dish and keep warm. Strain sauce, add water if needed, to make 1 cup. Melt butter, add flour and strained sauce. Cook, stirring constantly until thickened. Beat egg yolks with 1 tablespoon water and add to sauce. Cook for 1 minute, stirring vigorously. Place fillets in baking dish, pour sauce over them. Set in pan of boiling water in hot oven (400° F) for 3 minutes. Serve immediately.

Serves 6

QUAIL HASH

1 quail per person
good chicken stock
salt
pepper
flour
sprigs of parsley for garnish

Put quail into a saucepan and cover well with stock. Cook slowly for 15–20 minutes according to the size of the birds or until the meat can be removed from the bones easily. Reserve the stock. Strip the meat, dice it, and season to taste. With small amounts of additional stock, make your gravy with the flour and pour it over the diced quail. Cover and simmer for 10 minutes. Serve in casserole and garnish with the sprigs of parsley.

ROAST DUCK WITH ORANGE & PINEAPPLE

2	5 pound oven-ready ducks
2	oranges
4	slices canned pineapple
1	teaspoon tarragon
3	cloves garlic
2	tablespoons butter
1/2	cup brandy
1	cup Marsala wine
2	cups chicken bouillon
1	teaspoon tomato paste
1/2	cup currant jelly
3	tablespoons potato flour
1	teaspoon salt
	freshly ground black pepper

Peel the oranges and shred the rind. Set aside. Quarter the oranges and mix with pineapple, tarragon, and 2 chopped garlic cloves. Use mixture to stuff both ducks. Place ducks on rack in shallow baking pan and roast in slow oven (325° F) for 2 1/2 hours or until done. Meanwhile, sauté duck livers in butter for 10 minutes. Heat brandy, light it, and pour over livers. When flame dies, remove livers, chop and keep warm. To the sauce remaining in skillet, add shredded orange rind and 1 minced garlic clove and cook for 5 minutes. Combine Marsala and bouillon with tomato paste, jelly, potato flour, salt, and pepper. Add to sauce and cook, stirring constantly, until smooth. Add livers and simmer for 15 minutes. Pour into sauce boat, serve with duck.

Serves 6

WILD GOOSE IN WINE

1 wild goose, cut up (breast and thighs)
2 cups dry white wine
2 onions, sliced
2 tablespoons chopped parsley
1 teaspoon thyme
2 bay leaves, crumbled
2 slices bacon, minced
1 clove garlic
2 cups chicken bouillon
1 teaspoon salt
6 peppercorns

Marinate goose in the refrigerator overnight or for at least 8 hours in mixture of wine, onions, parsley, thyme, bay leaves, salt and peppercorns. Dry goose and save marinade. Put it in a casserole with the bacon and roast in a hot oven (425° F) for 25 minutes or until brown, turning the goose frequently. Add the marinade, garlic, and bouillon. Cover and bake in a moderate oven (325° F) for 1 hour or until goose is tender.

Serves 6

CHIPPED BEEF IN MUSHROOM SAUCE

- 3/4 pound dried chipped beef
- 2 cans condensed cream of mushroom soup
- 1/4 cup butter
- 2 cups milk
- 1 teaspoon Worcestershire sauce
- freshly ground black pepper
- 1/2 cup toasted almonds
- toast

Soak chipped beef in 2 cups of hot water for 10 minutes. Drain and discard water. Sauté beef in butter in chafing dish for 5 minutes, stirring constantly. Combine soup with milk and stir until smooth and thoroughly blended. Stir soup mixture and Worcestershire into beef. Season with pepper. Simmer for 10 minutes, stirring occasionally. Sprinkle with toasted almonds. Serve on toast.

Serves 6

SAUERBRATEN: WHITE HOUSE

3	pounds top round of beef
1	cup vinegar
1/2	cup chopped onion
2	bay leaves
1	tablespoon paprika
2	whole cloves
1/2	teaspoon thyme
1/2	cup flour
2	tablespoons shortening
1/4	cup sliced roasted carrot
1/4	cup chopped parsnips
1/4	cup chopped celery
1/4	cup dry red wine
2	teaspoons salt

Combine vinegar, 1 cup water, 1/4 cup onion, bay leaves, paprika, cloves, and thyme. Heat, but do not boil. Pour over meat. Cover and store in a cool place for several days, turning meat once each day. Remove meat, drain. Strain and save marinade. Coat the meat with 1/4 cup of flour and sear in shortening. Add carrot, parsnip, celery, and remaining 1/4 cup of onion and cook for 5 minutes, stirring constantly. Pour marinade over meat. Cover and simmer for 3 hours. Remove meat and keep hot. Mix remaining 1/4 cup of flour and the salt with 1/2 cup of water. Stir into sauce and cook until thickened. Strain gravy, add wine, and serve over meat.

Serves 6

GETTYSBURG FARM BEEF STEW

3	pounds stewing beef, cubed
2	tablespoons fat
2	large onions, sliced
2	cloves garlic, minced
1	cup chopped celery
1/4	cup chopped parsley
2 1/2	cups canned tomatoes
1	bay leaf, crumbled
1/2	teaspoon thyme
1	cup peas
12	small carrots
12	small onions
6	potatoes, quartered
1/2	cup flour
1	tablespoon salt
	freshly ground black pepper

Melt fat in saucepan and brown meat. Add sliced onions, garlic, celery, parsley, tomatoes, bay leaf, thyme, salt, pepper, and 2 1/2 cups water. Bring to a boil, reduce heat, cover, and simmer for 2 hours. Add remaining vegetables and simmer for 1 hour. Blend flour with 3/4 cup cold water and stir into stew. Simmer for 5 minutes.

Serves 6

BAKED GREEN LASAGNA: WHITE HOUSE

1-1/2	cups cooked spinach, drained and chopped
4	eggs
1	onion, finely chopped
1	small carrot, chopped
1/2	pound pork loin, diced
3	tablespoons tomato sauce
1	quart milk
	freshly ground black pepper
8 1/2	cups flour
1/4	cup finely chopped celery
1/2	pound lean beef, diced
1/4	cup dry white wine
	butter
	grated Parmesan cheese
	salt

First make the lasagna: Mix 8 cups of flour with the spinach and eggs. Knead on a lightly floured breadboard until a firm dough is formed. Roll out thin and cut into 4-inch squares. Cook squares in salted boiling water. Remove, dip into cold water, drain, and dry. While the lasagna is drying, make a meat sauce, or ragout, and a béchamel sauce.

For the meat sauce, sauté onion, celery, carrot, salt, and pepper in 2 tablespoons butter for 10 minutes or until the onion is lightly browned. Add beef, pork, wine, and tomato sauce and simmer for 10 minutes.

For the béchamel, melt 1/2 cup butter in a saucepan. Add 1/2 cup flour and a pinch of salt and stir until smooth. Add milk gradually, stirring constantly, and cook, stirring until thick and smooth. To make baked green lasagna, put alternate layers of lasagna, meat sauce, béchamel sauce and Parmesan cheese in a baking dish. Bake in a moderate oven (350° F) for 15 minutes.

Serves 6

TOMATO PUDDING

1	10 ounce can tomato puree
1/4	cup boiling water
6	tablespoons light brown sugar
1/4	teaspoon salt
1	cup white bread (cut into 1-inch cubes)
1/4	cup melted butter

Add the sugar and salt to the tomato puree and water, and boil for 5 minutes. Place bread cubes in casserole dish. Pour the melted butter over the bread and add the tomato mixture. Bake covered for 30 minutes at 375° F. Serve with the Quail Hash (see page 80) or other meats.

SLICED CUCUMBER PICKLES

1-1/2	teaspoons ground turmeric
20	medium cucumbers, sliced
12	onions, sliced
5	cups cider vinegar
4	cups sugar
1	teaspoon celery seed
4	pieces stick cinnamon, 1 inch each
1	tablespoon mustard seed
6	whole cloves
4	tablespoons salt
1	teaspoon peppercorns

Sprinkle sliced cucumbers and onions with salt and let stand at room temperature 1-1/2 hours. Drain well. Combine remaining ingredients in a large saucepan and bring to a boil. Add cucumbers and onions, reduce heat, and simmer 10 minutes. Remove cinnamon sticks. Ladle into hot sterilized jars and seal immediately.

Makes about 8 pints

CORN RELISH

5	cups cooked corn, cut from cob
1/2	cup chopped green pepper
1/2	cup chopped red pepper
3/4	cup chopped onion
1/2	cup chopped celery
1	tablespoon prepared mustard
1	tablespoon mustard seed
2	teaspoons celery seed
1/2	teaspoon ground turmeric
3/4	cup sugar
1	pint vinegar
2	teaspoons salt

Combine ingredients with 1/2 cup water, simmer for 30 minutes. Pack in hot sterilized jars to within 1/2 inch of top. Seal at once.

Makes 3-1/2 pints

Author's note: This is a must at harvest time. Make plenty! It'll last all year.

PRESIDENT EISENHOWER'S
FRENCH SALAD DRESSING

1 clove garlic, chopped
2 tablespoons green onion tops
1 tablespoon anchovy paste
1/2 cup sour cream
1 cup mayonnaise
2 tablespoons tarragon vinegar
1/8 teaspoon black pepper
1/2 tablespoon lemon juice
green food coloring

Mix the anchovy paste with the garlic and green onion tops. Add the remaining ingredients, plus one drop of green food coloring. Chill for 2 or 3 hours to blend flavors.

Serves 6

Author's note: Serve over lettuce, romaine, escarole, or mixed greens. Excellent with shrimp salad, crab meat or lobster salad.

GERMAN POTATO SALAD

6	hot boiled potatoes
6	strips bacon, diced
1/4	cup finely chopped onion
1/2	cup cider vinegar
2	tablespoons sugar
1	teaspoon salt

Fry bacon until crisp. Slice potatoes and add onion and salt. Add vinegar and sugar to bacon and fat in skillet and bring to a boil. Pour over potatoes and mix. Serve at once.

Serves 6

Author's note: A fine addition to this salad is to sauté sliced apples with skins on in a little butter or bacon fat.

PENNSYLVANIA DUTCH POTATO PANCAKES

4 pounds potatoes, peeled
2 large onions
1 egg
1-1/2 cups flour
2 teaspoons baking powder
1 teaspoon lemon juice
  ground nutmeg
  oil or vegetable shortening
1 tablespoon salt

Put raw potatoes and onions through food grinder, using fine blade. Drain thoroughly. Mix egg, flour, baking powder, lemon juice, a pinch of nutmeg, and salt. Drop mixture by tablespoonfuls into 2 inches of hot oil (375° F). Fry for about 10 minutes or until golden brown.

Serves 6

Author's note: For a tastier pancake, add 2 tablespoons of sour cream and 1 tablespoon of chopped chives.

STIRRED CABBAGE

      1   2 pound Chinese cabbage
   1/4 cup oil
      1   teaspoon salt

Cut cabbage in half lengthwise and remove stem. Slice cabbage crosswise into 1/2-inch strips. Chop stem. Fry stem in oil for 1 minute. Add salt and 1/2 cup water. Cover and cook over medium heat for exactly 3 minutes. Serve cabbage with any juice that remains.

Serves 6

Author's note: New American cabbage may be substituted for the Chinese. Quarter cabbage. Discard center stalk, then cut cabbage crosswise into 1/2-inch strips. Heat oil in a skillet, add cabbage, and cook for 1 minute. Add salt and water. Cook covered for 3 minutes.

CHIVE AND CHERVIL DUMPLINGS

2	tablespoons chopped chives
2	tablespoons chopped chervil
1-1/2	cups sifted flour
2	teaspoons double-acting baking powder
3/4	cup milk
3	teaspoons shortening
1	teaspoon salt
	freshly ground black pepper

Sift flour, baking powder, salt and pepper together. Cut in shortening with a pastry blender or two knives until the dough resembles coarse meal. Stir in chives and chervil. Add the milk, stirring only enough to blend. Drop by tablespoonfuls onto boiling beef or chicken stew. Cover and cook for 15 minutes.

Serves 6

Author's note: Very informal—goes well with heavy soups.

FROSTED MINT DELIGHT

        2 1 pound cans crushed pineapple
                (reserve 1 cup of the juice)
      3/4 cup pure mint apple jelly
        1 envelope unflavored gelatin
        1 pint whipping cream
                (reserve some for garnish)
        2 tablespoons confectioners' sugar

   Chill crushed pineapple and whipped cream. Melt the mint-flavored jelly and mix the crushed pineapple into it. Dissolve the gelatin and 1 cup of the pineapple juice. Mix the gelatin and fold into the pineapple mixture. Whip the cream, sweeten with confectioners' sugar, and fold into the combined mixture. Put into the freezer until firm, but do not freeze solid.

Author's note: This recipe should serve 10–12 and it should be served in a parfait glass topped with whipped cream. It is best eaten with cookies or wafers.

FROSTY STRAWBERRY SHORTCAKE

    1   pint strawberries, crushed
    6   individual sponge cake shells
    1   package vanilla frozen dessert mix
        light cream
    2   tablespoons curaçao
        sugar

Prepare frozen dessert mix as directed on the package, using cream instead of milk. Beat in curaçao. Pour into refrigerator tray and freeze until firm. Turn ice cream out into a chilled bowl and beat with a rotary beater until smooth. Return to tray and freeze until firm enough to serve. Spoon into cake shells and top with sugared crushed strawberries.

Serves 6

DOUBLE CHOCOLATE PIE

1-1/2	cups crumbled chocolate cookies
3	tablespoons butter
1	6 ounce package semisweet chocolate
3	eggs
2	tablespoons rum
1 1/4	cups cream, whipped

Line a buttered 7-inch pie plate with crumbled chocolate cookies mixed with butter. Bake the shell in a moderately hot oven (375° F) for 3 minutes.

For the filling, melt semisweet chocolate over hot water. Beat in 1 whole egg and 2 egg yolks, one at a time. Add 2 tablespoons rum. Beat 2 stiffly beaten egg whites into the chocolate mixture and fold in 1 1/4 cups cream, whipped. Spoon the mixture into the shell and chill well. Top with whipped cream and shavings of unsweetened chocolate.

BROWNIES

2	squares unsweetened chocolate
1/4	cup butter
1	cup sugar
2	eggs
1/2	teaspoon vanilla extract
2/3	cup flour
1	cup chopped nuts
	salt

Melt the chocolate in a mixing bowl over hot water. Remove from heat. Add the butter and stir until melted. Cool for 5 minutes. Add the sugar, eggs and vanilla and heat thoroughly. Mix in the flour and a pinch of salt. Stir in the nuts. Put into a greased 8-inch square pan and bake in a slow oven (300° F) for 40 minutes. Cut into squares.

John Fitzgerald Kennedy
Jacqueline Lee Bouvier Kennedy

"We observe today not a victory of party but a celebration of freedom—symbolizing an end as well as a beginning—signifying renewal as well as change. For I have sworn before you and Almighty God the same solemn oath our forbears prescribed nearly a century and three-quarters ago.

The world is very different now. For man holds in his mortal hands the power to abolish all forms of human poverty and all forms of human life. And yet the same revolutionary beliefs for which our forebears fought are still at issue around the globe—the belief that the rights of man come not from the generosity of the state but from the hand of God.

We dare not forget today that we are the heirs of that first revolution."

PRESIDENT JOHN F. KENNEDY INAUGURAL ADDRESS, JANUARY 20, 1961

JOHN F. KENNEDY BY AARON SHIKLER © WHHA (WHITE HOUSE COLLECTION)

With the world watching on a snowy January day in 1961, John Fitzgerald Kennedy became the thirty-fifth and youngest elected President of the United States, and Camelot was born. The 43-year-old Kennedy walked to the rostrum and delivered one of the shortest and most elegant inaugural addresses in over 175 years. Part of his address follows:

Let the word go forth from this time and place, to friends and foe alike, that the torch has been passed to a new generation of Americans, born in this century, tempered by war, disciplined by a hard and bitter peace, proud of our ancient heritage and unwilling to witness or permit the slow undoing of those human rights to which this nation has always been committed and to which we are committed today at home and around the world.

Let every nation know, whether it wishes well or ill, that we shall pay any price, bear any burden, meet any hardship, support any friend, oppose any foe, in order to ensure the survival and success of liberty. ...

In the long history of the world, only a few generations have been granted the role of defending freedom in its hour of maximum danger. I do not shrink from this responsibility—I welcome it. I do not believe that any of us would exchange places with any other people or any other generation. The energy, the faith, the devotion which we bring to this endeavor will light our country and all who serve it and the glow from that fire could truly light the world. And so, my fellow Americans, ask not what your country can do for you, but ask what you can do for your country.

The presidential battle between Nixon and Kennedy was, and still is, the closest popular election in history. Kennedy won by a slim 49.7% to Nixon's 49.5%. JFK often said that had Nixon done better in the debates, he would have won the election. Kennedy had a lot to prove to maintain his popularity. He was an idealist without illusions, a curious man who could be very irritable—his back gave him constant pain and he had other ailments that Americans knew nothing about at the time. Kennedy put together a very fine cabinet made up of accomplished individuals. The Harvard man strongly believed in hiring the best people for the job.

Kennedy was one of the wittiest of U.S. presidents. To a friend, he once gave a silver beer mug inscribed: "There are three things which are real: God, Human Folly and Laughter." He understood that the first two are beyond our comprehension, so we must do what we can with the third. Like Lincoln, Kennedy was bored with self-righteousness, false humility and garrulousness. "It's a gift," said some of his staff. "He doesn't know how to be stuffy."

When asked by a high-school boy how he became a war hero, the president replied, "It was absolutely involuntary; they sank my boat!"

Catholicism was still an issue for Kennedy when he ran for the presidency. So was the great influence his father had over him. Harry Truman was not an early supporter of JFK's and once said, "I'm not against the pope, I'm against the pop." When reporters at a dinner roast teased JFK about his father by presenting a skit featuring the songs "My Heart Belongs to Daddy" and "Just Send the Bill to Daddy," Kennedy commented in good spirit, "I just received a wire from my daddy and I quote him, 'Dear Jack, Don't buy a single vote more than necessary. I'll be damned if I'm going to pay for a landslide!'"

President Kennedy's high spirits, even during times of emergency, helped to give Americans a sense of hope. He sparkled at his press conferences, which he reinitiated on a weekly basis. The press had a field day with the Kennedy family and the new President. John Jr. and Caroline running in and out of the Oval Office, playing under JFK's desk, scooting downstairs to the kitchen, and running through the White House mess were common scenes. Everyone who worked at the White House remembered them with great affection.

Kennedy's humor became legendary. Unable to attend a testimonial luncheon for Postmaster General J. Edward Day, JFK sent his regrets and added, "I am sending this message by wire, since I want to be certain the message reaches you in the right place at the right time."

Even as a young man, Jack Kennedy had a great sense of humor. At dinner one night, the senior Kennedy complained about the amount of money his family spent. He said, "No one has the slightest concern for how much they spend," and proceeded to reprimand one of JFK's sisters so severely that she left the room in tears. When she returned, JFK looked up and said, "Well, Sis, don't worry. We have all decided that the only solution is to have Dad work harder."

Kennedy had his serious moments too; for example, the Cuban Missile Crisis—seventy-two hours of stand-down, the closest any country ever came to nuclear war.

When Kennedy finally met Kruschev at a summit meeting in Vienna regarding foreign policy, the encounter between the two most powerful men on earth was by no means friendly. Kruschev regarded Kennedy as a young, inexperienced upstart and was very frosty during their first meeting. When the two men began a serious discussion of U.S./Soviet relations, Kennedy couldn't help but notice two medals pinned to the chairman's lapel.

"What are those?" the President asked.

The chairman replied, "These are the Lenin Peace Medals." And then Kennedy said, "I hope you get to keep them."

I loved this president. He brought America and the world together and inspired others to do the same. America was getting bored before JFK, but the Kennedys inspired a new excitement in the nation. Young people stood in line to join the Peace Corps, and people of all walks of life took pride in themselves. Kennedy had a way of making everyone feel important and indeed they really were to him.

Speaking to a group of farmers in Sioux City, Iowa, Kennedy, in his Boston/Cape Cod accent, referred to the agricultural depression and cried out, "The rest of the country is doing very well. What's wrong with the American fah-mah today?"

As he paused dramatically, someone in the audience yelled out, "He's stah ving!" The audience, and JFK, roared with laughter.

Mrs. Kennedy also brought her own inimitable style to the White House, making the Kennedys the most elegant first couple in history. Planning a meal or a state dinner with Mrs. Kennedy was an event everyone looked forward to. A lovely, soft-spoken, young woman of 33, she really knew her stuff.

She had a flair for French cuisine and presentation, and hired none other than Rene Verdon, one of the finest chefs in the world. Verdon, the former chef of the Hotel Carlyle in New York City, brought to the White House exactly the panache Mrs. Kennedy wanted, but she also wanted to ease the severe formality.

Mrs. Kennedy's first reception was held on a Sunday afternoon. The formal receiving line was dispensed with, and she and the President mingled as they would have in their Georgetown home. Fireplaces blazed, beautiful flowers were everywhere, and waiters passed trays of hors d'oeuvres. Instead of dinners limited to diplomats, congressmen and judges, the First Lady mixed other prominent people from around the country into the guest lists.

Jacqueline Kennedy initiated some very unusual ways to serve official meals at the White House and even away from the White House. One state dinner was held at Mount Vernon The guest of honor was the President of Pakistan. The dinner was staged on the terrace of George Washington's home and the guests were brought to the party aboard the presidential yacht down the Potomac. The beautiful evening, the music of the fife and drum corps, and the historic significance of the setting all combined to make this dinner a huge success.

Once JFK entertained all the American Nobel laureates at a special dinner in the East Room of the White House. When it came time for the toast, Kennedy stood up and said, "The only time there was more intelligence in the White House was when Thomas Jefferson dined alone."

White House dinners became fun under the Kennedys and the White House menus were cut down to four or five courses, each more elegant than the last. This allowed ample time for toasts and socializing.

In addition to the state dinners, the Kennedys entertained twice as many visiting heads of state as previous administrations. The President was often the first at stag luncheons that he held for members of Congress. He personally reviewed the official guest list with his wife, and often tasted the wines and sauces before dressing for dinner. Jack Kennedy sipping sauce from a spoon was a common sight in the White House kitchens. In spite of his hands-on approach to all White House functions, he always made a point to emphasize that all aspects of White House social life were Mrs. Kennedy's responsibility.

The sheer vitality of President and Mrs. Kennedy makes his assassination in November 1963 even harder to understand. During my research, I came across the speech JFK was to give at the dinner in his honor on the day he was shot. I would like to share it with you, but let me preface it by quoting Senator Abraham Ribicoff, of Connecticut, in 1963: "More than any President before him, he committed the presidency to achieving full civil rights for every American. He opposed prejudice of every kind. There was no trace of meanness in this man. There was only compassion for the frailties of others. If there is a supreme lesson we can draw from the life of John Kennedy, it is a lesson of tolerance, a lesson of conscience, courage, and compassion."

From John Kennedy's undelivered speech:

What kind of peace do we seek? Not a pax Americana enforced on the world by American weapons of war. Not the peace of the grave or the security of the slave. I am talking about a genuine peace. The kind of peace that makes life on earth worth living. The kind that makes men and nations grow and hope to build a better life for their children, not merely peace for Americans but peace for all men and women, not merely peace in our time, but peace for all time. It should be clear by now that a nation can be no stronger abroad than she is at home. Only in America, which practices what it preaches about equal rights and social justice, will be respected by those whose choice affects our future.

Three hours before John F. Kennedy was shot in Dallas he said, "If anybody really wanted to shoot the President of the United States it is not a very difficult job. All one has to do is get on a high building someday with a telescopic rifle and there is nothing anyone can do to defend against such an attempt." In another strange twist, it has been recorded that John F. Kennedy's favorite poem was "I Have a Rendezvous with Death" by Allen Seeger.

INAUGURATION
CEREMONIES
PROGRAM

JANUARY TWENTIETH

NINETEEN HUNDRED SIXTY-ONE

PATÉ OF DUCK: WHITE HOUSE

1/4	pound paté de fois gras (goose liver), chopped fine
2 - 3	pound ducks, boned
1	pound veal
1	pound pork
2	onions, chopped
2	carrots, sliced
1/2	cup chopped parsley
1	teaspoon thyme
2	cups dry white wine
1/4	cup cognac
1	cup lard
1	cup butter
4	cups sifted flour
2	envelopes unflavored gelatin
1	teaspoon salt

Cube the ducks, 1/2 pound of veal, and 1/2 pound of pork. Combine cubed meat, onion, carrots, parsley, thyme, wine, and cognac and marinate in a cool place for 2 days. Drain. Save 4 cups of the marinade.

Chop remaining 1/2 pound of veal and 1/2 pound of pork. Mix drained meat with chopped meat and foie gras. Meanwhile, cut lard and butter into flour and salt until it resembles coarse meal. Add 6 tablespoons of water and mix lightly. Turn out on a floured board and roll thin. Line inside of a casserole with dough. Fill with meat mixture and cover with dough. Cut 2 dime-size holes in top. Bake in moderate oven (375° F) for 1 hour. Cool. Soften gelatin in 1 cup of the marinade. Bring remaining 3 cups of marinade to a boil and pour over gelatin stirring until gelatin is dissolved. Cool. Chill for 20 minutes. Pour through holes into paté. Chill for 2 hours.

Serves 12

PHEASANT BROTH: WHITE HOUSE

       2   hen pheasants
       1   large onion
     1/2   stalk celery
       2   medium carrots
           Ac'cent®
           freshly ground black pepper
           egg drops

Cover pheasants with water. Add onion, celery, carrots, Ac'cent®, and pepper. Bring to a boil, reduce heat, cover, and simmer for 45 minutes. Remove pheasants, cut off breasts, and save for another meal. Return pheasants to stock and simmer for 45 minutes or until meat falls from the bones. Remove pheasants and strain stock. Cut meat into small pieces and return to stock. Add egg drops before serving.

Serves 12

MRS. JOHN F. KENNEDY'S
ICED TOMATO SOUP

        6   large ripe tomatoes, coarsely chopped
        1   onion, chopped
      1/4   cup water
      1/2   teaspoon salt
             dash of pepper
        2   tablespoons tomato paste
        2   tablespoons flour
        2   chicken bouillon cubes, dissolved in 2 cups boiling water
        1   cup heavy cream

Combine tomatoes, onion, water, salt, and pepper in a saucepan. Cook over moderate heat 5 minutes. Combine tomato paste with flour and add to tomatoes with chicken bouillon. Simmer gently 3 minutes. Rub mixture through a fine sieve. Chill several hours. Before serving, add cream. Season to taste with more salt if necessary. Garnish each serving with a thin tomato slice if desired.

Serves 6

MRS. JOHN F. KENNEDY'S CONSOMME JULIENNE

2 small carrots, scraped
1 leek
1 stalk celery
2 slices turnip
1 tablespoon butter or margarine
3 cabbage leaves, shredded
1/2 medium onion, thinly sliced
1/8 teaspoon salt
   dash of pepper
1/8 teaspoon sugar
4 chicken bouillon cubes,
   dissolved in 4 cups boiling water
   chopped parsley

Cut carrots, leek, celery, and turnip into very thin strips about 2 inches long. Melt butter in a small saucepan over low heat. Add carrots, leek, celery, turnip, cabbage, onion, salt, pepper, and sugar. Cover and cook about 5 minutes until vegetables are tender. Combine with chicken bouillon, simmer 5 minutes. Serve with garnish of chopped parsley.

Serves 6

COD CHOWDER

2 pounds cod
2 ounces salt pork, diced
2 onions, sliced
4 large potatoes, diced
1 cup chopped celery
1 bay leaf, crumbled
1 quart milk
2 tablespoons butter
1 teaspoon salt
  freshly ground black pepper

Simmer cod in 2 cups water for 15 minutes. Drain. Reserve broth. Remove bones from cod. Sauté diced pork until crisp, remove and set aside. Sauté onions in pork fat until golden brown. Add cod, potatoes, celery, bay leaf, salt, and pepper. Pour in cod broth plus enough boiling water to make 3 cups liquid. Simmer for 30 minutes. Add milk and butter and simmer for 5 minutes. Serve chowder sprinkled with pork dice.

Serves 6

Author's note: JFK's favorite chowder.

BOSTON CLAM CHOWDER:
WHITE HOUSE

    3   dozen soft-shell clams, shucked
    2   ounces salt pork, diced
1-1/2   cups onion, sliced
    6   cups diced potato
    2   small bay leaves, crumbled
    4   cups milk, scalded
    2   cups cream, room temperature
    3   tablespoons butter
    2   tablespoons flour
    1   tablespoon salt
        freshly ground black pepper

Strain clams, keep liquor. Mince hard part of clams, chop soft part coarsely. Sauté salt pork until golden brown. Add minced clams, onion, potato, bay leaves, salt and pepper, and 3 cups of water. Bring to a boil, reduce heat, cover, and simmer for 15 minutes. Add clam liquor, plus enough water to make 3 cups. Add chopped clams, milk, cream, and butter blended with flour. Simmer for 20 minutes.

Serves 6

MRS. JOHN F. KENNEDY'S
NEW ENGLAND FISH CHOWDER

2 pounds haddock
2 onions, sliced
1 cup chopped celery
2 teaspoons salt
1 quart milk
2 ounces salt pork, diced
4 large potatoes, diced
1 bay leaf, crushed
  dash of pepper
2 tablespoons butter or margarine

Cook haddock in 2 cups boiling water over low heat 15 minutes. Drain and measure broth. Add enough water to make 3 cups broth. Remove bones and skin from fish, flake fish coarsely. Cook salt pork in a heavy saucepan over moderate heat until golden brown and crisp. Remove pork pieces. Add onions to fat in saucepan and cook until golden brown. Add fish, potatoes, celery, bay leaf, salt, pepper, and the 3 cups fish broth. Cover and simmer gently 30 minutes. Add milk and butter, simmer over very low heat 5 minutes longer. Serve chowder in warm bowls and sprinkle with crisp pork pieces.

Serves 6

BOULA - BOULA (AMERICAN SOUP)

       2 cups freshly shelled green peas
       2 cups canned green turtle soup
       1 cup sherry
     1/2 cup whipping cream
       1 tablespoon sweet butter

Cook the green peas in boiling, salted water and strain through a fine sieve or an electric blender to get a puree. Reheat. Add 1 tablespoon sweet butter, salt, and white pepper to taste. Blend with the green turtle soup and 1 cup sherry. Heat to just under the boiling point. Put the soup into serving cups. Cover each cup with a spoonful of unsweetened whipped cream and put the cups under the broiler to brown the topping. Serve immediately.

CLASSIC BOUILLABAISSE

2 - 2	pound lobsters
1	pound shrimp, pealed and deveined
1	pound eel
1-1/2	pounds striped bass or sea bass
2	tablespoons chopped parsley
3	pounds red snapper or mackerel (optional)
2	dozen mussels
2	dozen clams
1/2	cup chopped carrot
3	leeks, chopped
3/4	cup chopped onion
1/2	cup olive oil
12	thick slices French bread
4	cups canned tomatoes
3	cloves garlic
2	tablespoons chopped fennel
1/2	teaspoon saffron
1	bay leaf, crumbled
1/2	teaspoon thyme
1	tablespoon salt
	freshly ground pepper
1/2	cup butter, melted

Cut up lobster, leaving shell on. Cut eel, bass, and snapper into 1-inch slices. Scrub mussels and clams thoroughly to remove all outside sand and grit. Sauté carrot, leeks, and onion in olive oil for 10 minutes in a large pot. Add tomatoes, 2 minced garlic cloves, and other seasonings. Add lobster, eel, and 2 quarts of water and bring soup to a boil. Reduce heat and simmer for 15 minutes. Add bass and snapper and cook for 10 minutes. Add shrimp, mussels, and clams and cook for 20 minutes or until shells open. Mix butter and 1 crushed garlic clove. Spread some on one side of French bread slices and toast, buttered side up, in the broiler under moderate heat until brown. Turn slices, spread with rest of butter, and toast the other side. Serve the toast with the bouillabaisse.

Serves 12, generously.

MRS. JOHN F. KENNEDY'S
LOBSTER CARDINALE

6	1-1/2 pound lobsters
8	cups boiling water
3/4	cup butter or margarine
4	tablespoons flour
1-1/2	teaspoons salt
2	tablespoons dry white wine
4	tablespoons chopped canned mushrooms
1	tablespoon grated Parmesan cheese

Drop lobsters into rapidly boiling water. When water returns to a boil, cook lobsters 15 minutes; remove and cool. Boil the water rapidly until it is reduced to 2 cups. Place each lobster on its back and with a sharp knife cut membrane the entire length of the body. Remove and discard the stomach portion, which is under the head. Remove meat from claws and body and cut into 1-inch pieces. Place body shells in a shallow baking pan.

Melt 4 tablespoons of butter in a saucepan; add flour and salt. Gradually add 2 cups of the reduced liquid stirring constantly until smooth and thickened. Cook 15 minutes, stirring frequently. Add wine, mushrooms, and the remaining butter. Spread a little sauce in the bottom of each shell. Add lobster meat, top with rest of sauce, and sprinkle with cheese. Place 3 to 4 inches from heat in a preheated broiler and broil about 5 minutes, until mixture is hot and lightly browned.

Serves 6

MRS. JOHN F. KENNEDY'S
SALMON MOUSSE WITH CUCUMBERS

- 1 16 ounce can red salmon
- water
- 1 envelope unflavored gelatin
- 1 tablespoon onion juice
- 1/4 cup finely chopped celery
- 2 tablespoons chopped green pepper
- 1 cup heavy cream, whipped
- 1 large cucumber, thinly sliced
- 1 cup green-tinted mayonnaise

Drain salmon and measure liquid. Add water to make 1-1/2 cups. Sprinkle gelatin over 1/2 cup of the liquid. Stir over low heat until gelatin is dissolved. Remove from heat, stir in rest of liquid and onion juice. Chill to consistency of unbeaten egg white. Flake fish and combine with celery and green pepper. Fold into chilled gelatin with whipped cream. Turn into a 1-quart mold. Chill until firm. Unmold onto a serving plate. Garnish with cucumber. Serve with mayonnaise tinted pale green with food coloring.

Serves 6

Author's note: This is a great dish on a buffet table.

OLIVE SALMON LOAF:
WHITE HOUSE

3	cups flaked salmon
1/4	cup sliced ripe olives
3	cups bread cubes
3/4	cup milk
3	eggs, lightly beaten
2	tablespoons grated onion
1/2	cup minced parsley
1/4	cup lemon juice
1	teaspoon salt
	freshly ground black pepper

Combine all ingredients. Mix well. Pour into greased loaf pan or fancy mold. Bake in moderate oven (375° F) for 40 minutes.

Serves 6

SHRIMP CURRY:
WHITE HOUSE

3	pounds shrimp
3	coconuts
1/4	cup finely chopped onion
3/4	cup flour
2	tablespoons curry powder
2	tablespoons finely chopped ginger root or
	1 teaspoon ground ginger
2	cups milk
3/4	cup butter
3	tablespoons lemon juice
1	tablespoon salt

Before chopping whole ginger root, soak it in cold water to cover for 1 hour. Drain the ginger root and squeeze out all of the water. Shell and wash shrimp. Pierce eyes of 3 coconuts; drain coconut liquid. If yield is less than 3 cups, add enough water to make 3 cups. Crack coconuts and grate meat. Heat coconut liquid and pour over grated coconut. Let stand for 20 minutes and drain, saving coconut milk. (Keep grated coconut to serve with curry).

Sauté onion in butter in large saucepan for 5 minutes. Stir in flour and curry powder. Add coconut milk and fresh milk and cook over low heat until thickened, stirring constantly. Add shrimp, ginger, lemon juice, and salt. Simmer uncovered for 30 minutes, stirring frequently.

If you cannot get fresh coconut, combine 3 cups shredded coconut with 3 cups fresh milk in a saucepan and let stand at room temperature for 20 minutes. Bring to a boil, reduce heat and simmer for 10 minutes. Strain milk and substitute it for fresh coconut milk. Discard the coconut.

Serves 6

Author's note: Any lean fish or shellfish cut in small pieces can be substituted for shrimp. Hard-cooked eggs can be used instead of seafood—in this case, sauce should be prepared separately and quartered hard-cooked eggs added 10 to 15 minutes before serving.

MRS. JOHN F. KENNEDY'S
BAKED SEAFOOD CASSEROLE

1	pound lump crab meat
1	pound shrimp, cooked, shelled and deveined
1	cup mayonnaise
1/2	cup chopped green pepper
1/4	cup finely chopped onion
1-1/2	cups finely chopped celery
1/2	teaspoon salt
1	tablespoon Worcestershire sauce
2	cups coarsely crushed potato chips
	paprika

Heat oven to 400° F. Combine crab meat, shrimp, mayonnaise, green pepper, onion, celery, salt, and Worcestershire. Pour into a buttered 2-1/2 quart casserole. Top with crushed potato chips. Sprinkle with paprika. Bake 20 to 25 minutes, until mixture is thoroughly heated.

Makes about 8 servings

FROG LEGS PROVENCALE: WHITE HOUSE
(SAUCE OF GARLIC, OIL, AND ONION)

3 pounds frog legs
1 cup butter
3 tomatoes, peeled and chopped
1 cup sliced mushrooms
1/4 cup chopped parsley
2 cloves garlic, minced
1 cup heavy cream
1 cup flour
1 cup olive oil

Make tomato sauce: melt butter in skillet, add tomatoes, mushrooms, parsley and garlic and simmer for 10 minutes. Dip frog legs in cream, then flour. Sauté in oil in another skillet for 10 minutes or until brown. Serve with sauce.

Serves 6

Author's note: Be sure sauce Provencal is spooned on bottom of plate with frogs legs arranged on top. Lightly sprinkle some finely chopped parsley over dish for presentation.

ROAST DUCK IN ASPIC

2	5 pound oven-ready ducks
2	oranges, quartered
2	onions, quartered
8	whole cloves
2	envelopes unflavored gelatin
	orange slices
1/2	cup Cointreau
3	cans condensed consommé
1	teaspoon salt
	freshly ground black pepper
	watercress

Stuff ducks with orange quarters and onions studded with cloves. Place ducks on a rack in a shallow baking pan and roast in a slow oven (325° F) for 2 1/2 hours or until done. Cool ducks and discard stuffing. Cut ducks into serving pieces with poultry shears and arrange pieces in a shallow dish. Soften gelatin in Cointreau. Bring 1 can of consommé to a boil, pour into gelatin and Cointreau mixture, and stir until gelatin is dissolved. Stir in the remaining 2 cans of cold consommé, salt, and pepper and pour this mixture over duck. Chill in the refrigerator for at least 2 hours or until the aspic is set. Serve garnished with watercress and orange slices.

Serves 6

SALMIS OF PHEASANT

2	pheasants
1 1/3	cups beef bouillon
1	onion, quartered
1	carrot, cut up
1	cup chopped celery
1	cup mushroom caps
2	tablespoons chopped parsley
1	teaspoon salt
	freshly ground black pepper

Roast pheasants in a moderate oven (375° F) for 1 hour or until done. Slice breasts, cover them and keep hot over boiling water. Remove legs. Combine legs and carcasses with bouillon, onion, carrot, celery, salt and pepper. Bring to a boil, reduce heat, cover, and simmer for 15 minutes. Remove legs from stock, slice off meat, and keep it hot with breast slices. Strain stock, add mushroom caps and parsley, and simmer 15 minutes. Serve sliced pheasant meat with sauce.

Serves 6

BREASTS OF PHEASANT

     2 pheasants
1-1/2 cups beef or chicken bouillon
     1 onion, quartered
     1 carrot, cut up
     1 cup chopped celery
     1 cup mushroom caps
     2 tablespoons chopped parsley
     1 teaspoon salt
       freshly ground black pepper

Roast pheasants in a moderate oven (375° F) for one hour or until done. Slice breasts, cover them and keep hot over boiling water. Remove legs. Combine legs and carcasses with bouillon, onion, carrot, celery, salt and pepper. Bring to a boil, reduce heat, cover and simmer for 15 minutes. Remove legs from stock, slice off meat and keep it hot with breast slices. Strain stock, add mushroom caps and parsley, and simmer for 15 minutes. Serve sliced pheasant meat with sauce.

Serves 6

CHICKEN CASSEROLE BORDEAUX

3 pounds chicken breasts
1 pound white seedless grapes
2 cups Cabernet Sauvignon
1 cup red currant jelly
2 cups gooseberry jam
1 tablespoon horseradish
1 teaspoon salt
freshly ground black pepper
lemon pancakes

Crush grapes in a deep saucepan. Arrange chicken breasts on crushed grapes and pour wine over them. Add salt and pepper. Bring to a boil, reduce heat, cover and simmer for 1 hour. Remove breasts and cut meat from bones. Cut into pieces and keep hot. Strain broth from grapes, keep grapes hot. Add jelly, jam, and horse-radish to broth. Boil for 15 minutes. Arrange chicken in casserole surrounded with grapes. Pour sauce over. Serve with lemon pancakes.

Serves 6

CHICKEN KIEV: WHITE HOUSE

	breasts of three 3-pound chickens
9	tablespoons chilled sweet butter
1	cup flour
2	eggs, beaten
1/2	cup milk
3	cups sifted fresh bread crumbs
	vegetable shortening

Bone chicken breasts, leaving a joint of wing attached. Flatten the breasts with a cleaver, then stuff each one with 3 tablespoons of chilled butter. Carefully seal the edges with toothpicks. Dip the stuffed breasts in flour, then into egg beaten with milk, and roll them in bread crumbs. Then re-dip the breasts in flour, in egg and milk mixture, and bread crumbs. Fry in 3 inches hot vegetable shortening (375° F) for 8 to 10 minutes or until golden brown. Remove toothpicks; serve immediately.

Serves 6

CHICKEN IN WHITE WINE

3	3-pound chickens, cut up
1/2	cup plus 2 tablespoons dry white wine
4	tablespoons olive oil
1/4	pound mushrooms, sliced
1	cup sour cream
1/4	teaspoon Tabasco® sauce
2	teaspoons Ac'cent® (optional)
1-1/2	teaspoons salt
	freshly ground black pepper

Season chicken with Ac'cent®, 1 teaspoon salt and pepper. Sauté in olive oil for 10 minutes or until golden brown. Add 1/2 cup wine, cover and simmer for 30 minutes. Remove chicken and keep hot. Add mushrooms and remaining 2 tablespoons of wine to sauce remaining in skillet and simmer for 5 minutes, stirring frequently. Remove from heat, stir in sour cream, Tabasco®, and 1/2 teaspoon salt. Return to heat and simmer gently for 2 minutes or until thoroughly blended, stirring constantly. To serve, pour sauce over chicken.

Serves 6

POULET A L'ESTRAGON

1	3-pound chicken
2	tablespoons flour
	salt and pepper
	clarified butter for sautéing
3 or 4	shallots
1/2	cup dry white wine, preferably Chardonnay
1/2	cup chicken stock, reduced
1	bay leaf
1	pinch thyme
2	stems parsley
1	small bunch fresh tarragon

Cut chicken into 8 or 10 pieces, or leave whole if you wish. Combine flour, salt, and pepper. Coat the chicken with the flour mixture. Brown all sides in hot, clarified butter. Cut shallots very fine and spread over chicken. Simmer for a few minutes. Add wine, stock, and bouquet of herbs, using the stem only of the tarragon, saving the leaves. Cover and simmer cut up chicken for 25 minutes or until tender. Simmer the whole chicken for 45 minutes, turning frequently. When chicken is tender, remove and keep hot.

Sauce

1	cup light cream
1/4	cup grated Parmesan cheese

To the pan juices from the chicken, add the cream and cheese and any flour not used in coating the chicken. Simmer gently until sauce thickens. Strain the sauce over the chicken. Garnish with tarragon leaves, whole or chopped, preferably chopped.

TURKEY FILLETS: WHITE HOUSE

    6   fillets of turkey breast
        unbaked puff pastry
  1/2   cup butter
        white truffles, sliced
    6   thin slices Emmentaler cheese
        salt

Roll the puff pastry 1/8-inch thick and cut into 12 pieces large enough to fit turkey fillets. Bake. Meanwhile, flatten turkey fillets with a cleaver and season them with salt. Sauté fillets in butter over very low heat for 10 minutes. Do not brown the fillets. Set 1 fillet on a piece of baked puff pastry, top each fillet with truffles and 1 slice of cheese and cover with another piece of puff pastry. Arrange on baking sheets and bake in a moderate oven (375° F) for 10 minutes.

Serves 6

CURRIED LAMB: WHITE HOUSE

3	pounds lamb shoulder or neck
1/4	cup flour
2	cloves garlic, minced
4	large onions, sliced
3/4	cup butter
4	small apples, pared and chopped
4	tablespoons curry powder
4	tablespoons raisins
2	tablespoons Worcestershire sauce
2	lemons, sliced
4	tablespoons shredded coconut
3/4	cup chopped walnuts
1/2	teaspoon grated lime peel
1	tablespoon salt

Cut meat into 2-inch cubes. Roll in flour. Sauté garlic and onions in butter in large skillet for 5 minutes or until lightly browned. Add meat and sauté for 10 minutes, stirring occasionally. Add apples and curry powder. Simmer for 5 minutes, stirring occasionally. Add the remaining ingredients and 2 cups of water. Bring to a boil, reduce heat, cover and simmer for 1 hour.

Serves 6

Author's note: Beef, veal, or pork can be used instead of lamb. Fresh or leftover peas, string or wax beans, carrot slices, mushrooms, or quarters of green pepper may be added during the last 10 minutes of cooking.

VEAL CHASSEUR

2	pounds veal cutlet, sliced 1/4-inch thick
1/4	cup butter
2	shallots, minced, or 2 tablespoons onion
1	small clove garlic, minced
1	pound mushrooms, sliced
1/2	cup dry white wine
2	tablespoons chopped parsley
1	teaspoon salt
	freshly ground black pepper
	brown sauce

Trim fat from veal and cut the meat into 1-inch pieces. Sauté veal in butter for 10 minutes or until golden brown. Remove from skillet and keep hot. Sauté shallots and mushrooms in butter remaining in skillet for 5 minutes. Add wine and simmer for 15 minutes or until the liquid is reduced by one half. Stir in brown sauce, parsley, salt, and pepper. Add meat and simmer for 5 minutes.

Serves 6

MRS. JOHN F. KENNEDY'S
FILET DE BOEUF WITH SAUTEED VEGETABLES

    4   medium-size potatoes
    4   tablespoons butter or margarine
  1/2   pound mushrooms, sliced
    2   teaspoons salt
  1/4   teaspoon pepper
    4   tablespoons sherry
    4   6 ounce beef fillets

Peel potatoes and cut into balls with a melon ball cutter. Melt butter in a large skillet over moderate heat. Add potato balls; cook and stir about 10 minutes, until lightly browned. Add mushrooms and cook over low heat 5 minutes. Add salt, pepper, and sherry. Keep hot over very low heat. Place filets on broiler rack in preheated broiler 3 inches from heat. Broil 4 to 5 minutes on each side for rare; 6 to 7 minutes on each side for medium well done. Serve filets with the sautéed potatoes and mushrooms.

Serves 4

BEEF BOURGUIGNON: WHITE HOUSE

    3   pounds beef sirloin, cut in 1-inch cubes
    2   cups red Burgundy wine
  1/2   cup butter
    2   cups quartered mushroom caps
  1/4   cup chopped shallots
    1   tablespoon flour

Melt 6 tablespoons butter in a deep casserole. Add beef cubes, cover and braise in a hot oven (400° F) for 20 minutes. Meanwhile, sauté mushroom caps and shallots in remaining 2 tablespoons butter. Stir in flour. Add Burgundy and mix well. Pour over beef, cover and return to oven for 30 minutes.

Serves 6

Author's note: There is nothing wrong with adding finely chopped garlic and a bit of rosemary.

BEEF STROGANOFF

2	pounds sirloin of beef
2 1/2	tablespoons flour
2	tablespoons butter
2	cups beef stock, reduced
1/2	cup sour cream
2	tablespoons tomato juice or paste (preferably paste)
3	tablespoons grated onion
3	tablespoons butter for sautéing

Cut beef into thin strips. Sprinkle freely with salt and pepper and let stand covered for 2 hours in a cool place. Make a roux by blending flour with butter over gentle heat until the mixture bubbles and is smooth. Make sure that it is a light brown (caramel) color. Gradually stir in the beef stock and cook until mixture begins to thicken. Boil for 2 minutes and add the sour cream alternately with the tomato juice or the paste, stirring constantly. Simmer very gently without boiling for 1 minute. Brown the beef in 3 tablespoons butter with grated onion. When the meat is browned, pour the meat, onion, and butter into the sauce and taste for seasoning and simmer gently, or cook in double boiler over hot water for 20 minutes.

Author's note: I like to serve this dish over noodles with some very fine chopped parsley sprinkled on top. Also you may want to add a few mushrooms—JFK liked it that way.

MRS. JOHN F. KENNEDY'S
ENTRECOTE WITH WATERCRESS GARNISH

4	8-ounce entrecotes (rib steaks), cut 1 inch thick
	salt and pepper
1/4	cup butter or margarine
1/2	tablespoons chopped parsley
1	teaspoon lemon juice
	watercress

Cut a few bits of fat from meat and place in a heavy skillet over moderate heat until the fat melts. Add steaks; cook about 1-1/2 minutes on each side for a rare steak, about 2 minutes on each side for medium well done. Remove steaks to a heated platter. Season with salt and pepper. Add butter, parsley, and lemon juice to skillet and heat. Pour mixture over steaks. Garnish with watercress.

Serves 4

TOURNEDOS

6	tournedos of beef
2	shallots, finely chopped
2	tablespoons chopped tarragon
1-1/2	cups Madeira sauce
	freshly ground black pepper
3/4	cup butter
1/2	cup brandy
1	cup imported Madeira wine
3	large white truffles, thinly sliced
	salt

Tournedos are 2-inch thick slices of beef tenderloin trimmed of all fat. Sauté tournedos in 1/2 cup butter as desired—rare, medium, or well done. Add shallots and brown just a little, add brandy and flame it. Place tournedos on a platter and keep warm. To the sauce remaining in the skillet, add tarragon and 1/2 cup Madeira wine and cook until sauce is reduced to two-thirds of its original quantity. Add Madeira sauce and boil for 5 minutes. Season with salt and pepper. Remove from heat and blend in remaining 1/2 cup Madeira wine and 1/2 cup butter. Place the sliced truffles on the tournedos and pour the sauce over them.

Serves 6

MRS. JOHN F. KENNEDY'S
CASSEROLE MARIE - BLANCHE

1-1/2	pounds cooked drained noodles
1	cup cream-style cottage cheese
1	cup commercial sour cream
1/2	teaspoon salt
1/8	teaspoon pepper
1/3	cup chopped chives
1	tablespoon butter

Heat oven to 350° F. Combine noodles, cheese, sour cream, salt, pepper, and chives. Pour into a buttered 2-quart casserole and dot top with the 1 tablespoon butter. Bake about 30 minutes, until noodles begin to brown. Serve immediately.

Serves 6

MRS. JOHN F. KENNEDY'S
POMMES DE TERRE CHATOUILLARD

    4 medium-size baking potatoes
       vegetable oil
       salt

Peel potatoes and trim so that all surfaces are regular. Cut lengthwise into long, narrow, very even slices about 1/8-inch thick. Dry slices between pieces of paper toweling. Heat enough oil in a deep saucepan to fill pan half full. Heat oil to 350° F (use a deep-fat thermometer). Drop a handful of potato slices, one at a time, into the oil. Remove pan from heat and shake it to keep pieces moving constantly. When temperature reads 250° F, return pan to heat and shake it until slices begin to swell. Do not let the temperature of oil rise above 300° F Puffing will take about 8 minutes. Skim off potatoes and drain on a tray covered with paper toweling. Just before serving, heat the oil to 400° F. Drop the partially cooked slices into the hot oil. They will puff and rise to the surface. Turn constantly until browned. Drain. Sprinkle with salt. Serve hot.

Serves 4 to 6.

MRS. JOHN F. KENNEDY'S POTATOES SUZETTE

3	large baking potatoes
2	tablespoons butter
3	tablespoons heavy cream
1	egg yolk, well beaten
	salt and pepper to taste
1	tablespoon grated Parmesan cheese
1/8	teaspoon anchovy paste
1	tablespoon finely chopped chives

Heat oven to 400° F. Bake potatoes until fork-tender, about 1 hour. Cut in halves lengthwise, scoop out pulp without breaking shells. Mash pulp thoroughly. Add anchovy paste, chives, butter, cream, and egg yolk. Beat vigorously until light and fluffy. Season with salt and pepper. Spoon mixture into shells, sprinkle tops with cheese. Bake 15 minutes until tops are golden brown.

Serves 6

Author's note: Mix some Parmesan cheese with paprika and sprinkle over potatoes for a nice presentation. Add a dollop of butter and place under broiler until mixture turns reddish brown and crunchy for a nice presentation.

MRS. JOHN F. KENNEDY'S
MUSHROOMS WITH HERBS

1	pound mushrooms
1/2	cup olive oil
1	tablespoon onion, grated
1	tablespoon chives, chopped
1	tablespoon parsley, chopped
1	clove garlic, minced
3/4	teaspoon salt
3	tablespoons tarragon vinegar
3/4	teaspoon salt
	dash each: dried tarragon, dried thyme, and pepper

Wash and slice the mushrooms, combine with the remaining ingredients. Let stand 2 hours. Melt 4 tablespoons butter or margarine in a saucepan, add mushrooms and marinade. Simmer 10 minutes, stirring frequently.

Serves 4 to 6

Author's note: A fantastic side dish. Serve with steak or prime rib.

MRS. JOHN F. KENNEDY'S
GRILLED TOMATOES

3 large tomatoes
3 tablespoons fine dry bread crumbs
1 tablespoon grated Parmesan cheese

Cut 3 large tomatoes into halves crosswise. Arrange on a flat pan. Sprinkle top surfaces with a mixture of 3 tablespoons fine dry bread crumbs and 1 tablespoon grated Parmesan cheese. Dot with a little butter or margarine. Place in a preheated broiler about 4 inches from heat and broil until crumbs are browned. Sprinkle the edges with chopped parsley.

Serves 6

Author's note: Substitute bread crumbs with Italian seasoned bread crumbs for a nice touch.

MRS. JOHN F. KENNEDY'S
ASPARAGUS VINAIGRETTE

3	tablespoons	vegetable oil
4	tablespoons	parsley, chopped
2	tablespoons	chives, chopped
3	tablespoons	vinegar
1	teaspoon	salt
1/8	teaspoon	pepper
1-1/2	pounds	cooked and cooled fresh or frozen asparagus

Combine the first six ingredients. Beat with a rotary beater until well blended. Serve over asparagus.

Serves 6

Author's note: For a different flavor try adding balsamic vinegar in place of regular vinegar or a tablespoon of French Dijon mustard or 2 tablespoons finely chopped onion. Can't be beat for spring and summer.

ASPARAGUS PARMESAN: WHITE HOUSE

3	pounds asparagus
1	tablespoon grated Parmesan cheese
1/2	cup flour
1	egg
2	tablespoons dry white wine
1	cup dry bread crumbs
1/4	teaspoon garlic powder
1/2	cup olive oil
1	teaspoon salt
	freshly ground black pepper

Break off tough ends of asparagus stalks. Dip stalks first in flour, then in beaten egg mixed with wine, and then into crumbs combined with cheese, garlic powder, salt, and pepper. Sauté in olive oil for 10 minutes or until tender.

Serves 6

BOSTON BAKED BEANS

  2 cups dried navy beans
1/2 pound salt pork, halved
1/2 cup dark molasses
  2 teaspoons grated onion
1/2 teaspoon dry mustard

Soak beans overnight in water to cover. Bring to a boil in the same water, reduce heat, cover, and simmer for 1 hour. Drain, save water. Put half of pork in 6-cup bean pot. Add beans, molasses, onion, mustard, and 1/2 cup bean water. Put other pork half on top. Cover and bake in a slow oven (300° F) for 5 hours, adding bean water if needed. Uncover, bake for 1 hour.

Serves 6

Author's note: Try adding 3 tablespoons of chili sauce and 3 tablespoons of catsup or barbecue sauce. I also like to cover my beans with brown sugar.

MRS. JOHN F. KENNEDY'S
SALAD MIMOSA

  1/4 cup olive oil
    1 tablespoon wine vinegar
  1/2 teaspoon salt
       dash of pepper
  1/3 clove garlic, finely minced
    2 quarts crisp salad greens
    2 hard-cooked eggs, finely chopped

Combine oil, vinegar, salt, pepper and garlic in a jar with tight lid. Shake vigorously. Arrange greens in salad bowl, add dressing, and toss thoroughly. Sprinkle with chopped egg.

Serves 6

AVOCADO FRUIT SALAD

3 avocados
1 cup watermelon balls
1 cup honeydew melon balls
3 bananas, scored and sliced
1 grapefruit, sectioned
1 mango, cubed
1 cup fresh pineapple cubes
  mixed greens
  cherries
  salad dressing

Peel the avocados and cut them in half lengthwise. Slice the halves lengthwise into narrow wedges, then put the wedges back together to form avocado cups. Fill a salad bowl with mixed greens and arrange the avocado cups in a ring around the edge of the bowl. Fill each cup with one kind of cut fruit and arrange the remaining cut fruit in the center of the bowl. Garnish the salad with whole cherries. When the salad is tossed, the avocado cups will fall apart. Serve with hot spice, classic French, or sour cream dressing.

Serves 6

Author's note: Here's a great but simple sauce for dipping the fruit. Serve in individual ramekins:

2 cups whipped cream
1 cup Hellmann's mayonnaise
1 cup maraschino cherries

Blend well and chill before serving.

OPPOSITE: WHITE HOUSE CHINA PATTERN COLLECTION–
USED DURING THE GEORGE WASHINGTON ADMINISTRATION, 1789-1797

MRS. JOHN F. KENNEDY'S
HOT CHEESE CORN BREAD

           1   cup yellow cornmeal
           1   cup sifted all-purpose flour
        1/4   cup sugar
        1/2   teaspoon salt
           4   teaspoons baking powder
    1-1/2   cups shredded sharp American cheese
           1   egg
           1   cup milk
        1/4   cup soft shortening

Heat oven to 375° F. Sift together cornmeal, flour, sugar, salt and baking powder. Add cheese, egg, milk, and shortening. Beat with a rotary beater until smooth, about 1 minute. Do not overbeat. Pour into a greased 8-inch square pan. Bake 30 minutes. Cut into squares. Serve hot.

Serves 6

MRS. JOHN F. KENNEDY'S
HOT FRUIT DESSERT

   1 orange
   1 lemon
  1/2 cup light brown sugar, packed
  1/4 teaspoon ground nutmeg
   1 8-ounce can apricots
   1 8 3/4-ounce can pineapple tidbits
   1 8 3/4-ounce can sliced peaches
   1 17-ounce can pitted bing cherries
      commercial sour cream

Grate the rind from the orange and lemon; add to brown sugar with nutmeg. Cut orange and lemon into very thin slices. Drain and combine fruits. Butter a 1-quart casserole and arrange fruits in layers, sprinkling each layer with some of the brown sugar mixture. Bake 30 minutes at 350° F. Serve warm with a spoonful of sour cream on top.

Serves 6 to 8

Author's note: It's always best to use fresh fruit when in season.

MRS. JOHN F. KENNEDY'S
CRÈME BRÛLÉE

          3 cups heavy cream
          6 egg yolks
          6 tablespoons granulated sugar
        1/4 teaspoon vanilla extract
        1/2 cup light brown sugar, packed

Heat cream in top of double boiler over boiling water. In a bowl, beat egg yolks well. Gradually add granulated sugar and continue to beat until light and creamy. Slowly stir in hot cream. Place mixture in top of double boiler over gently simmering water. Cook, stirring constantly, until mixture heavily coats a silver spoon. Add vanilla. Pour into a heat-proof 2-quart casserole. Chill several hours. Just before serving, sprinkle top evenly with brown sugar. Place in preheated broiler 3 inches from heat. Broil 1 to 2 minutes. Watch carefully; sugar will burn easily. Serve at once.

Serves 6

MRS. JOHN F. KENNEDY'S
LEMON ICE

     4   cups water
 3 1/2   cups sugar
     1   cup fresh or frozen lemon juice
     1   tablespoon grated lemon rind

Combine water and sugar in a saucepan; bring to a boil and boil 5 minutes. Cool. Add lemon juice and rind. Pour into 2 refrigerator trays. Place trays in freezer. When mixture is frozen to a mush, remove to a cold bowl and quickly beat with a rotary beater until smooth. Return to trays and freeze again. Remove mixture to cold bowl and quickly beat until smooth. Return to trays and freeze until firm, about 2 hours.

Serves 6

MRS. JOHN F. KENNEDY'S
SOUFFLÉ FROID AU CHOCOLAT

- 2 1-ounce squares unsweetened chocolate, melted
- 1/2 cup confectioners' sugar
- 1 cup milk, heated
- 1 envelope unflavored gelatin, softened in 3 tablespoons cold water
- 3/4 cup granulated sugar
- 1 teaspoon vanilla extract
- 1/4 teaspoon salt
- 2 cups heavy cream, whipped

Combine chocolate and confectioners' sugar in a saucepan. Gradually add hot milk, stirring constantly. Place over low heat and stir until mixture reaches the boiling point. Do not boil. Remove from heat. Stir in softened gelatin, sugar, vanilla, and salt. Chill until slightly thickened. Beat with a rotary beater until light and fluffy. Fold in whipped cream. Pour into a 2-quart serving dish. Chill 2 to 3 hours.

Serves 6 to 8

MRS. JOHN F. KENNEDY'S
BABA AUX FRAISES

      1   package active dry yeast
    1/2   cup lukewarm water
      2   cups sifted all-purpose flour
    1/2   cup sugar
    1/2   cup soft butter or margarine
    1/2   teaspoon salt
      3   eggs, well beaten
      1   cup sugar
      1   cup water
    1/4   cup rum
      1   quart strawberries
    1/3   cup sugar
      3   tablespoons currants

Sprinkle yeast over water, stir until dissolved. Add 1/2 cup of the flour and 1 tablespoon of the sugar. Beat until smooth. Cover and let rise in warm place about 45 minutes until double in volume. Put butter in large bowl. Add rest of the 1/2 cup sugar gradually. Beat until fluffy. Add salt and eggs, rest of flour, currants, and yeast mixture and beat 5 minutes. Pour mixture into a well-greased 3-quart ring mold. Cover, let rise in warm place about 1 hour, until double in size.

Heat oven to 350° F. Bake 40 minutes. Cool 5 minutes. Invert cake on serving plate. Combine 1 cup sugar and water in a saucepan.

Boil 5 minutes over moderate heat. Cool and stir in rum. Spoon sauce over cooled cake. Slice the berries, reserving a few whole berries for garnish. Add 1/3 cup sugar. Place strawberries in center of cake and garnish with whole berries.

Serves 8

MRS. JOHN F. KENNEDY'S
HAZELNUT COOKIES

1   pound confectioners' sugar, sifted
8   egg whites, stiffly beaten
1   pound hazelnuts, finely ground
2   teaspoons ground cinnamon
    juice and rind of 1 lemon

Heat oven to 350° F. Gradually fold sugar into egg whites. Fold in nuts, cinnamon, lemon juice, and rind. Drop from a teaspoon onto greased and floured cookie sheets. Bake 10 minutes. Remove from pans immediately with a wide spatula.

Makes about 7 dozen

CHOCOLATE SOUFFLÉ: WHITE HOUSE

2 ounces sweet chocolate, cut into small pieces
1-1/2 cups milk
6 tablespoons sugar
6 egg yolks
6 tablespoons flour
2 tablespoons cornstarch
9 egg whites, stiffly beaten
butter
vanilla sauce
additional sugar for the soufflé dish

Bring chocolate, milk, and 6 tablespoons sugar to a boil, stirring constantly. Mix the egg yolks, flour, and cornstarch in a bowl. Add the boiling milk mixture gradually, stirring briskly. Return to the heat and bring to a boil, stirring constantly. Remove from heat and cool. Fold in the egg whites, then pour into a buttered and sugared soufflé dish. Bake in a hot oven (400° F) for 25 minutes. Serve with vanilla sauce (see page 232).

Serves 6

SOUFFLÉ FROID AU CHOCOLAT

    1 envelope unflavored gelatin, softened
    3 tablespoons cold water
    2 squares unsweetened chocolate
    1 cup milk
  1/2 cup confectioners' sugar
  3/1 cup granulated sugar
    1 teaspoon vanilla extract
  1/4 teaspoon salt
    2 cups heavy cream

Melt chocolate squares over hot (but not boiling) water, preferably in a double boiler. Heat milk just enough so that a foam shows on the surface then stir into the melted chocolate, very slowly. Add the confectioners' sugar, beat with a French whip until smooth. Cook, stirring constantly, over low, direct heat until mixture simmers. Remove from heat and mix into the softened gelatin, the granulated sugar, the vanilla extract, and the salt. Put this concoction in the refrigerator until slightly thick. Then beat the mixture until it is light and airy looking. In a separate bowl, beat the heavy cream until it holds a shape. Then combine the two mixtures by folding. Pour the soufflé into a 2-quart soufflé dish or a serving bowl.

Chill 2 or 3 hours in refrigerator until ready to serve.

Soufflé can be garnished with shaved semisweet chocolate, whipped cream, and chocolate cornucopias and chocolate discs. To make the chocolate decorations, spread melted semisweet chocolate on waxed paper and then place on a cookie sheet. Chill until firm, but not solid. Cut out discs with round cookie cutters. To make the cornucopias, cut 2-inch squares of chocolate and allow chocolate to stand at room temperature to soften slightly. Then roll into cornucopia shapes. Then chill them and fill with whipped cream.

Lyndon Baines Johnson
Claudia Alta Taylor "Lady Bird" Johnson

"For we are a nation of believers. Underneath the clamor of building and the rush of our day's pursuits, we are believers in justice and liberty and union, and in our own Union. We believe that every man must someday be free. And we believe in ourselves.

Our enemies have always made the same mistake. In my lifetime—in depression and in war—they have awaited our defeat. Each time, from the secret places of the American heart, came forth the faith they could not see or that they could not even imagine. It brought us victory. And it will again.

For this is what America is all about. It is the uncrossed desert and the unclimbed ridge. It is the star that is not reached and the harvest sleeping in the unplowed ground. Is our world gone? "

LYNDON BAINES JOHNSON INAUGURAL ADDRESS, WEDNESDAY, JANUARY 20, 1965

LBJ BY SHOUMATOFF © WHHA (WHITE HOUSE COLLECTION)

By all accounts, Lyndon Baines Johnson was a complex, fiercely competitive man. Lady Bird always said, "Lyndon was in such a hurry, he relished being at the pinnacle of power—a master manipulator who practiced his political instincts to achieve what he wanted." Lyndon Johnson, the consummate politician, learned his profession from none other than a fellow Texan, Speaker of the House Sam Rayburn. LBJ could be the great benefactor or he could be one of the most ruthless and deceptive individuals ever to take over the watch at the White House.

President Johnson got more legislation passed through Congress in one year than any other president. I remember he kept a large Rolodex in his private study. It contained the names of all the congressmen, senators, their wives, their children, their anniversaries, their birthdays, and any other pertinent information, especially whether he ever did a favor for them. On the appropriate date, LBJ would make a personal phone call, usually to the wife, to wish her a happy birthday or happy anniversary. Then a day or two later, another personal phone call to the husband at his office asking for support for whatever legislation he was trying to get passed. This was politics in its finest form. Most of the time the president got what he wanted.

The First Lady, Lady Bird Johnson, has always regretted that the public did not get to see the family side of her husband. A strong husband and a doting father to his two daughters, Linda Bird and Lucy Baines. Few would believe LBJ was such a family man, as he preferred to keep his family life private.

LBJ was a man who could get things done and was willing to do whatever it took. In his private study, called "no man's land" by his staff, there was a sign on a table. It read, "WYHTBTBTHAMWF"—When you have them by the balls, their hearts and minds will follow. He claimed this as his motto, and anyone who didn't know what it meant was told in no uncertain words. Believe me, I was on the receiving end of that lesson!

President Johnson's sense of humor was certainly one of the more earthy of any American president. When asked about getting rid of FBI Director J. Edgar Hoover, he decided it would be too difficult to bring off. "Well," he said philosophically, "it's probably better to have him inside the tent pissing out than outside the tent pissing in."

While selecting a running mate in 1964, and before he actually settled on Hubert Humphrey, his brother was inquiring about different people and asked about Gene McCarthy. The president said, "There's something sorta stuck up about Gene. You get the impression that he's got a special pipeline to God and that they only talk Latin to each other."

Once when LBJ was approached by a railroad executive who said, "I'm just a country boy…," Johnson interrupted, "Hold on there, wait a minute. When anybody approaches me that way, I know I'm going to lose my wallet."

An American diplomat once met then-Vice President Johnson at the Rome airport and, while on their way into the city, instructed him as if he were an ignoramus and backwoodsman on how to behave when he met the local dignitaries. Johnson listened patiently, and when they arrived at the hotel, the diplomat said, "Mr. Vice President, is there anything else I can do for you?" "Yes," said Lyndon Johnson sharply, "Just one more thing—button up your shirt!"

Lyndon Johnson was very aggressive and wanted to get things done. One night, while working late and keeping his staff late when Johnson was majority leader, one staff member said to the other, "What's the hurry? After all, Rome wasn't built in a day." "No," sighed one of the other staff members, "but Lyndon Johnson wasn't foreman on the job."

Johnson didn't care much for President Charles DeGaulle of France. When Vice President Johnson was in Paris and he met then-General Charles DeGaulle for the first time, the latter looked imperiously at Johnson and said loftily, "Now, Mr. Johnson, what have you come to learn from us?" Johnson beamed and replied, "Why, General, simply everything you can ever possibly teach me!"

In 1963, the cruel tragedy of President Kennedy's murder catapulted history's most qualified man into the presidency. The new President had more political experience than anyone, except when it came to following in the footsteps of one of the most glamorous administrations in the history of the executive mansion. The new First Lady was also one of the best qualified persons ever to step into that very difficult role. She had twenty-seven years of experience on the national scene, and a great personal knowledge of government and the protocols for entertaining in the White House.

During President Kennedy's funeral, Mrs. Johnson's expertise was invaluable. Just about every head of state of the free world, or their representatives, converged on Washington, D.C. The funeral procession was attended by the likes of Charles DeGaulle of France, Emperor Haile Selassie of Ethiopia, Prince Phillip of Great Britain, Queen Frederica and Princess Irene of Greece, Ludwig Eberhard of West Germany, and Prime Minister Lester Pearson of Canada, a few of the 109 dignitaries present. All of these people could have stayed at their individual embassies or missions or, if necessary, at Blair House (the official U.S. guest house). But all of them had to be officially received and, for the most part, fed by the White House.

The White House staff did a remarkable job. The chief usher, all the protocol officers, the chefs, the cooks, and everyone concerned made sure America, the deceased President, his family, and the new President were not embarrassed in any way.

The first state dinner hosted by the Johnsons was for President and Mrs. Antonio Segni of Italy. One hundred and forty people, politicians and diplomats, attended the black-tie affair. This was the first black-tie state dinner ever served. The dress prior to this was always white tie for official state functions, but LBJ detested wearing a white tie and tails. After the welcoming ceremony at the north portico of the White House, the Segnis were invited to the presidential quarters on the second floor. There, an exchange of gifts was made as a symbol of friendship between the two nations. After the exchange, the president and First Lady and the guests of honor assembled at the head of the grand staircase for the ceremonial entrance down the red-carpeted steps with the marine band playing "Hail to the Chief." The receiving line began just inside the door of the East Room.

The dinner menu—selected by Mrs. Johnson from suggestions by White House Chef Rene Verdon—featured Maryland crab meat, fillet of beef, waffled potatoes, string beans almandine, endive and watercress salad, cheese and coffee mousse. Spring flowers were set in green and gold china from the Truman collection and the blue and gold dinner china from FDR's administration. Coffee was served in the red and green rooms after the guests assembled and afterward the guests went back to the East Room, which had been set up for a concert featuring The New Christy Minstrels and Italian opera sung by American performers.

This state dinner became the prototype for many to follow. World leaders made their way to Washington, one right after the other, to reassure themselves of the new President. Indeed, Kennedy was a hard act to follow, but LBJ carried it off perfectly.

The President's personal taste in food did not require the fine talents of Chef Rene Verdon. Zephyr Wright, who had been cook to the Johnson family for many years, was installed in the family's private kitchen. There she prepared all of LBJ's meals. She cooked to please the president, and she tried to keep him on the low-calorie diet that was standard fare for family dinners.

Rene Verdon was in charge of all special occasions, and assisted by four other chefs with finely honed skills. Henry Haller took over as White House chef after Verdon complained to the press about the type of food the President preferred. Verdon was personally dismissed by LBJ.

Probably the most exciting social function at the White House of any administration is a wedding. In President and Mrs. Johnson's case, they hosted two of them.

The first wedding was Lucy's, on August 6, 1966 to Patrick Nugent. The bride and her new husband, along with both sets of parents, greeted guests in the

Blue Room. There were three buffet tables offering a feast of hot and cold dishes including steamship rounds, casserole of sliced chicken, shrimp and lump crab in Creole sauce, and sweetbreads and mushrooms in a heavy cream brandy sauce. The cold dishes included supreme of turkey, duck breast a l'orange, glazed northwest salmon and lobster En Bellevue. The seven-layer wedding cake was a summer fruit cake, a favorite of Lucy's.

When Linda was married to Charles Robb on December 9, 1967, it was the first wedding in the White House since Woodrow Wilson's daughter, Eleanor, married William McAdoo in 1914. A private ceremony for Linda and Charles was held in the East Room. As with Lucy's reception, Linda Bird's reception featured an elaborate buffet with lobster barquettes, crab meat bouchees, stuffed mushrooms, mini-lamb kabobs, and quiche Lorraine. The chilled platters included smoked salmon with capers, chicken liver pâté en mould, iced shrimp, assorted cheeses, and finger sandwiches. The wedding cake this time was an old-fashioned, five-layer pound cake, iced in white fondant and decorated with handmade sugar scrolls, loops and braids, pulled sugar roses, white lovebirds, and topped with a sugar basket filled with real white roses.

Both Lucy and Linda Bird entertained their wedding parties at the White House and each gave their guests mementos of the occasion. The menus may have varied for each occasion, but both brides-to-be chose the same dessert, Flower Pot Sundaes. These are made by using small ceramic flowerpots of green, white, and pink. Place a piece of yellow cake, split and spread with apricot jam, on the bottom of each. Fill with vanilla ice cream (or any flavor you wish; I prefer homemade apricot ice cream) to within a 1/2 inch of the rim.

Place another piece of cake, spread with the jam, on the top. Cut a paper straw, 3 inches long, and insert it in the pot so that two inches extends above the pot. Swirl very stiff meringue on top of the pot until it reaches the top of the straw. At the last minute, place in a very hot oven and brown the meringue. Just before serving, insert an appropriate flower in the straw to complete the presentation. Lucy used a sweetheart rose; while Linda Bird used a sprig of holly and a red rose.

The American people meant everything to President and Mrs. Johnson. They tried very hard to overcome difficult obstacles and opened the gates of the White House to the public, inviting them to share the President's home and walk through the gardens. Thousands of people from all walks of life toured the White House during LBJ's administration, and it has been said that his administration was the most open and friendly in the history of the mansion.

The Inaugural Committee

requests the honor of your presence

to attend and participate in the Inauguration of

Lyndon Baines Johnson

as President of the United States of America

and

Hubert Horatio Humphrey

as Vice President of the United States of America

on Wednesday the twentieth of January

one thousand nine hundred and sixty-five

in the City of Washington

Dale Miller

Chairman

CRAWFISH BISQUE: WHITE HOUSE

20	pounds fresh crawfish
1	cup chopped celery
1/2	cup chopped parsley
2	cups chopped onion
1/2	cup butter
8	stale buns, soaked in water
4	slices stale bread, crumbled
6	eggs, beaten
1/2	cup chopped scallion tops
	cayenne pepper
1	tablespoon salt
	freshly ground black pepper
1	cup hot cooked rice

Bring 2 quarts water to a boil, add crawfish, and 2 teaspoons salt. Reduce heat and simmer for 15 minutes. Drain and save stock. Pull out middle tail fin and with it the intestinal vein of each crawfish. Pick fat and meat from tails and heads and save it. Keep head shells for stuffing. Return tail shells to stock, and add 1/2 cup celery and 1/4 cup parsley. Bring to a boil, reduce heat, and simmer for 30 minutes. Strain. Chop crawfish meat and add half of it to this bisque. Remove from heat and cover to keep hot. Meanwhile sauté onion and remaining 1/2 cup celery and crawfish fat and butter in a heavy pot for 10 minutes. Combine drained soaked buns, crumbled bread, and eggs and stir into onion mixture. Add remaining chopped crawfish meat, remaining 1/4 cup parsley, scallion tops, remaining 1 teaspoon salt, a few grains of cayenne pepper, and black pepper. Cook over low heat for 10 minutes, stirring constantly. Stuff crawfish heads with this mixture. To serve, put 5 stuffed crawfish heads and a few spoonfuls of rice in each soup bowl. Pour bisque over each serving.

Serves 8

Author's note: A little secret—boil rice in fish broth or even chicken broth in place of water.

ZUPPA DI PESCE: WHITE HOUSE

3	pounds mixed haddock, trout, cod, salmon, red snapper, cut up
1	1-pound lobster, cut up
1/2	pound prawns or shrimp
1/2	pound squid, cut up
1	onion, cut up
1	stalk celery with leaves
2	tablespoons vinegar
1/2	cup olive oil
2	cloves garlic, minced
1	bay leaf
1/2	teaspoon thyme
1	teaspoon basil
2	tablespoons minced parsley
1/2	cup dry white wine
1-1/2	cups chopped peeled tomatoes
	whole saffron
1	tablespoon salt
	freshly ground black pepper
6	slices bread

Boil lobster and prawns for 5 minutes in 1 quart water with onion, celery, vinegar, and 2 teaspoons salt. Remove and shell lobster and prawns. Return shells to the broth with heads and tails of fish and simmer for 20 minutes. Strain and put broth aside.

Meanwhile, cut the fish, squid, and lobster meat into bite-size chunks. Sauté with prawns in 1/4 cup oil with garlic, bay leaf, thyme, basil and parsley for 5 minutes, stirring constantly. Add fish broth, wine, tomatoes, a pinch of saffron, the remaining 1 teaspoon salt, and the pepper. Bring to a boil, reduce heat, cover, and simmer for 10 minutes, stirring occasionally. Serve with slices of bread fried in the remaining 1/4 cup olive oil.

Serves 6

WATERCRESS SOUP:
WHITE HOUSE

2	bunches watercress
2	thick slices onion
1	3-inch piece of celery, cut up
1	tablespoon cornstarch
1	tablespoon sugar
3	cups chicken bouillon
1	large can evaporated milk
2	tablespoons butter
1	teaspoon salt

Remove leaves from stems of watercress. Place leaves, onion, celery, cornstarch, sugar, salt, and 2 cups bouillon in blender and blend until smooth. Place in saucepan, add remaining 1 cup bouillon. Bring mixture to a boil, reduce heat and cook for 10 minutes, stirring constantly. Add evaporated milk and butter and simmer for 5 minutes.

Serves 6

Author's note: Usually saved for light lunches for the ladies.

CHICKEN SOUP: WHITE HOUSE

      2   cans condensed cream of chicken soup
      2   cups light cream
      1   tablespoon curry powder
    1/4   cup lemon juice
      1   teaspoon salt
          freshly ground black pepper
          chopped chives or parsley

Combine chicken soup and cream in a saucepan and stir until smooth and well blended. Mix curry powder with 1/4 cup water and add to soup mixture. Simmer over low heat for 10 minutes, stirring frequently. Remove from heat and stir in lemon juice, salt, and pepper. Cool for 30 minutes. Chill in the refrigerator for at least 1 hour. Serve the soup garnished with chopped chives or parsley.

Serves 6

CORN CHOWDER

12	ounces salt pork, diced
1	cup onion, chopped fine
1-1/4	gallons milk
1/3	cup flour
1-1/2	tablespoons salt
1/4	teaspoon pepper
1	quart cooked potatoes, diced
1-1/2	quart whole kernel corn, drained

Fry the finely diced salt pork until crisp. Add the chopped onion and cook until light brown. Remove the meat and onions from the fat. Use the fat, flour, and milk to make a thin white sauce. Combine this with the meat, onion, potatoes, corn, and seasonings.

Serves 25

Author's note: Goes great as a choice with barbecue beef, pork or chicken. Served often at the LBJ ranch.

CREOLE CRAB GUMBO

1	pound cooked crab meat
1	pound okra, cut up
1/2	cup sliced onion
4	tablespoons butter
4	tablespoons flour
5	cups canned tomatoes
1	cup diced green pepper
2	cloves garlic, crushed
1	teaspoon ground nutmeg
2	teaspoons salt
	freshly ground black pepper

Sauté onion in butter 10 minutes. Stir in flour and brown. Add crab meat and other ingredients plus 2 cups water. Bring to a boil. Reduce heat, cover, simmer for 1 hour.

Serves 6

LOBSTER BARQUETTES

1	tablespoon finely chopped shallots
2	tablespoons butter
2	cups diced, cooked Maine lobster meat
1/2	cup cream sauce
24	barquettes (oval pastry shells)
1	cup whipped cream
1	cup hollandaise sauce
	pinch cayenne pepper
	grated Parmesan cheese to taste

Sauté the shallots in butter until clear. Add the lobster meat and the cream sauce. Mix thoroughly and fill each barquette about 3/4 of the way. Fold whipped cream into hollandaise sauce and add a pinch of cayenne pepper. Spread over lobster mixture and dust with the grated Parmesan cheese. Place under hot broiler until sauce is bubbly and slightly browned.

Makes 24 and is a wonderful appetizer

Author's note: Always served when the Johnson's entertained.

BROILED DOVES

    6 doves
       butter
    6 slices bacon
       salt
       freshly ground black pepper toast
       chopped parsley lemon wedges

    Season doves inside and out with salt and pepper and rub skins with butter. Wrap each dove in a slice of bacon held in place with a toothpick. Broil under low heat for 20 minutes, turning frequently. Serve on toast with parsley and lemon.

Serves 6

SHRIMP WITH REMOULADE SAUCE

3 pounds cooked shrimp
1 cup mayonnaise
2 hard-cooked eggs, finely chopped
6 stuffed olives, chopped
1 tablespoon green pepper, chopped
1 clove garlic, minced
1 tablespoon anchovy paste
1 teaspoon Worcestershire sauce
1 teaspoon dry mustard (preferably Coleman's)
salt
freshly ground black pepper

Shell shrimp and chill for at least 1 hour. Combine the rest of the ingredients to make the sauce and mix thoroughly. Chill for at least 1 hour. Serve sauce with shrimp.

BARBECUED CHICKEN:
WHITE HOUSE

   3 2-pound chickens, cut up
1/2 cup dry white wine
1/2 cup oil
   1 teaspoon chopped chives
   2 tablespoons chopped parsley

Marinate chicken at room temperature for 1 hour in combined wine, oil, chives, and parsley. Turn chicken once or twice and baste with the marinade. Broil for 30 minutes or until done, turning frequently and basting with tomato-wine sauce.

Serves 6

Tomato-wine sauce

   1 can crushed tomatoes, drained
   1 cup red wine

Pour tomatoes into a sauce pan, stirring until reduced and thick.

CHICKEN MEXICAN

1	6-pound oven ready chicken (capon)
3	large onions, chopped
1	tablespoon sesame seeds
3/4	cup dry red wine
1	cup blanched almonds
3	tablespoons olives, sliced
1	teaspoon salt
4	tablespoons oil
3	cloves garlic, minced
1/4	teaspoon marjoram
2	cups chicken bouillon
1/2	cup sliced, stuffed
1	tablespoon chili powder
	freshly ground black pepper

Season chicken with salt and pepper. Sauté chicken in oil for 15 minutes or until brown on all sides. Remove chicken, keep hot. Add onions and garlic to oil remaining in skillet and sauté for 10 minutes or until lightly browned. Add sesame seeds, marjoram, and wine and simmer for 5 minutes. Put chicken, onion mixture, and bouillon in a deep casserole. Add almonds, olives and chili powder. Cover and bake in a moderate oven (350° F) for 30 minutes. Uncover and bake 15 minutes.

Serves 6

SOUTHERN FRIED CHICKEN

3	2-pound chickens, cut up
1/4	cup flour
	butter
	vegetable shortening
1	teaspoon salt
	freshly ground black pepper

Mix flour, salt, and pepper in a paper bag, put chicken in bag and shake. Melt enough butter and vegetable shortening to cover the bottom 2 inches of a large skillet. Add chicken, cover skillet, and cook slowly for 30 minutes. Uncover, drain fat, and add enough water to cover bottom of skillet. Cover skillet again, simmer for 30 minutes.

Serves 6

PEDERNALES RIVER CHILI

4	pounds chili meat
8	tablespoons bacon drippings
1	large onion, chopped
2	cloves garlic
1	tablespoon ground oregano
1	teaspoon comino seed
1	string dried mushrooms
6	teaspoons chili powder
1-1/2	cups canned whole tomatoes
2	2-1/2 pound cans kidney beans, light or dark
2	6 generous dashes liquid hot pepper sauce
	(i.e., Tabasco®, preferably the green Tabasco®)
	salt and pepper to taste
2	cups hot water

Chili meat is coarsely ground round steak or well-trimmed chuck meat. If specially ground, ask the butcher to use 3/4-inch plate for coarse grind. Place the ground meat, onions, garlic, and bacon drippings in a large heavy frying pan or Dutch oven. Cook until light colored. Add the oregano, the comino seed, chili powder, tomatoes, kidney beans, hot pepper sauce, dried mushrooms, salt, and hot water. Bring to a boil, lower heat and simmer about 1 hour. Skim off the fat during the cooking. Serve hot in individual casseroles.

Author's note: Instead of hot water, I prefer 2 cups chicken stock or 2 cups beef stock or 2 cups veal stock. I also let the chili sit overnight, at least for 24 hours, preferably 48 hours, before serving. This chili can also be served by taking a large hard roll and cutting out the center and then pouring the chili in the hard roll and baking it in the oven. When it comes out, top it with shredded cheddar cheese and a dollop of sour cream.

PORK AND CORN BREAD RING

3	cups diced cooked pork
1	package corn muffin mix
1	cup sliced mushrooms
2	tablespoons minced onion
4	tablespoons butter
4	tablespoons flour
2	cups milk
2	egg yolks, well beaten
1/2	teaspoon salt

Prepare mix as directed on the package. Bake in a ring mold in a hot oven (400° F) for 30 minutes. Meanwhile, sauté mushrooms and onion in butter for 5 minutes. Add flour, stir until smooth. Add milk and cook, stirring until thickened. Stir some of this sauce into egg yolks. Stir egg yolk mixture into sauce. Add pork and salt and cook over hot (not boiling) water for 20 minutes stirring occasionally. Serve in hot corn bread ring.

Serves 6

Author's note: Unusual Texan dish. Most often served at the LBJ ranch.

BARBECUED LEG OF LAMB: WHITE HOUSE

1	6-pound leg of lamb, boned and flattened
1	cup oil
1/4	cup wine vinegar
2	cloves garlic, crushed
1	tablespoon salt
	freshly ground black pepper
	hot barbecue sauce

Marinate lamb at room temperature for 2 hours in combined oil, vinegar, garlic, salt, and pepper. Turn the lamb once or twice and baste occasionally with the marinade. Remove from marinade and broil for 2 hours or until done, turning frequently and basting with hot barbecue sauce.

Serves 6

Author's note: This sauce is so much better than the standard one we usually used.

ROAST SUCKLING PIG

1	10-pound suckling pig
1/2	cup chopped celery
1/4	cup chopped onion
1	clove garlic, cut
3	tablespoons butter
3	cups soft bread crumbs
1/4	teaspoon thyme
	apple juice
1/2	teaspoon salt
	apple

Sauté celery, onion, and garlic in butter for 5 minutes. Combine with bread crumbs, thyme, and salt and enough apple juice to moisten. Stuff pig and close cavity. Place piece of wood in pig's mouth. Cover ears and tail with foil to prevent burning. Roast in a moderate oven (325° F) for 4 hours, basting frequently.

To serve, remove piece of wood and insert apple.

Serves 6

BARBECUED PORK CHOPS

6   1-inch-thick pork chops
1   cup soy sauce
1   clove garlic, crushed
    freshly ground black pepper
1   cup chili barbecue sauce

Marinate pork chops at room temperature for 1 hour in combined soy sauce, garlic, and pepper. Turn chops once or twice and baste with the marinade. Broil for 30 minutes on each side, basting frequently with chili barbecue sauce.

Serves 6

PEPPER STEAK:
WHITE HOUSE

        3   pounds tenderloin steak, sliced
        3   green peppers, sliced
        3   onions, sliced
        9   large mushrooms, sliced
        3   tomatoes, quartered
    1-1/2   cups Espagnole sauce
      3/4   cup butter
      1/2   cup flour
        6   tablespoons
            Burgundy wine
            salt
            freshly ground black pepper

First make green pepper sauce: sauté green peppers, onions, mushrooms, and tomatoes in 1/2 cup butter for 5 minutes. Add Espagnole sauce and simmer for 10 minutes. Salt and pepper the sliced steak. Dip in flour and sauté in remaining 1/4 cup butter for 2 minutes. Add sauce and simmer for 15 minutes, stirring frequently. Add wine and simmer for 3 minutes.

Serves 6

STUFFED SQUASH A LA WHITE HOUSE

3	medium-size squash, yellow or zucchini
1	onion, minced
1/2	cup butter
	seeds of 1 cardamom pod, crushed
1/3	cup almonds, blanched and ground
1-1/2	teaspoons coriander seed
	freshly ground black pepper
	whole saffron
1/4	cup yogurt
1	cup cream
2	teaspoons lemon juice
1/2	teaspoon salt

Split squash lengthwise and scoop out center, leaving wall 1/2-inch thick, and chop. Add onion and a pinch of saffron. Sauté in 1/4 cup butter for 5 minutes. Add yogurt and cardamom and simmer for 10 minutes. Add cream mixed with ground almonds, lemon juice, and salt. Simmer for 5 minutes. Place the mixture in squash shells, dot with remaining 1/4 cup butter, and sprinkle with coriander and pepper. Bake in a moderate oven (350° F) for 20 minutes.

Serves 6

MRS. LYNDON JOHNSON'S
LIMA BEAN & MUSHROOM CASSEROLE

1	package frozen baby lima beans
1	teaspoon salt
1	tablespoon butter
1	cup fresh sliced mushrooms
1/2	cup grated Parmesan cheese
1/4	teaspoon chili powder
1/4	teaspoon ground black pepper

Cook baby lima beans in salted water. Drain thoroughly. Put small amount of butter in saucepan and melt. Add mushrooms and sear for 5 minutes. Add flour and milk to make thick sauce. Add grated cheese and let melt. Season with salt, chili powder, and pepper. Add lima beans and serve very hot.

MRS. LYNDON JOHNSON'S SPINACH SOUFFLÉ

      3 eggs, separated
      1 cup chopped cooked spinach
    1/2 cup thick white sauce
    1/4 cup chopped onions
    1/2 cup grated cheese

Sauté onions in small amount of butter. Make white sauce of 2 tablespoons butter, 2 tablespoons flour, 1 cup whole milk (rich or light cream), 1/2 teaspoon salt, and 1/8 teaspoon pepper. Beat yolks until thick and lemon colored. Stir into white sauce and add spinach and cheese. Fold in stiffly beaten egg whites and turn into greased casserole. Set in pan of hot water and bake in moderate oven (350° F) about 50 minutes. Serve at once.

SPINACH PARMESAN

      3 pounds fresh spinach, carefully washed and stemmed
      6 tablespoons Parmesan cheese, freshly grated
      6 tablespoons onions, minced very fine
      6 tablespoons heavy cream
      5 tablespoons butter, melted
    1/2 cup cracker crumbs

Cook the spinach until tender and drain thoroughly. Be sure that it is stemmed and chopped coarsely. Add the cheese, onion, cream, and 4 tablespoons butter. Pour into shallow, well-greased spring-form pan. Sprinkle with crumbs mixed with remaining butter. Bake for 10–15 minutes at 350°. Garnish spinach ring with puff pastry.

MRS. LYNDON JOHNSON'S
TURKEY DRESSING

	medium-size pan of corn bread
4	slices toasted bread
1	stalk chopped celery
3	large onions, chopped
6	eggs
1/4	cup butter
	salt, pepper, sage
	stock from turkey

Mix together bread and corn bread that has been crumbled with stock from turkey. Be sure to use enough stock so it will not be stiff. Add eggs and remaining ingredients. Bake slowly for one hour.

Serves 8

MRS. LYNDON JOHNSON'S POPOVERS

 1   cup sifted flour
 1   cup milk
 2   eggs, beaten
 1/4 teaspoon salt
 2   tablespoons melted shortening

Grease pans. Mix and sift flour and salt. Combine eggs, milk, and shortening. Gradually add to flour mixture, beating about one minute or until batter is smooth. Fill greased sizzling hot pans about three-quarters full and bake in very hot oven (450° F) about 20 minutes. Reduce heat to moderate (350° F) and continue baking for 15 or 20 minutes.

Makes 6

MRS. LYNDON JOHNSON'S SPOON BREAD

        3 cups sweet milk
        3 eggs
        1 scant cup cornmeal
           pat of butter the size of a walnut
        3 level teaspoons baking powder
        1 level teaspoon salt

Stir cornmeal into 2 cups milk and let mixture come to a boil, making a mush. Add balance of milk and well-beaten eggs. Stir in salt, baking powder, and melted butter. Bake 30 minutes in oven at 350° F.

MRS. LYNDON JOHNSON'S BROWNIES

     1   cup sugar
     2   eggs
   3/4   cup flour
     1   teaspoon vanilla
   1/2   cup melted butter
   1/2   cup coarsely chopped nuts
     2   squares Baker's chocolate

Mix all together and spread in buttered 8 x 8 x 2 tin. Bake 25 minutes and cut in 2-inch squares while still warm.

FROM THE WHITE HOUSE COLLECTION DURING THE ANDREW JACKSON ADMINISTRATION—1829 TO 1837

MRS. LYNDON JOHNSON'S
STRAWBERRY ICE BOX PIE

- 1 17-ounce package marshmallows
- 1 box frozen strawberries OR 2 cups fresh strawberries, sweetened to taste
- 1 cup whipping cream
- 1 cool pastry shell

Put marshmallows in double boiler. Add 2 tablespoons strawberry juice. Cook until marshmallows are dissolved. Mix strawberries and marshmallows thoroughly. Chill about 2 hours. Fold whipped cream into marshmallow mixture and pour into pastry shell. Chill until firm.

Pastry Shell

- 1 cup flour
- 2 tablespoons shortening
- 1 teaspoon salt
- 3 tablespoons cold water
- 1 tablespoon sugar

Roll into 10-inch pie pan. Bake at 350° F for 10 minutes.

BAKED ALASKA: WHITE HOUSE

1	8-inch cake layer
4	egg whites
1/2	cup sugar
1	quart firm ice cream

Beat egg whites until foamy, add sugar and beat until stiff but not dry. Place cake on heavy, unfinished wooden tray or heat-proof platter. Spoon ice cream on the cake leaving a 1-inch border all around. Cover ice cream and cake completely with egg whites (meringue). Brown meringue lightly in a very hot oven (500° F) for 2 minutes. Serve immediately.

Serves 6

MRS. LYNDON JOHNSON'S
DOUBLE DIVINITY

2 cups sugar
2/3 cup water
1/2 cup light corn syrup
2 egg whites, slightly beaten
1 teaspoon vanilla
dash of salt

Combine 1/2 cup sugar and 1/3 cup water and cook until small amount of syrup forms soft ball in cold water (240° F). Cook remaining 1-1/2 cups sugar, 1/3 cup water and corn syrup until it forms a hard ball in cold water (254° F). Cool first syrup slightly. Add slowly to egg whites, beating constantly about 1 to 2 minutes, or until mixture loses its gloss. Add second syrup in same way. Add vanilla and turn into greased pan. Cut in squares when cold. This candy is softer and creamier than the regular divinity.

Approximate yield: about 40 pieces.

MRS. LYNDON JOHNSON'S CHESS PIE

       1/2 pound butter
         2 cups sugar
         4 eggs
         1 heaping tablespoon flour
       1/2 teaspoon vanilla
         1 unbaked pie shell

   Mix sugar and flour together, add to butter and blend until light and fluffy. Add eggs one at a time, beating after each addition. Add vanilla and pour into unbaked pie shell. Bake in 300° F oven until knife inserted comes out clean—about 1 hour.

PEACH ICE CREAM

1	package frozen peaches
1	cup milk
1/2	cup sugar
2	eggs yolks, beaten
1	cup heavy cream
1	teaspoon vanilla extract
	salt

Defrost and drain the peaches. Put milk in the top part of a double boiler and cook over very low heat until a light film forms on top of the milk. Add the sugar and salt to the milk and stir until the sugar dissolves. Remove from heat and beat slowly into the egg yolks. Set over hot water and cook, stirring constantly for 5 minutes or until the mixture coats a spoon. Remove from heat and cool the custard. Then chill it for 30 minutes. Whip the cream until thick, add the peaches, vanilla, and chilled custard. Pour into a freezer and freeze for 1 hour. Turn the ice cream out into a chilled bowl and stir well. Return it to the tray and freeze until it is firm enough to serve.

Makes about 1 quart

SUMMER FRUIT CAKE

1-1/2	cups white seedless raisins
	apple juice
1-3/4	cups sifted cake flour
1	teaspoon double-acting baking powder
1/4	teaspoon salt
1/2	cup butter
3/4	cup sugar
5	egg whites
3/4	cup chopped candied pineapple
1	cup chopped pecans
1/2	teaspoon almond extract
1/2	teaspoon vanilla extract

Cover the raisins with apple juice and let soak in the refrigerator for 2 or 3 days, or until the raisins are really nice and plump and very soft. Drain them. Start heating the oven to 300° F. Grease an 8" x 4" x 3", line with heavy paper, and grease again. Sift the flour once and measure. Add baking powder and salt and sift together three times. Cream butter thoroughly, gradually adding the sugar. Cream until light and fluffy. Add egg whites, one at a time, beating thoroughly after each. Add fruits, nuts, and flavoring and mix well. Add flour, a little at a time, beating after each addition until smooth. Pour into the greased pan. Bake in the 300° F oven for 1 hour and 15 minutes, or until done. It should produce 8 to 10 servings.

MRS. LYNDON JOHNSON'S PRUNE CAKE

- 1/2   cup Crisco®
- 1   cup sugar
- 2   whole eggs
- 1-1/3   cup flour
- 2/3   cup chopped prunes
- 2/3   cup sour milk (buttermilk)
- 1/2   teaspoon soda
- 1/2   teaspoon salt
- 1/2   teaspoon cinnamon
- 1/2   teaspoon nutmeg
- 1/2   teaspoon allspice
- 1/2   teaspoon baking powder

Cream shortening, add sugar and eggs, beat well. Mix dry ingredients and add alternately with sour milk to creamed mixture. Add chopped prunes. Bake in 2 waxed paper-lined cake pans for 25 minutes at 350° F.

Frosting

- 2   tablespoons butter
- 2   tablespoons prune juice
- 1   tablespoon lemon juice
- 1/2   teaspoon cinnamon
- 1/2   teaspoon salt
- 1-1/2   cups powdered sugar

Cream butter, add prune juice and lemon juice, salt, and cinnamon. Beat in powdered sugar gradually.

OPPOSITE: PRESENTATION CHINA FROM THE AUTHOR'S COLLECTION

MRS. LYNDON JOHNSON'S TEXAS COOKIES

1/2	cup butter
1	cup sugar
1	egg
1	tablespoon cream
1/2	teaspoon of lemon flavoring
	rind of one lemon, grated
1-1/2	cups flour
1/2	teaspoon salt
1	teaspoon baking powder

Blend together 1/2 cup butter and 1 cup sugar. Add 1 egg and 1 tablespoon cream. Grate rind of lemon and 1/2 teaspoon of lemon flavoring and add to mixture. Add 1-1/2 cups flour, 1/2 teaspoon salt, and 1 teaspoon baking powder. Chill for 2 to 3 hours (better when chilled overnight). Roll very thin and cut with dough cutter. Bake 8 to 10 minutes in 375° F oven.

Makes approximately one dozen

MRS. LYNDON JOHNSON'S
WHEATIES® COCONUT COOKIES

	1	cup shortening (or 1/2 cup butter)
	1	cup brown sugar
	1	cup white sugar
	2	eggs
	2	cups coconut
2 to 2-1/2		cups flour
	1	teaspoon baking soda
	1/2	teaspoon vanilla
	2	cups Wheaties® cereal

Sift and measure 1/2 teaspoon baking powder, 1/2 teaspoon vanilla, and 2 cups Wheaties®. Blend shortening and sugar. Add beaten eggs. Add coconut. Sift flour, soda, baking powder, and salt together and add to mixture. Blend in vanilla and then Wheaties®. Roll in balls the size of a walnut and bake 12 minutes in 400° F oven.

Richard Milhous Nixon
Patricia Thelma Ryan Nixon

"What kind of nation we will be, what kind of world we will live in, whether we shape the future in the image of our hopes, is ours to determine by our actions and our choices.

The greatest honor history can bestow is the title of peacemaker. This honor now beckons America—the chance to help lead the world at last out of the valley of turmoil, and onto that high ground of peace that man has dreamed of since the dawn of civilization.

If we succeed, generations to come will say of us now living that we mastered our moment, that we helped make the world safe for mankind.

This is our summons to greatness. I believe the American people are ready to answer this call."

RICHARD MILHOUS NIXON FIRST INAUGURAL ADDRESS, MONDAY, JANUARY 20, 1969

RICHARD NIXON BY WILLS © WHHA (WHITE HOUSE COLLECTION)

*P*at and Richard Nixon entered the White House with an intimate knowledge acquired during the Eisenhower administration, where he served as Ike's vice president. People called the Nixon administration the "Imperial Presidency" because of the pomp and circumstance he so enjoyed, going so far as to dress the White House guards in special brightly colored uniforms. It made them look like they were members of the Foreign Legion. Although that didn't last long, the title "Imperial" stuck throughout the administration.

Nixon's public image was terrible, but when with friends or in small groups, he really was quite witty. He was also a man who was greatly concerned about his country and the role it would play, worldwide, in the future.

When he ran against Kennedy, the election was so close he could have demanded a recount, but explained, "The order of transfer of responsibilities from the old to the new could be delayed for months. The situation within the entire federal government would be chaotic."

When it came to light in the New York Herald Tribune that there had been voting frauds, Earl Mazo, a reporter for the Tribune launched an investigation by running a series of articles. Early in December 1960, one month before JFK's inauguration, Nixon invited Mazo to his home for a chat.

"Earl," he said as they shook hands, "these are interesting articles you are writing, but NO ONE steals the presidency of the United States." He went on to say, "The country would be torn by partisan bitterness if there was an official challenge of the election results, and the damage to America's foreign relations might be irreparable."

"Our country," he told Mazo, "can't afford the agony of a constitutional crisis and I damn well will not be a party to creating one just to become President." Mazo agreed to drop the editorials.

Nixon's problem was that he was elusive, inexplicable, strange, and hard to understand. To Harry Truman, however, there was no mystery. Truman's anger was understandable. Nixon launched his career in the late 40's charging that the Truman administration was riddled with Communists and traitors. Indeed, he even started a whisper campaign against his opponents, finally winning the election.

Nevertheless, the people got what they voted for and America survived. One night on CNN's Larry King Live, the former president was asked by King, "Is it hard to drive by the Watergate?"

"Well," said Nixon, "I've never been in the Watergate."

"Never been in the Watergate!" cried King, somewhat surprised.

"No," replied Nixon, "other people were in there, though—unfortunately!"

After hearing JFK's inaugural address, Nixon ran into Ted Sorenson, an aide to Kennedy. Said Nixon to Sorenson, "I wish I had said some of those things."

"What part?" asked Sorenson, "The part about 'Ask not what your country can do for you?'"

"No," replied Nixon, "the part that starts 'I do solemnly swear.'"

At an autograph reception in 1962 when Nixon's book Six Crises was published, he asked one purchaser to whom he should address his greeting. The purchaser, knowing what a challenge his name would be, said, "You've just met your seventh crisis. My name is Stanaslaus Wojechzleschki."

Knowing he had not done well in the first-ever televised debates against Kennedy, Nixon referred to himself as a dropout from the electoral college because he flunked debating.

President Nixon was either loved or loathed. Speaker of the House Tip O'Neill said, "The irony about Nixon is that his pre-Watergate record is a lot better than most liberals realize. It was Nixon, after all, who opened the doors of China and who eventually brought the troops home from Viet Nam."

In contrast, Harry Truman said, "Richard Nixon is a no-good, lying bastard. He can lie out of both sides of his mouth at the same time and if he ever caught himself telling the truth, he'd lie just to keep a hand in."

And Governor Jimmy Carter once said, "In two hundred years of history, he is the most dishonest President we've ever had. I think he was a disgrace to the presidency."

All I can say is draw your own conclusions, there is good and bad in everyone.

In spite of it all, the President and Mrs. Nixon knew how to throw a bash.

Pat Ryan met her future husband at a little theater group in Whittier, California. In 1938, she was playing the female lead in a play titled The Dark Tower. The leading man, Richard Nixon, had just returned to town to practice law. Two years later they were married and very soon after moved to Washington, D.C., where Nixon had accepted a job as an attorney in the Office of Economic Management. After the war, Mr. Nixon ran for Congress as a Republican candidate of California's 12th Congressional District. The year was 1946, and this marked the beginning of one of the most controversial political careers of anyone who has ascended to the presidency. Nixon's political career spanned twenty-nine years, and lasted until the day he resigned the presidency, August 9, 1974.

Although Nixon was never really accepted by the moneyed Eastern establishment, through hard work he fared very well, especially after he ran against JFK and moved to New York City to practice law. It was then that Nixon grew wealthy. It's a shame he could never trust people; he would have been a great president, especially in foreign affairs, had he not been quagmired in scandal, losing his Vice President, Spiro Agnew, and himself resigning in disgrace.

The social highlight of Nixon's first administration was the wedding of their daughter, Tricia, to Edward Finch Cox, in the Rose Garden of the White House. A lavish buffet included smoked Pacific Rim salmon, prime ribs of beef, sautéed shrimp in coconut, and a seven-tier, 350 lb. wedding cake that was five-feet wide at the bottom, decorated with lovebirds and the initials of the bride and groom.

During the first year in office, President and Mrs. Nixon entertained over 50,000 guests, which is a record. The kitchen was kept very busy in those days and some of the recipes follow.

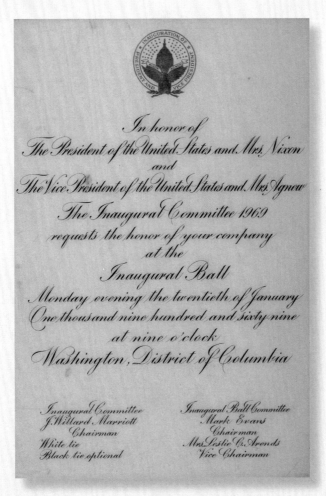

CRAB MEAT IN CANAPE SHELLS

1/2	cup cooked crab meat
48	packaged canapé shells
1	tablespoon butter
2	tablespoons flour
2	tablespoons grated Parmesan cheese
3/4	cups light cream
1	egg yolk
2	tablespoons dry sherry
1/2	teaspoon salt
	freshly ground black pepper

Melt butter over low heat. Add flour and stir until smooth. Add cheese and cream and cook until thickened, stirring constantly. Remove from heat. Stir in crab meat, salt, and pepper. Beat egg yolk with sherry and add to crab meat mixture. Spoon into canapé shells and broil under medium heat for 3 minutes or until brown on top.

Makes 48

CAMEMBERT ALMOND BALLS

          8 ounce Camembert cheese
          1 cup salted almonds, ground
          1 cup dry white wine
        1/2 cup sweet butter, softened
             toasted crackers

Place whole cheese in bowl, pour wine over it, and let stand at room temperature overnight or for at least 8 hours, turning cheese once or twice. Drain and discard liquid. Press cheese through a coarse sieve or food mill and blend in softened butter. Chill for at least 3 hours. Shape the cheese into about 24 small balls. Roll the balls in ground almonds, and serve them at once with toasted crackers.

STUFFED CELERY

	celery stalks
2	8-ounce packages cream cheese
1/2	cup sour cream
1/2	cup butter, softened
2	tablespoons minced capers
1	teaspoon anchovy paste
1	teaspoon minced onion
1	teaspoon dry mustard
1	teaspoon paprika

Combine cream cheese, sour cream and butter and stir until smooth. Add capers, anchovy paste, onion, mustard, and paprika. Fill celery stalks with cheese mixture. This cheese mixture can be kept in a covered container in the refrigerator for at least 1 week.

Makes about 3 cups

Author's note: Take the time to peel the celery stalks for an entirely different flavor. For a special treat add 2 tablespoons of softened bleu cheese to mixture.

MANHATTAN CLAM CHOWDER

2	dozen hard-shell clams, shucked
2	ounces salt pork, diced
1/2	cup thinly sliced leeks
1/2	cup chopped onion
1	clove garlic, minced
1/2	cup chopped green pepper
1/2	cup diced carrot
1/4	cup chopped celery
3	cups diced potato
1	cup canned tomatoes
1/4	cup catsup
1/4	cup chopped parsley
1-1/2	teaspoons thyme
1	bay leaf, crumbled
4	whole cloves
2	teaspoons salt
	freshly ground black pepper

Strain clams, keep liquor. Mince hard part of clams, chop soft part coarsely. Sauté salt pork until golden brown. Add leeks, onion, and garlic and sauté for 5 minutes. Add minced clams, green pepper, carrot, celery, potato, salt, and 6 cups of water. Bring to a boil; reduce heat, cover and simmer for 10 minutes. Add chopped clams and clam liquor plus enough water to make 3 cups. Add tomatoes, catsup, parsley, thyme, bay leaf, cloves, and pepper. Simmer for 20 minutes.

Serves 6

LOBSTER TIENTSIN

1	3-pound lobster
4	cups finely chopped Chinese cabbage
	peanut oil
2	tablespoons cornstarch
2	tablespoons dry sherry
1/4	teaspoon ground ginger
2	egg whites
1/4	cup chicken bouillon
1	teaspoon soy sauce
	freshly ground black pepper

Blanch cabbage in hot oil. Rinse with cold water and drain. Remove meat from raw lobster and cut into 1/2-inch pieces. Combine egg whites and cornstarch and marinate lobster in this mixture for 30 minutes. Stir in two tablespoons of bouillon, sherry, soy sauce, ginger, and pepper. Cook in 2 tablespoons oil in a large skillet over high heat for 5 minutes stirring constantly. Remove lobster mixture and keep hot. Cook cabbage, remaining 6 tablespoons of chicken bouillon, and 2 tablespoons of oil in skillet over high heat for 5 minutes, stirring constantly. Add lobster mixture and cook for 5 minutes, stirring constantly.

Serves 6

POMPANO EN PAPILLOTE (IN PAPER BAG): WHITE HOUSE

      3   medium-size fillets of pompano
      1   stalk celery, cut up
      1   onion, cut up
      2   cups dry white wine
      6   tablespoons butter
      2   tablespoons flour
      2   cups cooked shrimp, chopped
          salt
      2   cups cooked crab meat
      3   shallots, chopped
      1   clove garlic, minced
      1   bay leaf, crumbled
          thyme
          Tabasco® sauce
          freshly ground black pepper

First make the stock. Combine heads and bones of the pompanos with celery, onion, 1 teaspoon salt, and 3 cups water. Bring to a boil, reduce heat, and simmer for 30 minutes. Strain stock. Measure 1 cup of stock and set it aside. Pour remaining stock into skillet and add 1/2 cup wine. Season fillets with salt and pepper and fold in half. Place in hot stock and simmer for 8 minutes. Remove from heat and allow fillets to cool in stock. Remove fillets and drain.

Meanwhile make the fish velouté. Melt 2 tablespoons butter, add flour, and stir until smooth. Add 1 cup fish stock and cook until thickened, stirring constantly. Set aside. Sauté shallots in remaining 4 tablespoons butter for 5 minutes. Add shrimp, crab meat, garlic, bay leaf, a pinch of thyme, and a dash of Tabasco®. Mix well. Add the remaining 1-1/2 cups wine and cook for 15 minutes, stirring frequently. Cool.

To make pompano en papillote, cut 6 parchment paper hearts about 8 inches long and 12 inches wide. Brush them with oil. Place a spoonful of sauce on one side of each heart. Put 1 pompano fillet on top and cover with a little sauce. Fold paper hearts over and around to seal in fish and sauce. Arrange them on an oiled baking sheet and brush them with oil. Bake in a hot oven (450° F) for 15 minutes or until the paper is browned. Serve pompanos immediately in their paper covers. Rip the paper open at the table.

Serves 6

BALTIMORE OYSTER LOAF

    3 dozen oysters, shucked
    3 small loaves French bread
    1 clove garlic
    4 tablespoons melted butter
       milk

Split the loaves of bread lengthwise, leaving a hinge along one side. Scoop out the soft centers, leaving a 1-inch shell, and break center into coarse crumbs. Set crumbs aside. Rub the inside of the loaves with cut garlic, then brush inside and crust with 2 tablespoons of the butter. Drain oysters and save liquor. Sauté the oysters in the remaining 2 tablespoons butter for 5 minutes or until the edges curl. Stuff the oysters into the hollow loaves. If additional filling is needed, use 1/2 cup oyster liquor mixed with crumbs. Close the loaves and wrap each one in cheesecloth dipped in milk. Twist the ends of the cheesecloth tightly and tuck them under the loaves. Bake on a baking sheet in a moderate oven (350° F) for 30 minutes. To serve, unwrap loaves and cut them in half.

Serves 6

SALMON: WHITE HOUSE

    6   salmon steaks
    1   tablespoon balsamic vinegar
    1   teaspoon salt
  3/4   cup butter, melted

Combine vinegar, salt, and 2 quarts water in a skillet. Bring to a boil. Add salmon, reduce the heat and simmer for 12 minutes. Drain salmon and serve with melted butter.

Serves 6

CHINA FROM WHITE HOUSE COLLECTION OF PRESIDENT FRANKLIN PIERCE, 1853-1857

COLD POACHED SALMON

6	salmon steaks
2	onions
	lemon or lime wedges
	cucumber slices
1/4	cup butter
1/4	cup vinegar
2	cloves
1	tablespoon salt
	watercress
2	carrots, chopped
2	stalks celery with leaves, cut up
2	tablespoons chopped parsley
1/2	bay leaf, crumbled
10	peppercorns
	mayonnaise verte

Sauté onions, carrots, and celery in butter in a large skillet for 5 minutes or until onion is soft. Add vinegar, parsley, cloves, bay leaf, salt, and peppercorns, and 2 quarts of water. Bring to a boil and cook for 10 minutes, stirring occasionally. Reduce heat and add salmon steaks. Cover skillet and simmer for 10 minutes. Cool salmon in the stock. Remove salmon and discard stock. Chill salmon in the refrigerator for at least 1 hour. Serve with mayonnaise verte. Garnish with watercress, lemon or lime wedges, and cucumber slices.

Serves 6

Author's note: Mayonnaise verte is flavored and colored green with finely minced herbs such as spinach, sorrel, watercress, parsley, chervil, and tarragon. If desired these herbs may be blanched first.

OYSTER - STUFFED CHICKEN: WHITE HOUSE

3	broiler chickens, split in half
3	tablespoons chopped green pepper
3	tablespoons chopped parsley
1	clove garlic, crushed
	bread crumbs
1	teaspoon salt
	cranberry or lingonberry preserves
1	pint oysters
2	tablespoons chopped celery
2	tablespoons chopped onion
	butter
1/4	teaspoon cayenne pepper
	freshly ground black pepper

Drain and chop oysters and save their liquor. Sauté oysters and vegetables with seasonings in 4 tablespoons butter for 10 minutes. Add 1 cup bread crumbs and 1/2 cup oyster liquor. Meanwhile, place chickens in shallow baking pan, skin side up, and dot with butter. Add 1/2 cup of water to pan. Bake in a moderate oven (375° F) for 30 minutes or until brown. Remove chicken from oven. Turn chicken skin-side down and fill each cavity with oyster stuffing. Sprinkle stuffing with bread crumbs and melted butter. Bake 20 minutes or until crumbs are golden brown. Serve with cranberry or lingonberry preserves.

Serves 6

LAMPS OF CHINA DELIGHT

- 1/2 cup finely chopped cooked chicken
- 1/2 cup cooked crab meat
- 1/4 cup finely chopped canned bamboo shoots
- 1/4 cup chopped mushrooms
- 1 tablespoon chopped parsley
- 1/4 cup finely chopped scallions
- 6 eggs, lightly beaten
- 4 tablespoons cornstarch
  peanut oil
- 1 teaspoon salt
  freshly ground black pepper

Combine chicken, crab meat, vegetables, eggs, salt, and pepper. Spoon into 18 buttered Chinese porcelain spoons or heat-proof custard cups. Steam on rack in covered pan over 1 inch of boiling water for 10 minutes. Cool. Remove cakes from spoons and roll in cornstarch. Fry in 1 inch hot oil (375° F) for 5 minutes or until brown. Serve with Lamps of China sauce.

Serves 6

CHICKEN BREASTS IN GELATIN:
WHITE HOUSE

2   3-pound chickens
1   bay leaf, crumbled
2   onions, cut up
1   tablespoon salt
1   stalk celery with leaves
1   clove garlic
3   envelopes unflavored gelatin
6   peppercorns

Place chickens in a saucepan and add water to cover. Add celery, bay leaf, garlic, onions, salt, and peppercorns. Bring to a boil, reduce heat, cover, and simmer for 1 hour. Remove the chickens from broth. Drain and cool. Cut the chickens in quarters. Chill the chicken for at least 1 hour. Strain the broth and set aside 1 quart. Soften the gelatin in 1 cup cold water. Add this to the hot, strained broth and stir until the gelatin is dissolved. Cool. Chill for 1/2 hour or until slightly thickened. Spoon very carefully over the chilled chicken to coat it completely. Return to refrigerator and chill for 1 hour. When chicken is glazed, garnish it with anything from artichokes to mushrooms.

Serves 6

SWEETBREADS EN BROCHETTE

          3 pairs sweetbreads
          1 tablespoon dry white wine
          6 slices bacon, cut in pieces
          3 medium green peppers, cut in 1-inch squares
        1/2 cup butter, melted
             freshly ground black pepper
          1 egg, beaten
        1/2 cup bread crumbs
         24 mushroom caps
        1/2 teaspoon salt
             chateau sauce

Cut each parboiled sweetbread into 4 pieces, dip into egg beaten with wine, salt and pepper. Then dip into bread crumbs. Thread on skewers, alternating sweetbreads with bacon, mushrooms, and peppers. Broil under low heat, basting with melted butter, until golden brown. Serve with chateau sauce.

Serves 6

Author's note: An excellent preparation for sweetbreads—one of the best recipes ever.

KOTTBULLAR: WHITE HOUSE

        1   pound ground lean beef
      1/4   pound ground veal
      1/2   pound ground lean pork
      1/2   cup heavy cream
        2   eggs
            cayenne pepper
            freshly ground black pepper
        2   slices white bread
      1/2   cup slightly browned chopped onion
        4   egg yolks
      1/4   cup butter
        1   teaspoon salt

Remove crust from bread and crumble bread into cream. Soak for 10 minutes. Put beef, pork, veal, and onion through a food grinder. Add soaked bread, eggs, egg yolks, a few grains of cayenne pepper, salt and black pepper and mix well. Shape into balls and sauté in butter.

Serves 6

Author's note: Great for the cocktail table.

FILET OPALESCENCE

1	pound top sirloin of beef, sliced 1-inch thick
1/4	cup dry sherry
2	tablespoons cornstarch
2	tablespoons peanut oil
1/2	cup thinly sliced mushrooms
1/2	cup snow peas, cut in 1/2 inch pieces
1	cup chicken bouillon
	chow mein noodles
1	teaspoon soy sauce
1/8	teaspoon ground ginger
1/2	cup thinly sliced asparagus
1/2	cup finely chopped chives

Cut beef into 2-inch strips and slice strips across grain about 1/8-inch thick. Combine sherry, soy sauce, cornstarch, and ginger. Marinate beef in this mixture for 1 hour. Fry in oil in large skillet on high heat for 5 minutes, stirring constantly. Remove beef and keep hot. Add vegetables and bouillon to liquid remaining in skillet and cook over high heat for 5 minutes, stirring constantly. Add beef to vegetables and cook for 5 minutes more, stirring constantly. Serve the filet opalescence with chow mein noodles.

Serves 6

STUFFED TOMATOES

8	large tomatoes
1-1/2	cups chopped onions
1/2	pound mushrooms, chopped
6	ounces Canadian bacon
2	tablespoons chopped chives
2	tablespoons chopped parsley
3/4	cup olive oil (best to use a good quality oil)
2	eggs, beaten
1	package dry bread crumbs
	salt and pepper to taste

Wash the tomatoes. Remove about 3/4 of the centers, being careful not to break the walls. For the stuffing, mix together the onions, mushrooms, bacon, chives, and parsley. Start heating the oven to 400° F. Heat 1/2 cup of the oil in a large skillet and sauté the mixture for 10 minutes. Remove the pan from the heat and stir in the beaten egg, salt and pepper. Fill the tomatoes with the stuffing and place in a greased baking dish. Sprinkle with bread crumbs and remaining oil. Bake for about 20–40 minutes, depending on how well done you like your tomatoes.

BOUILLABAISSE SALAD

    1   cup cooked crab meat
    1   cup cooked lobster meat
  1/2   pound cooked shrimp
    1   cup cooked whitefish
    2   tomatoes, sliced
    6   ripe olives, halved
        mixed greens
        salad dressing

Arrange crab, lobster, shrimp, whitefish, and tomatoes on a bed of mixed greens. Garnish with olives. To serve, toss with classic French or hot spicy dressing.

Serves 6

Author's note: Wonderful for an outdoor tea in the summer.

HERBED COTTAGE CHEESE SALAD

- 1 tablespoon minced chives
- 1 tablespoon minced basil
- 1 pound cottage cheese (small curd)
- 1 cucumber, diced
- 1 tablespoon minced onion
  freshly ground black pepper
- 1 tablespoon minced dill
- 1 tablespoon minced tarragon
- 1 cup sour cream
- 1 green pepper, diced
- 1 teaspoon salt
  mixed greens
  salad dressing

Combine cottage cheese with sour cream, herbs, cucumber, green pepper, onion, salt, and black pepper. Arrange greens on plate and spoon the herbed cottage cheese mixture on top. Serve with your favorite salad dressing (Thousand Island is very good with this recipe).

Serves 6

Author's note: One of President Nixon's favorites. He made this dish famous by pouring ketchup over it.

SESAME BREAD

2	tablespoons sesame seed
1	large loaf French bread
1/4	cup butter
1/4	cup finely chopped parsley
1/4	cup finely chopped chives

Slice bread lengthwise. Combine butter, parsley, and chives and spread on cut surfaces of bread. Sprinkle with sesame seed and bake in a moderate oven (350˚ F) for 20 minutes or until loaf is crisp. For a variation try adding garlic to the spread.

Serves 6

VANILLA SOUFFLE A LA WHITE HOUSE

        4   tablespoons butter
        2   tablespoons flour
        1   cup light cream, scalded
        5   egg yolks
     1/4   cup sugar
     1/4   cup vanilla
     1/2   teaspoon salt
        6   egg whites, stiffly beaten

Start heating the oven to 450° F. Butter and sugar a 1-1/2-quart soufflé dish or casserole. In medium-size saucepan, melt the butter. Stir in the flour and cook until mixture starts to turn brown. Gradually stir in scalded cream and cook over medium heat, stirring constantly for about 5 minutes. Beat egg yolks and sugar together in a large bowl and stir in the cream mixture. Add vanilla and salt. Fold in the egg whites. Pour mixture into sugared soufflé dish and bake at 450° F for 10–12 minutes. Then lower the heat to 350° F and bake for an additional 20 minutes. Serve immediately with the vanilla sauce.

Vanilla Sauce

         3/4   cup sugar
  1-1/2 to 2   teaspoons vanilla
            6   egg yolks
            1   cup milk
                 pinch of salt

Beat the sugar, yolks, vanilla, and salt together on the top of a double boiler and stir in the milk. Cook over the boiling water, stirring constantly until mixture coats a spoon. Chill.

Makes about 6 servings

CHINA PATTERN USED DURING THE ADMINISTRATION OF JAMES K. POLK

WALNUT CLUSTERS

    1/2   cup sifted all purpose flour
    1/4   teaspoon baking powder
    1/4   teaspoon salt
    1/4   cup soft butter
    1/2   cup sugar
      1   egg
  1-1/2   teaspoons vanilla
  1-1/2   squares semisweet chocolate
      2   cups coarsely chopped walnuts

Start heating the oven to 350° F. Sift the flour, baking powder, and salt together and reserve. Mix the butter and sugar together until creamy. Add egg and vanilla and mix well. Melt chocolate on top of double boiler and stir into mixture. Add flour mixture and fold in the nuts. Drop by teaspoonfuls on greased cookie sheets, 1 inch apart. Bake in 350° F oven for 10 minutes. Cool if desired. A bit of melted chocolate may be spread on the top of each.

CREAM CARAMELS

         2 cups sugar
      1/4 cup butter
         1 cup chopped nuts
      1/2 teaspoon salt
         1 cup light corn syrup
         2 cups heavy cream
         2 teaspoons vanilla extract

Combine sugar and corn syrup in large saucepan. Set candy thermometer in pan. Place pan over low heat and cook, stirring constantly, until the mixture comes to a boil. Boil, without stirring, until thermometer reads 305° F. Remove saucepan from the heat and add 1 tablespoon of butter. Return the pan to the heat and stir in the remaining butter, adding only a little butter at a time so that the mixture will not stop boiling. Warm the cream and add it slowly and continue boiling, stirring vigorously until the thermometer reads 250° F. Remove from heat and let stand for 5 minutes. Add nuts, salt, and vanilla, stirring only enough to blend. Pour the candy into a greased 8 x 11-inch pan. Let stand for at least 8 hours. Turn candy out of pan, cut with a heavy knife. Wrap each piece in waxed paper.

Makes about 2 pounds

CREPES SUZETTE

2	eggs
2	egg yolks
6	tablespoons flour
	sugar
2	cups milk
3/4	cup butter
1/4	cup Cointreau
1/2	cup orange juice
1	tablespoon grated lemon rind
1/4	cup brandy
1	teaspoon salt

Beat eggs and egg yolks together lightly. Sift in flour, 2 tablespoons sugar, and salt. Add milk and beat well. Strain through a fine sieve. For each crepe, melt 1 teaspoon butter in a small skillet, add 2 tablespoons batter and cook over high heat for 2 minutes on each side. Makes 12.

To serve, melt remaining 1/2 cup butter in chafing dish. Add Cointreau, orange juice, and lemon rind and cook for 5 minutes or until mixture comes to a boil. Add a few crepes and cook them for 2 or 3 minutes, basting frequently with the Cointreau sauce. Fold each crepe in quarters and push to one side. Repeat until all crepes are used. Pour brandy into a ladle and warm it over a match. Light the brandy and pour it over the crepes to flame them. When the flame dies, serve the crepes with the sauce.

Serves 6

Author's note: Canned crepes and their sauce may be used if desired. Heat them in a chafing dish and flame with 1/2 cup brandy.

COEUR A LA CREME: WHITE HOUSE

   1 8-ounce package cream cheese
   1 pound cottage cheese
   1 cup heavy cream
   1 quart fresh strawberries, hulled
      confectioners' sugar

Let cream cheese stand at room temperature for at least 1 hour. Beat until smooth. Add cottage cheese and heavy cream slowly, beating constantly until thoroughly blended. Spoon into 6 individual heart-shaped baskets lined with cheesecloth. Set on tray and chill overnight or for at least 8 hours. To serve, unmold coeurs and arrange fresh strawberries around them. Sprinkle berries with sugar if desired.

Serves 6

APRICOT COCONUT BALLS

1	cup dried apricots
1	cup flaked coconut
3/4	cup chopped nuts
1	teaspoon grated lemon rind
1	tablespoon lemon juice
1	tablespoon orange juice
	confectioners' sugar

Heat apricots in the top of a double boiler over boiling water for 10 minutes. Put apricots, coconut, and nuts through food grinder, using fine blade. Knead ground mixture with lemon rind, lemon juice, and orange juice. Add enough confectioners' sugar to make a firm mixture. Form into small balls and roll in confectioners' sugar. Allow to dry at room temperature for at least 4 hours.

Makes about 1 pound

Author's note: I made these for President Nixon and they became his favorite. Illustrated in "Ladies Home Journal" Christmas Edition, 2006.

OPPOSITE: CHINA PATTERN USED DURING THE GEORGE WASHINGTON ADMINISTRATION, 1789-1797

Gerald Rudolph Ford
Elizabeth Bloomer Ford

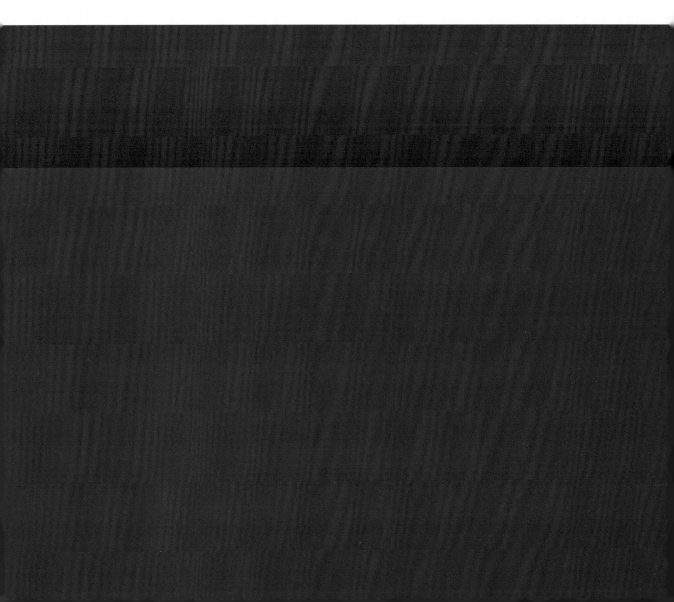

"My fellow Americans, our long national nightmare is over.

Our Constitution works; our great Republic is a government of laws and not of men. Here the people rule. But there is a higher Power, by whatever name we honor Him, who ordains not only righteousness but love, not only justice but mercy.

As we bind up the internal wounds of Watergate, more painful and more poisonous than those of foreign wars, let us restore the golden rule to our political process, and let brotherly love purge our hearts of suspicion and of hate. ...

God helping me, I will not let you down."

GERALD R. FORD'S REMARKS ON TAKING THE OATH OF OFFICE AS PRESIDENT, AUGUST 9, 1974

GERALD FORD BY KINSTLER © WHHA (WHITE HOUSE COLLECTION)

*P*resident Gerald Ford's road to the White House was singular in American history. Richard Nixon appointed Ford Vice President after the departure of Spiro Agnew. He chose Ford over several others because of Ford's forthright, honest and considerate reputation as a person and as a congressman. He seemed to be a humble man who said, after becoming President, "I'm a Ford, not a Lincoln." And that's the way he orchestrated his presidency. The country needed the calming effect that Gerry Ford could offer.

Lyndon Johnson once said, "Gerry Ford played too much football without a helmet." Some Washingtonians thought this was true, but the fact is Gerry Ford graduated from Yale Law School in the top twenty-five percent of his class. Among his classmates were Supreme Court Justice Potter Stewart, Secretary of State Cyrus Vance and Peace Corps Director Sargent Shriver. His was a bridge presidency. He appointed New York's Governor Nelson Rockefeller as his Vice President, but Americans were very aware that neither one had been elected to the office. Ford's tenure was short and lacked the milestones that marked other administrations.

Betty Ford took an active role in the social life of the White House. She planned menus and worked closely with the chefs. She brought her own style of gracious hospitality to the role of First Lady. Both she and the President showed a personal interest in and concern for their guests, and this was reflected in even the most formal affairs.

One of Ford's first state dinners was given for President and Mrs. Leone of the Italian Republic on September 25, 1974. The state dining room, in which all official dinners are held, had two round head tables surrounded by twelve other round tables. Yellow table cloths, flowers in shades of yellow, vermeil flatware from several different administrations and china decorated with wildflowers all contributed to the warmth and friendliness of the President and First Lady.

One of Ford's first presidential acts was the pardon of Richard Nixon for "any and all crimes" and it stirred up a storm. The President hoped it would heal the nation, but, according to Attorney General John Mitchell, the public as a whole, objected to pardoning Nixon when the men who acted on his behalf were disbarred or sent to jail (although Nixon was also disbarred).

Ford was sixty-two when he entered the White House and in fabulous physical condition. He still golfed, skied, swam, and played tennis. He was an artful ballroom dancer as was his wife, but the press made him out to be a clumsy buffoon, which couldn't be farther from the truth. Unfortunately, his spill down the ramp of Air Force One on arriving in Salzburg didn't help. Reporters noted the fall as an important event, and CBS even opened their news story about a campaign trip he was on as "remarkably free of gaffs." Ford's so-called newsworthy clumsiness even made him the brunt of a special program at a dinner in March 1976. Chevy Chase, the comedian, was the entertainment at the annual banquet of the Radio and Television Correspondents Association in Washington, D.C. Chase came out first and as the band played "Hail to the Chief," he stumbled and fell across the entire width of the stage. He bumped his head on the rostrum and then said, "I have asked the Secret Service to remove the salad fork embedded in my left hand." Ford laughed with everyone else but showed his own sense of humor. When it was his turn, he got up and pretended to get tangled in the tablecloth, dropping dishes and silverware on the floor. As he approached the podium, he scattered the text of his speech all over the place. The audience went crazy with laughter.

Once on a trip to Japan, Ford was scheduled to meet Emperor Hirohito. Protocol dictates a visiting head of state to call on the emperor in a mourning suit— black tie, tails and striped pants. President Ford's valet forgot to pack the suit, so Ford had to borrow one from an officer at the American embassy. This would have been just fine except the officer was much shorter than the president, the cuffs of the trousers stopped at Ford's ankles. Of course, the press had a field day at Ford's expense.

Once Ford got lost in the White House, much to the dismay and embarrassment of the Secret Service. The family's golden retriever, Liberty, was usually kept in a kennel on the first floor. Because she was about to deliver her puppies, they moved her to a room on the third floor. One evening, Liberty's trainer had to leave the White House, so President Ford offered to keep the dog in his bedroom. "Mr. President," said the trainer, "she's no trouble at all. If she needs to go to the bathroom, she'll just come and lick your face." About 3 a.m., the president was awakened by a very wet kiss. President Ford got up, slipped on his robe and slippers, and took the elevator to the ground floor, went outside with Liberty, and waited until she returned. Going back to the mansion, he pressed the button for the elevator but nothing happened, the power had been cut off. So Ford and Liberty walked. He opened a door to the left of the elevator and climbed the stairs to the private quarters. At the top of the stairs was a door, but when he turned the knob, he found that it was locked. The third-floor door was also locked. Traipsing back downstairs to the first floor, he found the door had locked behind him. After going up and down the steps several times, looking in vain for some help, the President finally started pounding on the walls. The place at once sprang to life. Lights went on and Secret Service agents appeared, although a bit chagrined after finding out the problem. Ford told them not to worry—all he missed was a little bit of sleep.

President Ford left the White House never having won his own election to the office. He did leave the country intact though and President Carter, on his inaugural day, deeply moved Gerry and Betty Ford with his opening remarks. "For myself and for our nation," said Carter after taking his oath, "I want to thank my predecessor for all he has done to heal our land."

FRENCH FRIED DEVILED EGGS

12	eggs, hard cooked
4	tablespoons crumbled bleu cheese
1/4	cup minced celery
1	teaspoon grated onion
1	tablespoon Worcestershire sauce
1/4	cup dry white wine
1/2	teaspoon salt
1	egg, beaten
1/2	cup heavy cream
1	tablespoon minced parsley
	cayenne pepper
1	cup dry bread crumbs
	oil or vegetable shortening
	tomato celery sauce

Cut eggs in half lengthwise. Remove yolks and mash them. Add cheese, cream, celery, parsley, onion, Worcestershire, a few grains of cayenne pepper, and salt. Stir until thoroughly mixed. Fill egg whites with yolk mixture and press halves together. Roll eggs in crumbs. Add wine to beaten egg and dip the eggs in it. Roll again in crumbs. Fry in 3 inches of hot oil (375° F) for 5 minutes or until lightly browned. Serve immediately with tomato celery sauce.

Serves 6

CHILLED CUCUMBER SOUP

2-1/2 cups chopped, pared seeded cucumbers
   1 cup chicken broth
   1 teaspoon salt
   1 dash white pepper to taste
   4 drops red pepper seasoning
   1 tablespoon lemon juice
   1 cup sour cream
 1/2 cup finely diced cucumbers

Combine the chopped cucumbers, chicken broth, salt, pepper, red pepper seasoning, and lemon juice in electric blender container and cover. Blend until smooth. Add sour cream to the mixture and blend well. Chill for several hours. Garnish each serving with finely diced cucumbers.

8 servings

Author's note: Soup looks much nicer and the presentation is much better if you leave the skin on the diced cucumbers.

GAZPACHO

4	cups diced tomato
1-1/2	cups chopped green pepper
3/4	cup chopped onion
1	clove garlic, minced
2	cups beef bouillon
1/2	cup lemon juice
1/4	cup olive oil
1	tablespoon paprika
1/2	cup sliced cucumber
1	tablespoon salt
	freshly ground black pepper

Combine all ingredients except cucumber. Let stand at room temperature for 1 hour, stirring frequently. Chill for at least 2 hours. Add cucumber just before serving.

Serves 6

SUPREME OF SEAFOOD NEPTUNE

1-1/2	cups mayonnaise
3/4	cup chili sauce
1	tablespoon chopped shallots
3	drops red pepper seasoning
1	teaspoon salt
1	dash white pepper to taste
1	teaspoon unflavored gelatin
1	tablespoon boiling water
	parsley
	hearts of palm
2	tablespoons white horseradish, drained
1-1/2	teaspoons Worcestershire sauce
2	cups cooked crab meat, diced
2	cups cooked tiny shrimp
1	cup cooked scallops, diced
	finely minced green pepper
	whole shrimp
	sliced hard-cooked egg
	red caviar
	cherry tomatoes
2	tablespoons oil and vinegar

Combine the mayonnaise, chili sauce, shallots, horseradish, Worcestershire sauce, red pepper seasoning, salt, and pepper and mix until smooth. Dissolve the gelatin in boiling water, stir into sauce mixture, and fold in the crab meat, shrimp, and scallops. Spoon into 1-3/4-quart ring mold. Chill for several hours or overnight until firm.

Unmold the ring onto a platter. Decorate the center with hearts of palm and green pepper. Trim the mold with whole shrimp, egg slices topped with caviar, tomatoes, and parsley. Spoon oil and vinegar dressing over the hearts of palm.

10 first-course servings

Author's note: This is one of my favorite recipes! Mrs. Ford served this for a luncheon entrée.

OYSTER POULETTE (SAUCE OF STOCK)

2	dozen oysters, shucked
1/4	pound mushrooms
3	tablespoons butter
1	tablespoon lemon juice
2	tablespoons flour
	dash of nutmeg
2	egg yolks
1/2	cup heavy cream
1/2	teaspoon salt
	freshly ground black pepper
6	slices toast
2	tablespoons minced parsley

Remove mushroom caps. Slice and save them. Cook mushroom stems in 3/4 cup water for 20 minutes. Strain and save mushroom liquor. Discard stems. Meanwhile, drain oysters and save liquor. Simmer oysters in 1 tablespoon butter, lemon juice, salt, and pepper until edges curl. Remove from heat and set aside. Melt remaining 2 tablespoons butter in top part of double boiler. Add flour and stir until smooth. Add 1/2 cup mushroom liquor and 1/2 cup oyster liquor and cool, stirring constantly, until thickened. Add oysters and their sauce, mushrooms, and nutmeg. Simmer for 5 minutes, stirring occasionally. Place over hot (not boiling) water and stir in egg yolks beaten with cream. Cook over hot water for 10 minutes, stirring occasionally. Serve over toast and sprinkle with parsley.

Serves 6

OYSTERS ROCKEFELLER: WHITE HOUSE

36	freshly opened oysters on the half shell
6	tablespoons butter
6	tablespoons finely minced raw spinach
3	tablespoons minced parsley
5	tablespoons bread crumbs
1/2	teaspoon Herbsaint®
3	tablespoons minced onion
3	tablespoons minced celery
	Tabasco® sauce
1/2	teaspoon rock salt
6	pie tins

Melt butter in saucepan. Add all the rest of the ingredients except the oysters. Cook, stirring constantly, for 15 minutes or until soft. Press through sieve or food mill. Cool. Place rock salt in pie tins. Set oysters on half shell on top and put a spoonful of sauce on each oyster. Broil under medium heat until sauce begins to brown. Serve immediately in the pie tins.

Serves 6

Author's note: The exact recipe for Antoine's Oysters Rockefeller is a secret of the house. Owner Roy Alciatore gives this as a close facsimile.

LOBSTER THERMIDOR: WHITE HOUSE

3	2-pound lobsters
3/4	cup butter
2	cups heavy cream
1	cup milk
	salt
1/4	cup olive oil
1/4	cup prepared mustard
3	tablespoons flour
1/2	cup grated Parmesan cheese
	freshly ground black pepper

Split the lobsters. Brush with oil and sprinkle with salt and pepper. Broil under medium heat for 5 minutes. Remove from broiler and dot with 6 tablespoons of butter. Bake in a hot oven (400° F) for 10 minutes. Remove lobster meat from shells and slice it. Save coral. Brush inside of each shell lightly with mustard. Meanwhile, simmer cream over low heat for 30 minutes, stirring occasionally. Melt 4 tablespoons of butter, stir in flour and 1/2 teaspoon salt. Add milk slowly, cook until sauce thickens, stirring constantly. Mix in cream and lobster coral. Return lobster meat to shells and cover with sauce. Sprinkle with Parmesan cheese and dot with remaining 2 tablespoons of butter. Bake in hot oven (400° F) for 10 minutes.

Serves 6

Author's note: Decadent! To say the least, guests love it, not just for the taste but for its scarcity.

RUBY RED GRAPEFRUIT CHICKEN

2	ruby red grapefruits
1	tablespoon honey
1/4	teaspoon salt
3	tablespoons butter or margarine
1/2	cup whole cranberry sauce
1/4	teaspoon cloves, ground
1	frying chicken, disjointed

Peel and section the grapefruit, squeezing all juice from membranes into a saucepan. Add cranberry sauce, honey, cloves, and salt, mixing well, then bring to a boil. Stir in the grapefruit sections. Brown your chicken in butter in a frying pan, then place in a shallow baking dish. Baste with grapefruit sauce. Bake in a 350° F oven for about 45 minutes, basting frequently. Serve the chicken with the remaining grapefruit sauce.

Serves 4 people

Author's note: An especially popular dish, not only in the Ford administration, but also in the Johnson and Kennedy administrations. Chef Henry Haller originally got this recipe from Rene Verdon and when Haller presided over the kitchens of the White House, he used it often.

BREASTS OF CHICKEN WITH HAM

6	6 ounce chicken breasts, boned and skinless
6	slices of cooked ham
6	tablespoons butter
1	cup canned sliced mushrooms
1/4	teaspoon savory
1/4	teaspoon rosemary
1/4	teaspoon thyme
1/2	cup dry sherry
1/4	cup dry white wine
1	tablespoon cornstarch
1	cup heavy cream
1	teaspoon salt
	freshly ground black pepper
6	slices toast

Bone and skin chicken breasts and cut them in half. Season with salt and pepper. Sauté breasts in 4 tablespoons of butter for 10 minutes or until golden brown. Drain mushrooms and add 1/2 cup of mushroom liquid to chicken. Set mushrooms aside. Add herbs to chicken, cover and simmer for 20 minutes. Add sherry and wine and simmer for 10 minutes. Add mushrooms and cornstarch dissolved in cream and simmer for 5 minutes or until sauce is thickened, stirring constantly. Sauté ham in remaining 2 tablespoons of butter. Place ham on toast, top with chicken, and spoon sauce over.

Serves 6

HAM WITH BRANDIED PEACHES

    1   8-pound, precooked, boned ham
    6   canned brandied peaches
        whole cloves
    1   cup honey
    1   teaspoon dry mustard
        cayenne pepper

Score ham and stud with cloves. Combine 1/4 cup of the brandied peach juice, honey, mustard, and a few grains of cayenne pepper. Spread mixture over top and sides of ham. Bake in a hot oven (425° F) for 15 minutes or until well glazed, basting once or twice with pan juices. Cool. Chill in the refrigerator for at least 1 hour. Serve the ham with chilled brandied peaches.

Serves 6

BEEF BELMONT: WHITE HOUSE

8	pounds short ribs of beef with bone
	bouquet garni (parsley, bay leaf,
	and thyme tied in piece of cheesecloth)
6	celery stalks
3	leeks, diced
4	ounces egg noodles
	freshly ground black pepper
1/4	cup freshly grated horseradish
4	carrots, diced
12	pearl onions
	salt
1	cup sour cream
	pickled green tomatoes

Place meat in 4 quarts of cold water and bring slowly to a boil. Skim top until clear. Add bouquet garni and simmer for 1-1/2 hours. Remove bouquet garni. Season with salt and pepper to taste. Add celery, carrots, leeks, and onions. Simmer for 15 minutes Add egg noodles and simmer for 10 minutes. Serve the soup with vegetables and noodles in a large soup plate. Then serve the meat separately, accompanied by a sauce of sour cream and horseradish combined, and the pickled green tomatoes.

Serves 6

Author's note: Best served on a sideboard so guests can help themselves. A real winner.

CHINA FROM THE WHITE HOUSE COLLECTION OF JOHN QUICY ADAMS, 1825-1827

VEAL CUTLETS A' LA BOLOGNESE

6   veal cutlets
1   egg, beaten
1   cup bread crumbs
1/2   cup grated Parmesan cheese
1/2   cup lard
6   slices boiled ham
1   cup milk
1   cup canned tomato sauce
1/2   teaspoon salt
    freshly ground black pepper

Beat egg with 2 tablespoons of water. Dip cutlets into the egg mixture and then into bread crumbs that have been combined with 2 tablespoons cheese, salt, and pepper. Sauté in boiling hot lard for 10 minutes. Top cutlets with ham and sprinkle with remaining cheese. Combine milk and tomato sauce and add to cutlets in skillet. Cover and simmer for 25 minutes.

Serves 6

STRAWBERRY MOUSSE

1-1/2	pint fresh strawberries
1/2	cup sugar
1	tablespoon Kirshwasser
1	tablespoon lemon juice
3/4	cup water
2	envelopes unflavored gelatin
2-1/2	cups whipping cream

Place one pint of strawberries, sugar, Kirshwasser, lemon juice and 1/4 cup water in an electric blender; cover. Blend this mixture until smooth. Sprinkle the gelatin over remaining 1/2 cup water, heat until dissolved, and stir in the strawberry puree. Chill until this mixture begins to thicken. Whip 1-1/2 cups cream until stiff and fold into the thickened strawberry puree. Spoon into 1-1/2-quart mold. Chill several hours or overnight until firm. Unmold onto a serving plate. Decorate with the remaining 1 cup cream, whipped, and remaining whole strawberries.

10 servings

Author's note: An easy dish for entertaining—make it the night before and place in the refridgerator.

GLAZED APPLE SLICES

2	pounds cooking apples
1	lemon
2	cups brown sugar
1/4	teaspoon ground nutmeg
1/8	teaspoon ground cloves
1/2	teaspoon ground cinnamon

Peel, core, and slice apples. Grate the lemon peel and squeeze the lemon. Arrange apple slices in a shallow baking dish. Combine 1 cup sugar, lemon peel and juice and spices with 1-1/2 cups of water. Pour over apples. Bake in a moderate oven (375° F) for 25 minutes. Sprinkle with the remaining 1 cup sugar and broil under low heat for 5 minutes. Serve warm or chilled.

Serves 6

Author's note: What a great fall dish—either served warm with a pork roast or chilled as an hors d'œuvre with cheese—yummm!

RUM CAKE: WHITE HOUSE

4	eggs
1/2	cup sugar
1/2	teaspoon vanilla extract
1	cup minus 2 tablespoons sifted cake flour
7	tablespoons butter, melted and cooled
	rum mustard cream
2	tablespoons dark rum
	semisweet chocolate frosting

Combine eggs, sugar, and vanilla in deep bowl. Beat with electric or rotary beater until thoroughly mixed. Set in another bowl containing very hot (not boiling) water and beat about 15 minutes or until mixture is high, light and fluffy. Remove from hot water and continue beating until mixture is cool. Sprinkle 1/3 of the flour over egg mixture and fold in gently with slotted spoon. Repeat until all flour is used. Fold in butter. Pour into buttered and floured 9-inch spring-form pan (or in 2 deep 9-inch layer pans) and bake in a moderate oven (350° F) for 35 minutes. Turn out onto cake-cooling rack. When cold, cut into 2 layers. Put layers together with rum custard cream. Sprinkle top of cake with dark rum and then spread top with semi-sweet chocolate frosting.

INDIAN PUDDING

       1/4   cup yellow cornmeal
         1   quart milk
         1   cup molasses
       1/2   teaspoon ground ginger
       1/2   teaspoon ground cinnamon
         1   teaspoon salt

    Scald milk in the top of a double boiler. Place over hot water, stir in cornmeal and cook for 15 minutes or until thickened, stirring frequently. Mix in the rest of the ingredients. Pour into a greased casserole, set the casserole in a pan of hot water. Bake in a slow oven (325° F) for 2 hours. Stir the pudding once after 1 hour of baking.

Serves 6

CHOCOLATE SOUFFLÉ: WHITE HOUSE

2	ounces sweet chocolate cut into small pieces
1-1/2	cup milk
	sugar
6	egg yolks
6	tablespoons flour
2	tablespoons cornstarch
9	egg whites, stiffly beaten
	butter
	vanilla sauce

Bring chocolate, milk, and 6 tablespoons sugar to a boil, stirring constantly. Mix the egg yolks, flour, and cornstarch in a bowl. Add the boiling milk mixture gradually, stirring briskly. Return to the heat and bring to a boil, stirring constantly. Remove from heat and cool. Fold in the egg whites, then pour into a buttered and sugared soufflé dish. Bake in a hot oven (400° F) for 25 minutes. Serve with vanilla sauce (see page 232).

Serves 6

CHOCOLATE WALNUT FUDGE

2 squares unsweetened baking chocolate
1/2 cup chopped walnuts
2 cups sugar
3/4 cup milk
2 tablespoons corn syrup
1 tablespoon butter
1 teaspoon vanilla extract

Combine sugar, milk, corn syrup, and chocolate in a saucepan. Set candy thermometer in pan. Place pan over low heat and cook, stirring constantly, until mixture comes to a boil. Continue cooking without stirring until candy thermometer reads 238° F. Remove from the heat and add butter. Let the mixture cool until thermometer reads 110° F. Add vanilla and beat the mixture until thick and creamy. Stir in walnuts. Pour into a buttered pan. Refrigerate for at least 2 hours.

Makes about 1 pound

James Earl "Jimmy" Carter
Eleanor Rosalynn Smith Carter

"And I join in the hope that when my time as your President has ended, people might say this about our Nation:
* – that we had remembered the words of Micah and renewed our search for humility, mercy, and justice;*
* – that we had torn down the barriers that separated those of different race and region and religion, and where there had been mistrust, built unity, with a respect for diversity;*
* – that we had found productive work for those able to perform it;*
* – that we had strengthened the American family, which is the basis of our society;*
* – that we had ensured respect for the law, and equal treatment under the law, for the weak and the powerful, for the rich and the poor;*
* – and that we had enabled our people to be proud of their own Government once again."*

JIMMY CARTER INAUGURAL ADDRESS, THURSDAY, JANUARY 20, 1977

JIMMY CARTER BY ABRAMS © WHHA (WHITE HOUSE COLLECTION)

*W*ith only a single term as governor of Georgia and two terms in the state senate on his political resume, Jimmy Carter, the ultimate longshot, became President of the United States in 1977. He was so unknown that when he appeared in 1974 on the TV show "What's My Line," he almost stumped the panel.

When he told his mother, "Miss Lillian," that he was going to run for President, she asked, "President of what?"

Carter's personality is very different from the other men who have held this awesome job. He is introspective, always ready to confront his own shortcomings and seek self-improvement. He is a strong believer in the power of positive thinking. His greatest strength is his own inner peace. Very unpretentious, he and the First Lady brought a new kind of informality to the White House that, frankly, did not please the press or the American public. He would often carry his own luggage aboard Air Force One and he eliminated the playing of "Hail to the Chief" when he entered a room for a formal occasion. For a simple man, Carter is a complex personality and has been described variously as shy, yet supremely self-confident, compassionate and tender, yet at times, steely and very inconsiderate. Very rarely did he show his temper in front of others - usually he expressed his displeasure with an icy stare or sarcasm. Once he left a top aide on the tarmac and would not allow the plane to turn around and pick him up. With an order to the pilot to take off, he commented, "If he can't get here on time, he should take another plane."

Jimmy Carter's family was very close-knit. When he was sworn in to office, a reporter asked Miss Lillian, "I bet you're very proud of your son." To which Miss Lillian answered, "Which one?" The matriarch of the Carter family was a powerful woman in her own right. She became the oldest person ever to join the Peace Corps, and instilled that sense of humanitarianism in her children.

The Carter administration was a real partnership—the first such partnership since FDR's administration. Mrs. Carter even had an office on the first floor of the White House instead of the small study on the second floor in the family quarters. She decided to do this because she wanted total privacy for the President without any interruptions.

Carter's reign was lackluster. In the spring of 1979, when he flew to New Hampshire, he and his administration were coming under heavy fire from the press. When a newsman in Portsmouth asked him whether his daughter Amy ever bragged about her father being president, Carter replied, "No, sir, she probably apologizes."

Plagued by double-digit inflation, Carter seemed to run into a brick wall wherever he turned. A very bright man, he had a difficult time governing because he majored in minors. The hostage situation in Iran was escalating, and with the election for his second term around the corner, the 52 hostages, held captive for more than a year, were more than a great concern to the president and contributed to his defeat. Carter saw no resolution to the situation and found no help through the UN and other diplomatic circles. He made a single-minded decision and dispatched a special team from the U.S. military to rescue the hostages. The unit commander, by the way, was an old friend and high school pal of mine named Colonel Ned Seifert of the United States Marine Corps. When the team landed in Iran, they were hampered by the unexpected malfunction of three helicopters, causing the commander to abort the final assault on Teheran. During the evacuation, two of the aircraft collided, killing eight servicemen. It seemed that if the president didn't have bad luck, he wouldn't have had any luck at all.

In November 1980, the militants holding the hostages relinquished them to none other than the Ayatollah Khomeini himself and with Algeria acting as an intermediary, a deal was struck with the United States. Khomeini agreed to release the hostages in exchange for unfreezing Iranian assets in the United States and he dropped all his other demands. The hostages left Iran on January 20, 1981, ending 444 days of captivity just after President Carter turned over the reins of government to Ronald Reagan.

Perhaps the greatest feat of Carter's presidency was the Camp David Accord. In 1978, the Middle East peace process began with a bold gesture from Egypt's Anwar Sadat, in his historic visit to Israel in 1977. At that time, Carter united Sadat and Israel's Menachim Begin at Camp David, the presidential retreat in Maryland's Catoctin Mountains. Thirteen days of intense and personal negotiations resulted in the three heads of state hammering out the first two documents of peace between the Arab nation and Israel. This eventually led to a formal peace treaty ending a 31-year state of war between the two countries. Fate had its revenge again, though. Sadat and Begin were awarded the Nobel Peace Prize—and rightfully so—but Carter was nominated too late to share in the award.

Chicago Mayor Richard Daly once said, "Carter talks about true values."

Speaker of the House Tip O'Neill said, "When it came to understanding the issues of the day, Jimmy Carter was the smartest public figure I've ever known. The range and extent of his knowledge was astounding. He could speak with authority about energy, the nuclear issue, space travel, Middle East, Latin America, human rights, American history, and just about any other topic that came up."

On the other hand, Henry Kissinger, the former secretary of state, said, "The Carter administration has managed an extraordinary feat of having, in the same time, the worst relations with our allies, the worst relations with our adversaries and the most serious upheaval in the developing world since the end of World War II."

Ronald Reagan said, "We must overcome something the present administration has cooked up. A new and altogether indigestible economic stew, one part inflation, one part high unemployment, one part recession, one part runaway taxes, one part deficit spending, seasoned by an energy crisis. It's an economic stew that has turned the national stomach. He would be better off offering you the Jimmy Carter sandwich. On two slices of white bread, spread some peanut butter and add lots of bologna."

For what it's worth, I personally think Kissinger was completely out of order and Reagan was posturing. Human rights have also been the first priority in Carter's life and he has always been a great humanitarian.

"Jimmy's greatest anguish was the aborted mission to rescue the American hostages in Iran. He was sick with fear the hostages would be tortured and killed," Mrs. Carter said, summing up Carter's policy of putting people over politics.

Carter acknowledged his defeat while the votes were still being counted. In some parts of the country people were still voting when he made a very gracious concession speech. It went like this:

"I promised you four years ago that I would never lie to you," he said, "so I can't stand here and say it doesn't hurt. I wanted to serve as President because I love this country and because I love the people of this nation…

"Finally, let me say that I am disappointed tonight but I have not lost either love."

And so the greatest humanitarian to hold the presidency retired. Carter quickly overcame his disappointments and plunged into a myriad of activities. He wrote his memoirs, built his presidential library, and founded the Carter Center Foundation to sponsor projects on behalf of human rights and the peaceful settlement of conflicts around the world. He often flew to foreign countries at the request of the incumbent American President to monitor free elections in various parts of the world. Time magazine declared him to be a superb ex-president. He taught Sunday school, built homes for the Habitat for Humanity and wrote a book of poems titled Always a Reckoning. If this President cannot be remembered for the political accomplishments of his administration, may he be remembered for his heart and selflessness.

BRANDIED PATÉ

1	cup canned liver paté
1/4	cup brandy
1	cup finely chopped mushrooms
1/2	cup butter
2	tablespoons chopped parsley
	salt to taste
	freshly ground black pepper to taste
	chopped chives to taste

Sauté mushrooms in butter over low heat for 5 minutes or until lightly browned. Add mushrooms and butter to paté and mix well. Stir in brandy, parsley, salt, and pepper and blend thoroughly. Let stand at room temperature for at least 1 hour. Chill in the refrigerator overnight or for at least 4 hours. Serve sprinkled with chopped chives.

Serves 6

CLAMS CASINO

36	cherrystone clams on the half shell
3	slices of bacon, diced
1/4	cup diced green pepper
1/2	cup diced pimento
1	teaspoon minced shallots
3	cloves minced garlic

Arrange clams and shells on a bed of rock salt (this prevents the clams from spilling over). Sprinkle with bacon, green pepper, pimento and shallots. Bake in a hot oven (400° F) for 15 minutes or until bacon is brown.

Serves 6

Author's note: This dish is favored all over the world, but this simple recipe is one of the best.

MEXICAN MENUDO SOUP

1	teaspoon coriander seed
3	pounds tripe
1	pound veal, cubed
3	large onions, chopped
3	cloves garlic, minced
1	teaspoon chili powder
1	teaspoon oregano
2	cups canned whole hominy
1/4	chopped parsley
1	tablespoon salt
	freshly ground black pepper to taste

Cut tripe into thin strips. Combine with veal cubes, onion, garlic, chili powder, coriander, oregano, salt, and pepper in 4 quarts water in a large saucepan. Bring to a boil and continue boiling for 5 minutes. Skim. Reduce heat, cover and simmer for 5 hours. Add the hominy and simmer for 30 minutes. Sprinkle with parsley.

Serves 12

Author's note: Not well known outside Mexico, but one of my favorites.

FRIED SHRIMP CURLS

    3   pounds shrimp (any size shrimp will do)
 1/2   cup Hoy Sien Jeung sauce
    6   tablespoons vinegar
    1   dozen scallions, cut in 1-inch pieces
    3   1-inch pieces gingerroot, minced
    2   teaspoons soy sauce
        freshly ground black pepper to taste
    2   tablespoons sugar
 1/2   cup oil
    3   cloves garlic, minced
    1   teaspoon cornstarch
    2   salt

Wash the shrimp. Pull off legs, but not shells and tail. Make sauce of Hoy Sien Jeung, sugar, vinegar, salt and pepper. Fry the shrimp in oil for 1 minute on each side. Add the sauce, scallions, ginger, and garlic. Fry for 5 minutes, stirring constantly. Add cornstarch mixed with soy sauce and 1 tablespoon of water. Fry for 2 minutes.

Serves 6

Author's note: 1/2 teaspoon of garlic salt mixed with 2 tablespoons bouillon may be used instead of the Chinese flavoring Hoy Sien Jeung.

CRAB MEAT EN BROCHETTE:
WHITE HOUSE

3 pounds fresh crab meat
3 cups soft bread crumbs
1/2 cup dry sherry
1 tablespoon dry mustard
1 tablespoon chopped chives
  bacon slices, cut in half

Combine the crab meat, bread crumbs, sherry, mustard, and chives. Mix well. Shape into balls the size of walnuts. Wrap each ball in 1/2 slice bacon and fasten bacon with toothpick. Thread on skewers and broil under medium heat for 15 minutes or until well browned, turning frequently.

Serves 6

Author's note: Instead of using soft bread crumbs, try using Italian seasoned bread crumbs

DEVILED PIG'S FEET

- 6 pig's feet, split
- 1 large onion
- 2 cloves garlic
- 1/2 cup chopped celery, with leaves
- 6 tablespoons chopped parsley
- 1 teaspoon thyme
- 1 teaspoon sage
- 1 bay leaf
- 1/2 cup flour
- 2 beaten eggs
- 2 tablespoons dry white wine
- 1 tablespoon A-1® sauce
- 1/4 teaspoon Tabasco® sauce
- 1 cup dry bread crumbs
- 1/4 teaspoon dry mustard
- 1/2 cup butter
- 1-1/2 teaspoons salt
- freshly ground black pepper
- applesauce

Scrub the pig's feet thoroughly. Put them in a heavy saucepan and add onion, garlic, celery, 4 tablespoons parsley, thyme, sage, bay leaf, and 1 teaspoon salt plus enough water to cover. Bring to a boil. Reduce heat, cover pan and simmer for 2 hours or until pig's feet are tender. Drain and discard stock. Cool the pig's feet.

To devil the pig's feet, roll them in flour and dip into an egg mixed with wine, A-1® sauce, Tabasco® sauce, remaining 1/2 teaspoon salt, and pepper to taste. Dip into bread crumbs seasoned with mustard and remaining 2 tablespoons parsley. Sauté in butter for 10 minutes or until golden brown. Serve with cold applesauce, preferably chunky.

Serves 6

Author's note: I would use a French mustard rather than a domestic mustard. I would serve with warm applesauce, mixed with just a little bit of cinnamon.

VEAL CUTLET CORDON BLEU

        12 thin slices veal
         6 thin slices Swiss cheese (preferably imported)
         6 thin slices Virginia ham (use water-added ham only)
         3 eggs, beaten
            flour
       3/4 cup bread crumbs (Italian, seasoned crumbs)
       3/4 cup butter
            salt and black pepper to taste
        24 cooked asparagus tips

Flatten the veal slices with a cleaver and sprinkle with salt and pepper. Put one slice cheese and one slice ham on each of the 6 veal slices and cover with the remaining veal slices. Pound edges together. Dip in flour, then in egg, then in crumbs. Fry in butter for about 8 minutes. Serve hot with the asparagus tips.

Serves 6

CORN CRISPED PORK CHOPS

        3/4 cup cornflake crumbs
        1/2 teaspoon salt
        1/4 teaspoon pepper
          4 center cut or rib pork chops
        1/2 cup evaporated milk

   Combine the cornflake crumbs, salt, and pepper. Dip pork chops into
evaporated milk then in crumb mixture, turning to coat both sides. Place on aluminum foil lined baking sheet and bake at 375° F for 50 minutes.

Serves 4

ROAST FRESH PORK WITH APRICOTS

1   4-pound pork shoulder
6   canned apricots and juice
2   tablespoons chopped onion
2   tablespoons chopped celery
2   tablespoons butter
2   cups toasted bread cubes
1   dash ground nutmeg
1/2 teaspoon salt

Have the butcher bone and cut pockets into the pork shoulder. Sauté onion and celery in butter for 5 minutes or until onion and celery are clear. Add 1/4 cup canned apricot juice, bread cubes, salt, and pinch of nutmeg. Stuff the pork shoulder with this mixture. Roast in slow oven (325° F) for 3 hours. Add the apricots and cook for 15 minutes.

Serves 6

Author's note: This is a very old country recipe. An addition to enhance this dish—cut and saute pears and mix with chunky apple sauce.

PEPPER STEAK:
WHITE HOUSE

3	pounds tenderloin steak, sliced
3	green peppers, sliced (preferably julienne style)
3	onions, sliced
9	large mushrooms, sliced (preferably portabellos)
3	fresh tomatoes, quartered
1-1/2	cups Espanol sauce
3/4	cup butter
1/2	cup flour
6	tablespoons red Burgundy
	salt and black pepper to taste

First make green pepper sauce by sautéing the green peppers, onions, mushrooms, and tomatoes in 1/2 cup butter for 5 minutes. Add the Espanol sauce and simmer for 10 minutes. Salt and pepper the sliced steak. Dip in the flour and sauté in the remaining 1/4 cup butter for 2 minutes. Add the sauce and simmer for 15 minutes, stirring frequently. Add the wine and simmer for 3 minutes.

Serves 6

SWEET AND SOUR MEATBALLS

1-1/2 pounds ground beef
   3 tablespoons flour
1-1/2 cups chicken bouillon
   6 large cans of pineapple, drained
   2 tablespoons soy sauce
 3/4 cup vinegar
 3/4 cup sugar
   2 eggs
 3/4 cup oil
   3 large green peppers, diced
   2 tablespoons cornstarch
   1 teaspoon Ac'cent® (optional)
 3/4 cup pineapple juice
 1/2 teaspoon salt
    freshly ground black pepper

Shape ground beef into 18 balls. Combine eggs, flour, salt, and pepper. Dip the meatballs in batter and fry in oil until brown. Remove meatballs and keep hot. Pour all but 1 teaspoon of oil from the skillet. Add 1-1/2 cups bouillon, green pepper, and pineapple. Cover and cook over medium heat for 10 minutes. Mix remaining ingredients and cook. Cook, stirring constantly, until mixture comes to a boil and thickens. Add the meatballs and simmer for 15 minutes. Serve with rice.

Serves 6

CHILI CON CARNE

4	cups canned red kidney beans
	(light or dark, preferably dark)
2	pounds ground beef
2	cups sliced onion
3	cloves garlic, minced
1/4	cup oil
2-1/2	cups canned tomatoes
4	tablespoons chili powder
1/2	teaspoon crushed red pepper
3/4	teaspoon oregano
1	teaspoon salt
1/2	teaspoon cumin

Sauté onion and garlic in oil for 10 minutes. Add beef and brown. Add other ingredients, cover and simmer for 30 minutes or until done.

Serves 6

SEAFOOD SALAD: WHITE HOUSE

1	2-pound lobster, boiled
1-1/2	cups cooked, shelled shrimp
24	mussels, steamed
3/4	cup chopped mushrooms
6	tomatoes, sliced
1/2	cup cooked small green peas
	French salad dressing
	shredded lettuce

Remove meat from the lobster and cut into pieces. Chill lobster, shrimp, and mussels. To serve, combine seafood, mushrooms, tomatoes, peas, and dressing. Toss well and serve on top of lettuce.

Serves 6

HERBED GREEN SALAD

        romaine lettuce
        chicory
        Belgian endive
        freshly chopped parsley
        freshly chopped tarragon
        freshly chopped chervil
        freshly chopped dill
        champagne dressing (or any other light dressing)

Arrange the romaine, chicory and endive in a salad bowl. Sprinkle generously with the chopped herbs.

To serve, toss well with champagne or classic French dressing. Fresh basil, watercress, chives, or rosemary may be added to the salad or substituted for the other herbs.

MEXICAN CORN CASSEROLE

Cornmeal Strips
- 1 cup yellow cornmeal
- 1 teaspoon salt
- freshly ground black pepper to taste

Bring two cups water to a boil in a saucepan. Mix cornmeal, salt, and pepper with 1 cup cold water. Pour into boiling water, stirring constantly. Cook until thickened, stirring frequently. Pour into greased, 10-inch-square baking pan. Chill overnight, or for at least 4 hours. Cut into 1 x 2-inch strips.

Meat Filling
- 2 pounds ground beef
- 1 can condensed cream of chicken soup
- 2-1/2 cups canned whole kernel corn
- 1/2 cup sliced stuffed olives
- 1 teaspoon salt
- 1 cup finely chopped onion
- 2 cloves garlic, minced
- 1 teaspoon chili powder
- 1 green pepper, sliced thin (julienne)
- freshly ground black pepper to taste

Combine beef, 1/2 cup chicken soup, 1/2 cup onion, garlic, chili powder, salt, pepper, and 2 cups water in a saucepan. Bring to a boil, reduce heat and simmer for 15 minutes, stirring occasionally. Combine the canned corn, remaining chicken soup, and remaining 1/2 cup onion in a bowl and mix well. Stir in 1/4 cup olives. Line large casserole with cornmeal strips. Pour in the meat mixture Top with the corn and olive mixture. Arrange green pepper slices and remaining 1/4 cup olive slices on top. Cook in a hot oven (400° F) for 30 minutes.

Serves 6

PEARL BARLEY CASSEROLE

    1 cup pearl barley
1/2 cup pine nuts
1/2 cup butter
    1 cup finely chopped onions
    1 cup finely chopped parsley
1/2 cup finely chopped chives
    6 cups beef bouillon
    1 teaspoon salt
       freshly ground black pepper

Sauté the pine nuts in butter for 5 minutes or until golden brown. Remove nuts and sauté onion in butter remaining in skillet for 5 minutes. Add barley and brown, lightly stirring constantly. Add parsley, chives, bouillon, salt, and pepper and half of the pine nuts and pour into casserole. Bake in moderate oven (350° F) for 1 hour, stirring once after 30 minutes. Sprinkle the rest of the sautéed pine nuts over the top and bake for 20 minutes more.

Serves 6

EGGPLANT PARMESAN

1	large eggplant
1/4	cup grated Parmesan cheese
1/4	pound mozzarella cheese, sliced
1	egg, lightly beaten
1/4	cup dry white wine
1	cup cracker crumbs
1	clove garlic, minced
1/4	cup olive oil
2	cups canned tomato sauce
2	tablespoons minced parsley
1/4	teaspoon basil
1/4	teaspoon oregano
1	bay leaf, crumbled
1	teaspoon salt

Pare the eggplant and cut crosswise into 1/4-inch slices. Beat egg with wine. Dip eggplant slices in egg and wine and dip them in cracker crumbs. Sauté garlic in oil for 5 minutes. DO NOT BURN GARLIC. Add eggplant and sauté for 10 minutes or until golden brown. Remove the eggplant and keep hot. Add the tomato sauce, parsley, basil, oregano, bay leaf, and salt to oil remaining in skillet and simmer for 15 minutes, stirring frequently. Arrange alternate layers of eggplant, Parmesan, mozzarella cheese, and sauce in casserole. Top with mozzarella. Bake in moderate oven (350° F) for 30 minutes.

Serves 6

CHILI BARBECUE SAUCE

1-1/2	tablespoons chili powder
2	cloves garlic, finely chopped
6	tablespoons butter
3/4	cup red wine
3/4	cup beef bouillon (strong, reduced)
1	teaspoon sugar
	freshly ground black pepper to taste
3/4	cup finely chopped onion
3/4	cup finely chopped green pepper
4	cups canned tomatoes
2	tablespoons cornstarch
1	tablespoon salt

Sauté onions, garlic, and green pepper in butter for 5 minutes. Add chili powder, tomatoes, wine, salt, and pepper. Combine cornstarch, cold bouillon, and sugar and stir into chili mixture. Bring to boil; reduce heat and cook until thickened, stirring constantly. Cover and simmer for 10 minutes. Serve with hot dogs, ham, or spare ribs. Sauce may be kept in refrigerator for at least one week.

Makes about 6 cups

Author's note: This sauce is perfect on any meat—just baste often—it's not too hot.

MASHED ACORN SQUASH

    3   acorn squashes
  1/4   cup butter
    1   tablespoon minced onions
    1   cup heavy cream
  1/4   teaspoon ground nutmeg
        salt
    2   tablespoons maple syrup

Cut the squashes in half lengthwise, and remove the seeds and fibers. Put 1 teaspoon butter, 1/2 teaspoon minced onion, and a dash of salt in each half. Cover and bake in 350° F oven for 30 minutes or until tender. Scoop the cooked squash from shells and mash with cream and the remaining 2 tablespoons of butter, nutmeg, and the maple syrup.

Serves 6

Author's note: Just to be different try adding 1/4 teaspoon ground cinnamon and 1 tablespoon dark brown sugar—wow!

POLENTA (CORN APLENTY)

1 cup yellow cornmeal
4 tablespoons grated Parmesan cheese
2 tablespoons butter
1 teaspoon salt
  freshly ground black pepper to taste

Bring 4 cups salted water to a boil in top part of double boiler. Slowly add cornmeal and cook until slightly thickened, stirring constantly. Place over boiling water and cook for 45 minutes. Add the cheese, butter, and black pepper. Cook for 5 minutes.

Serves 6

HUSH PUPPIES

            2   cups water ground white cornmeal
            1   teaspoon double-acting baking powder
            3   tablespoons sugar
        1/4   cup butter
            1   tablespoon salt

Combine cornmeal, baking powder, sugar, and salt. Add slowly to 3-1/2 cups boiling water, stirring briskly. As soon as mixture is smooth, remove from heat. Stir in butter. Cool. Form into finger-shape rolls and fry in 2 inches hot fat (375° F) until golden brown.

Makes about 3 dozen

POTATO ROLLS

2	large potatoes, boiled and mashed (approximately 1 cup)
2	envelopes granular yeast
1	cup milk
2/3	cup butter
1/2	cup sugar
5-1/2	cups sifted flour
2	eggs, beaten
1-1/2	teaspoons salt

Dissolve the yeast in 1/2 cup lukewarm water. Scald milk and add butter, sugar, and salt. Stir until sugar is dissolved. Add mashed potatoes and mix well. Cool the mixture until it is lukewarm. Add the yeast and half of the flour. Mix well. Beat in the eggs. Add remaining flour and mix thoroughly. Knead the dough on lightly floured board for 10 minutes or until smooth and elastic. Place in greased bowl turning once to bring the greased side up. Cover with damp cloth. Let rise in warm place, about 80–85° F for an hour, or until dough is doubled in bulk. Punch dough down. Form into 36 rolls. Place in greased muffin pans, and let rise in warm place for 30 minutes. Brush the rolls with melted butter. Bake in moderate oven (375° F) for 20 minutes.

RED CABBAGE

1	3-pound red cabbage
2	green apples, peeled and chopped (preferably Granny Smith variety)
1	onion, finely chopped
1/4	cup sugar
1/4	cup vinegar (cider or white)
2	tablespoons bacon fat
1	teaspoon salt
	freshly ground black pepper
1/2	teaspoon ground allspice

Shred cabbage. Put in saucepan with apples, onion, allspice, sugar, vinegar, bacon fat, salt, and pepper and 1/4 cup boiling water. Bring to boil, reduce heat. Cover and simmer for 1 hour, stirring occasionally.

Serves 6

Author's note: Keep in crock for 2 or 3 days, covered tightly in refrigerator, then serve.

PINTO BEAN CAKES

       2 cups dried pinto beans
     1/4 teaspoon crushed red pepper or
            1 chili pepper, minced
       2 cloves garlic, chopped
     1/2 cup butter
       1 teaspoon salt

Soak the beans overnight in water and keep covered. Simmer them in morning in the same soaking water with salt for 2 hours. Drain beans and chop them coarsely or put them through food grinder using a coarse blade. Add red pepper and garlic. Shape into 12 cakes and sauté in butter for 10 minutes or until golden brown.

Author's note: Lima, navy, or great northern beans may be substituted for pinto beans. 4 cups of canned pinto or lima beans, heated and drained, may be substituted for 2 cups dried beans, soaked and cooked.

SAUTÉED VIDALIA ONION SLICES

    6 large Vidalia onions
1/2 cup butter

Peel the onions. Cut into 1/2-inch slices. Sauté very slowly in butter for 10 minutes, or until tender, turning once.

This is a very seasonal dish and will feed 6 people

BLACK BEANS IN GARLIC SAUCE

2 cups dried black beans
2 ounces salt pork, diced
2 cloves garlic, sliced
1 teaspoon cumin seed
1 teaspoon salt

Soak the beans overnight in water and keep covered. Simmer them in the morning in the soaking water for 2 hours with salt. Drain beans and keep hot. Sauté diced pork for 5 minutes. Add garlic and sauté for 5 more minutes or until pork dices are crisp and garlic slices are golden brown. Stir in cumin seeds and the beans.

Serves 6

Author's note: 4 cups canned lima beans, heated and drained, may be used instead of 2 cups dried beans, soaked and cooked.

RICE PILAF STUFFING

    1/2 pound rice (equivalent to 1 cup)

      2 cups good strong reduced-beef stock

    1/4 cup onions, finely chopped

    1/2 cup mushrooms, finely sliced

    1/2 medium-size bay leaf

    1/3 cup butter and oil (1/6 and 1/6)

        salt and pepper to taste

      4 apples, peeled and sliced

After boiling rice, add the first seven ingredients, and bake at 400° F. Remove from oven and add apples and mix together and serve.

Author's note: White rice will work fine in this recipe, but brown rice will add a richer, nuttier flavor.

PEANUT STUFFING

- 3 cups shelled roasted peanuts
- 4 cups dry bread crumbs
- 1 medium onion, finely chopped
- 1/2 cup dry white wine
- 1/2 cup chicken bouillon
- 1 egg, beaten
- 3 tablespoons butter, melted
  freshly ground black pepper to taste

Chop the peanuts and brown them in moderate oven (375° F) for 15 minutes. Add remaining ingredients and toss lightly together.

Makes about 8 cups

SPOON BREAD

    1   cup white cornmeal
    1   quart milk
    2   tablespoons butter
    4   eggs, well beaten
  1/4   teaspoon salt

Scald the milk in top of double boiler. Place over hot water, stir in cornmeal, butter, and salt. Cook for 15 minutes, or until thickened, stirring frequently. Pour over eggs. Bake in greased casserole in hot oven (400° F) for 45 minutes.

Serves 6

Author's note: Use only whole milk.

PEANUT BRITTLE

1-1/2	cups salted peanuts
1-1/2	cups sugar
1	cup light corn syrup
1	teaspoon baking soda
1	tablespoon butter
1/2	teaspoon vanilla extract

Combine sugar, corn syrup and 1/3 cup water in a large saucepan. Set candy thermometer in pan. Cook, stirring constantly until the syrup boils. Boil until the thermometer reads 300°. Remove from heat, add baking soda (which should be free of lumps) and stir until the mixture bubbles. Stir in butter, vanilla, and peanuts. Pour into two buttered cookie sheets. When cold, break into pieces. This candy will get sticky unless kept in a tightly covered tin.

Makes about 1 pound

Author's note: Obviously a Carter family favorite.

BLUE ROOM, 1999, CLINTON ADMINISTRATION BY BRUCE WHITE - WHITE HOUSE HISTORICAL ASSOCIATION © WHHA

Ronald Wilson Reagan
Nancy Davis Reagan

"Can we solve the problems confronting us? Well, the answer is an unequivocal and emphatic 'yes.' To paraphrase Winston Churchill, I did not take the oath I have just taken with the intention of presiding over the dissolution of the world's strongest economy.

In the days ahead I will propose removing the roadblocks that have slowed our economy and reduced productivity. Steps will be taken aimed at restoring the balance between the various levels of government. Progress may be slow—measured in inches and feet, not miles—but we will progress. Is it time to reawaken this industrial giant, to get government back within its means, and to lighten our punitive tax burden. And these will be our first priorities, and on these principles, there will be no compromise."

RONALD REAGAN FIRST INAUGURAL ADDRESS, TUESDAY, JANUARY 20, 1981

RONALD REAGAN BY KINSTLER © WHHA (WHITE HOUSE COLLECTION)

*T*he oldest person ever elected to the presidency, Ronald Reagan was 70 years young upon his ascendancy. It's often been said that in our media-crazed nation, it was only a matter of time before an actor became President. But, without a doubt, Reagan did a wonderful job of making Americans proud again, often to the dismay of his adversaries who thought Bonzo truly went to Washington.

Reagan earned the name "The Great Communicator" for his skilled and effective use of television. He was a gifted orator and raconteur with an endless supply of anecdotes from his days in Hollywood. He has been described as aloof, intensely private, and reluctant to reveal much about himself to those outside his family. Several books have been written about Reagan's time in office by former administration officials.

One man, Secretary of State Alexander Haig, said, "The President was portrayed as a remarkably passive figure, disengaged from day-to-day operations, timid about asserting his authority, inept at personal confrontation and lacking, at times, even a basic understanding of major issues."

Other people in the know say he was by all accounts affable, cheerful, even-tempered, and forever optimistic. According to Hedrick Smith of The New York Times, "His 'aw shucks' manner and charming good looks disarm those who, from a distance, thought of him as a far right fanatic."

On the other hand, Nancy Reagan really staged the show. She wrote the script and Ronny, as she called him, followed it like a Hollywood movie. She called the shots. I once heard, but never verified, that Reagan wanted my old friend, Congressman Jack Kemp, as his vice presidential running mate. Nancy put her foot down and said absolutely not because he was too good looking and much younger than Reagan. She thought Kemp would detract from Reagan's image.

Without a doubt, Ronald Reagan has had a charmed life. His high school yearbook caption reads, "Life is just one grand sweet song, so start the music." I just loved that attitude. A great American, President Reagan believed intensely in free will.

He once said, "We are given a certain control of our destiny because we have a chance to choose."

He also said, "We are given a set of rules or guidelines in the Bible by which to live and it is up to us to decide whether we will abide by them or not."

When Reagan took office, the country was a mess. Inflation had reached double digits, apathy was at an all-time high, but to all Americans, young and old alike, President Reagan returned a confidence and sense of hope.

Early on, before his presidency, coached by Congressman Jack Kemp, Reagan became a supply-sider—an economic philosophy designed to reduce the plague of double-digit inflation, and therefore prompt businesses to reinvest profits and create jobs.

A right-wing conservative, Reagan was endorsed by the voting Americans and in 1984 won a second term by the largest electoral vote in history. He ran against Walter Mondale and won 525 electoral votes to Mondale's 13.

But at least one person wasn't pleased with Reagan's economics. In March 1981, barely two months into Reagan's first term, a 25-year-old drifter from a wealthy family fired six rounds from his revolver as the President emerged from the Washington, D.C., Hilton. One bullet ricocheted off the presidential limousine and entered Reagan's left side, bounced off the seventh rib, punctured and collapsed a lung, and lodged one inch from his heart.

Fortunately, an ever-present and alert Secret Service agent, Jerry Parr, shoved the President into the limousine and threw himself over the president as a shield. Neither Parr nor Reagan realized that Reagan had been shot. When Reagan started coughing up blood, Agent Parr ordered the limousine to George Washington Hospital, where an emergency team, already alerted, awaited the President's arrival. Mr. Reagan walked into the hospital under his own power, but rapidly grew weak and complained about difficulty breathing. Doctors reported later that his blood pressure had dropped so rapidly that had treatment been delayed 5 minutes more, he probably would have died.

"I forgot to duck," the President joked, and then said to the doctors and surgical team before he went into surgery, "I hope you're all Republicans!" When he awoke after surgery, he borrowed a line from W.C. Fields, "I'd rather be in Philadelphia!"

Although Ronald Reagan escaped the assassination attempt, press secretary James Brady and a D.C. police officer were not so lucky. Brady suffered severe brain damage and has been struggling through rehabilitation ever since. He and his wife Sarah have spearheaded much of the anti-firearms legislation that has been presented to Congress since that incident.

Reagan's tenure in office was not without controversy. Critics believed his ultra-conservative views sometimes interfered with his common sense. Reagan knew how to use the presidency as a tool to run the government. Agree or disagree with him, the president hired some good men as cabinet secretaries. For the most part, they were leaders and captains of industry and knew their job well. The problem was, Reagan gave them too much rope. Take, for example, the Iran-Contra scandal or the fact that the Reaganomics program left America the largest creditor nation in the world after being the largest debtor nation in the world.

There were many people, however, who, through the private and public sector, swore by Reagan. One of my favorite people is Jeane Kirkpatrick, the former ambassador to the United Nations. She once said, "Ronald Reagan brought to the presidency, confidence in the American experience."

A friend of mine, a former congressman from Rochester, New York, and former president of the World Bank, Barber Conable, said, "He may not be strong on some details, but he knows how to sketch out broad outlines for his objectives and to provide a sense of direction."

Quoting Secretary of State Alexander Haig, "He has contributed greatly to the revival of America's confidence and pride."

Ronald Reagan's own wish as President was, "What I really would like to do is to go down in history as the President who made Americans believe in themselves again." Personally, I think he did just that.

Ronald Reagan thoroughly enjoyed being President. He loved the pomp and circumstance that went with the position, presiding over ceremonial functions, hosting dinner parties with Mrs. Reagan, elaborate receptions and dinners at the White House, and executing snappy salutes as commander in chief of the Armed Forces, even though he was a civilian and not in uniform.

The official White House receptions were star-studded events and people clambered for invitations. You will see by the recipes in this chapter that the food was at least part of the attraction.

Reagan did like to joke and could dish it out as well as take it. He once said, "It's true that hard work never killed anybody, but I figure why should I take a chance. I'll see you after my nap."

Reagan loved his naps and at the White House Correspondent's Association Dinner he said he had been working very hard burning the midday oil. Toward the end of his second term, he teased about his plans for retirement. "As soon as I get home to California, I plan to lean back, kick up my feet, and take a long nap." Then he added, "Ah, come to think of it, things won't be all that different after all."

Reagan also loved to joke about his age. After taking over the White House in January 1981, he turned 70 years old—the oldest man ever to occupy the Oval Office. He thanked people for celebrating his thirty-first anniversary of his thirty-ninth birthday. Three years later, when he turned seventy-three and was planning to run again, he told some senior citizens that he was still so active that he planned to "campaign in all thirteen states."

In another speech about the trade deficit, he pointed out that the United States has had a trade deficit almost every year between 1790 and 1875 and then added, with a deadpan expression, "I remember them well." He added, "Of course, I was only a boy at the time."

President Reagan never tired of poking fun at himself. In a speech to a business group, he said, "George Washington gave an inaugural address of just 135 words and became a President. Of course, there was William Henry Harrison. He spoke at his inauguration for nearly 2 hours, caught pneumonia, and died within a month." Then came the zinger: "I told him to keep it short!"

When the Reagans moved into the White House, jelly beans were immediately elevated to the esteemed position of America's First Candy. Ronald Reagan said, "We can hardly start a meeting or make a decision without passing around the jar of jelly beans. You can tell a lot about a fella's character by whether he picks out all of one color, or just grabs a handful."

President Reagan was called many names while in office in addition to "The Great Communicator"; "The Teflon President" and "Dr. Feel Good" among them, but he was also known as the "Chief of the One Liners."

"When you go to bed with the federal government, you get more than a good night's sleep."

Criticizing the Salt II Conference, he cracked, "Too much salt isn't good for you."

He also commenced a speech in Moscow in 1986 by saying, "As Henry VIII said to each of his six wives, 'I won't keep you long.'"

President Reagan made a hobby of collecting jokes from his cabinet secretaries. George Schultz, his secretary of state, sometimes inserted a joke in his cables and communications when he was overseas. This was Secretary Schultz's way of making sure that Reagan read the cable. When he was stateside, if the President said, "George, that was a great joke you inserted," then Schultz knew that his message had gotten through.

Mr. Reagan's favorite jokes were about the Soviet Union, and he liked to kid their officials about the shortcomings of their system. "What are the four things wrong with Soviet agriculture?" The answer: "Summer, Fall, Winter and Spring."

When Reagan extolled the benefits of free speech in the United States to Mikhail Gorbachev at their first meeting in Geneva, he said, "Why, people can even stand in front of the White House and yell 'To hell with Ronald Reagan.'"

Gorbachev, who had a great sense of humor replied, "That's nothing, Mr. President. Russians can stand at the Kremlin wall and yell 'To Hell with Ronald Reagan,' too!" The President and the Soviet leader both broke up laughing and became great personal friends—much to the advantage of the United States.

Once, when he was talking about economic recovery during his 1980 campaign, Reagan said, "I publicly declare that there is a depression in this country."

President Carter answered by saying, "There is no depression in the country; it is a recession."

Reagan said, "That shows how little Mr. Carter knows. If the President wants a definition, I'll give him one. Recession is when your neighbor has lost his job; a depression is when you have lost yours." Then he paused, laughed, and said, "A recovery is when President Carter loses his!"

President Reagan suffered his share of gaffes while living in the White House. He called Liberia's President Samuel Doe, Chairman Mo and addressed Oklahoma Senator Don Nichols as Don Rickles. But the best was at a dinner in honor of the Prince and Princess of Wales. Reagan introduced them as the Prince of Wales and his lovely lady, Princess David.

The ballerina sitting next to actor Peter Ustinov gasped. "What?" she whispered, "Did he really say Princess David?"

"Don't worry," replied Ustinov. "He's just thinking of next weekend at Camp Diana."

After surgery following the assassination attempt, Reagan quoted Sir Winston Churchill in a note to aides, "There is no more exhilarating feeling than being shot at without result."

Years later, when asked about his health, President Reagan said, "Since I came to the White House, I got two hearing aids, a colon operation, skin cancer, a prostate operation, and I was shot. The damn thing is, I never felt better in my life!"

In November 1994, when the annual Ronald Reagan Freedom Award Dinner was held in Beverly Hills, California, plans had been made for the former president to confer the medal on Israel's Prime Minister Yitzhak Rabin. But Mr. Reagan was unable to attend. A few days before, he had announced to the country that he was suffering from Alzheimer's disease and would not be making any more public appearances.

"When the Lord calls me home," he said in his final, open letter to the American people, "whenever that may be, I will leave with the greatest love for this country of ours and eternal optimism for its future."

The Presidential Inaugural Committee
requests the honor of your presence
to attend and participate in the Inauguration of

Ronald Wilson Reagan

as President of the United States of America

and

George Herbert Walker Bush

as Vice President of the United States of America

on Tuesday the twentieth of January

one thousand nine hundred and eighty one

in the City of Washington

HAMBURGER SOUP

1	cup butter
2	pounds lean ground beef
2	cups diced onion
4	cloves garlic, finely diced
1-1/2	cups diced carrots
2	cups diced celery
1	cup diced green bell pepper
3	quarts hot beef broth
4	large ripe tomatoes, peeled and chopped
	(or one 14-1/2 ounce can stewed tomatoes)
1/2	teaspoon freshly ground black pepper
2	bay leaves
1	15-ounce can hominy
2	tablespoons chopped fresh parsley

Melt the butter in heavy skillet and add meat; brown quickly over high heat. Add the diced vegetables; cover and simmer over medium heat for 10 minutes, stirring occasionally. Add the hot broth, tomatoes, pepper, and bay leaves. Cover and simmer over medium heat for 35 minutes, stirring occasionally. Stir in the hominy. Simmer over medium/high heat, cover slightly ajar, for 10 minutes. Remove bay leaves and add chopped parsley. Serve at once with thick slices of toasted French bread.

Soup will freeze well and can be kept refrigerated for several days in a covered container.

Makes 4 quarts

VEAL AND VEGETABLE SOUP

- 2 tablespoons butter
- 1 cup diced onions
- 1 cup diced leeks (white part only)
- 4 cloves garlic, finely chopped
- 1 cup halved thinly sliced carrots
- 2 cups finely diced lean veal
- 1/4 teaspoon freshly ground white pepper
- 2 quarts hot chicken stock
- 1 bay leaf
- 1 cup heavy cream
- 1 tablespoon chopped fresh parsley

Melt the butter in a 4-quart saucepan and add onions, leeks, garlic, and carrots. Cover and simmer over medium heat for 10 minutes. Add diced veal and sprinkle with pepper. Sauté for 3 minutes, stirring constantly. Add hot stock and bay leaf. Cover and simmer over medium heat for 30 minutes, stirring occasionally. Stir in heavy cream and chopped parsley and bring just to the boiling point over high heat. Remove from heat and serve at once with cheese toast triangles and wedges of pita bread.

Makes 3 quarts

CHICKEN POT PIE

    1   4-pound roasting chicken
    1   medium-size onion, quartered
    2   cloves garlic, crushed
    2   medium-size carrots, peeled and chopped
    3   stalks of celery, chopped

In a tied cheesecloth, make a spice bag containing 24 black peppercorns, 1 bay leaf, 2 cloves, 1/4 teaspoon each dried marjoram, thyme, and rosemary.

    2   tablespoons salt
        juice of 1 lemon
    3   cups dry white wine
  2–3   cups cold water
    1   cup 1" x 1/8" carrot sticks, cooked tender-crisp
        (al dente)
    1   cup 1" x 1/8" celery sticks, cooked tender-crisp
        (a dente)
  1/2   cup pearl onions, boiled and drained
    1   cup fresh button mushrooms, boiled and drained
  1/2   cup shelled fresh green peas
    3   cups chicken velouté sauce
    1   tablespoon chopped fresh parsley

Cut the chicken into 6 pieces, cut off the wings, remove the back, and set aside for stock. Cut off the legs and thighs and slice the breast in half. In a large soup pot, combine the onion and garlic with carrots and celery. Add the spice bag and arrange the chicken pieces on top. Sprinkle with salt and lemon juice. Pour on the wine and add enough cold water to cover. Cut a circle of waxed paper the size of the soup pot and set atop the chicken. Top with a heat-proof plate of the same size to weigh down the ingredients. Bring to a boil over medium/high heat and reduce to medium/low and simmer for 5 minutes. Remove from the heat and let stand for 10 minutes. Preheat oven to 350° F. Butter the inside of a 2-quart casserole dish. Remove and bone the cooked chicken and slice it into bite-size pieces. Arrange half of the chicken pieces in the casserole dish. Cover with a vegetable layer consisting of half of the carrot and celery sticks, half of the pearl onions and button mushrooms, and half of the peas. Layer the remaining chicken on top of the vegetable layer. Cover

CHICKEN POT PIE (CONTINUED)

with half of the chicken velouté sauce. Cover with a layer of the remaining vegetables and pour the rest of the chicken velouté sauce over all. Sprinkle with chopped parsley and top with the pot pie crust. Press the edges of the pie crust to the sides of the casserole dish to seal well and flute them. Prick the top 10–12 times with a fork to allow steam to escape.

Brush the crusts lightly with an egg/water mixture. Bake on upper half of the preheated oven for 20 minutes. Brush again with more egg wash and bake for 20 minutes more or until crust is golden brown and pot pie is steaming hot throughout.

Serve at once with Belgian endive salad or other crisp greens.

Chicken Velouté Sauce

(Makes about 3 cups)

3	tablespoons butter
3	tablespoons flour
3	cups hot chicken stock
1/2	cup heavy cream
1	tablespoon Worcestershire sauce
1/4	teaspoon salt
1/4	teaspoon freshly ground white pepper
1/8	teaspoon nutmeg

In a 2-quart saucepan, melt the butter; add the flour and work into a roux. Cook for 1 minute over medium heat, stirring constantly with a wire whisk. Be very careful not to burn the roux.

Stir in hot stock and bring to a boil stirring constantly. Simmer over medium heat for 10 minutes stirring often. Add the heavy cream and bring to a boil stirring constantly. Remove sauce from heat and stir in the Worcestershire sauce, salt, pepper and nutmeg.

Keep warm until ready for use.

CHICKEN POT PIE (CONTINUED)

Pot Pie Crust

(Makes 1 pie crust)

3	cups flour
1	teaspoon salt
1/2	teaspoon baking powder
1/4	cup vegetable shortening
1	egg
2	tablespoons white wine vinegar
5 to 6	tablespoons cold water

Sift the flour with salt and baking powder into a mixing bowl. Use a pastry cutter to cut in shortening until well distributed. Beat egg with vinegar and 5 tablespoons of water. Add to the mixing bowl and blend quickly by hand until dough is smooth. Add more water if needed and handle dough as little as possible. Form by hand into a smooth ball. Wrap tightly in plastic and refrigerate for 2 hours to ease the handling.

On a lightly floured board, roll out dough to fit the casserole dish allowing an extra inch or two for fluting edges.

TOMATO CONCASSE

- 1 tablespoon extra-virgin olive oil
- 1 tablespoon finely minced shallots
- 1 clove garlic, finely minced
- 3 medium-size ripe tomatoes, peeled and coarsely diced
- 1/2 teaspoon salt
- 1/4 teaspoon freshly ground white pepper
- 1 tablespoon chopped fresh parsley

In a sauté pan, heat the oil over medium/high heat and add the shallots and garlic and sauté for 1 minute, being careful not to burn garlic. (If the garlic burns, start over.) Add the diced tomatoes; sprinkle with salt and pepper. Simmer over medium heat, stirring gently with a wooden spoon for 3 minutes. Do not allow to brown. Serve at once, sprinkled with chopped parsley. This dish is best served hot over rice or pasta and is usually served with veal.

Serves 6

PAELLA A LA VALENCIANA

1	3-1/2 pound chicken
1	tablespoon salt
1/2	teaspoon freshly ground white pepper
1/4	cup extra virgin olive oil
1	cup diced onions
4	cloves garlic, finely minced
2	cups diced red and green bell peppers
1/2	pound sliced chorizo (spicy, red, Spanish sausage)
2	cups long grain rice, raw
1	teaspoon saffron
1	tablespoons tomato paste
2	cups dry white wine
3	cups hot chicken stock
1	cup fresh green peas
1	pound large fresh shrimp, peeled and deveined (preferably prawns)
1/2	pound small fresh scallops
12	fresh mussels, thoroughly scrubbed
2	tablespoons chopped fresh parsley

Cut the chicken into 10 pieces and cut off the wings, remove the back and reserve for stock. Separate the legs and thighs and quarter the breast. Mix together salt and pepper; season the chicken pieces lightly and reserve the extra seasoning. In a large sauté pan or paella pan (a large heavy skillet with 2 handles), heat the olive oil, brown the chicken on all sides, and let drain on paper towels. Add the onions, garlic, and peppers to the hot oil and sauté for 3 minutes. Stir in the sliced sausage and sauté for 3 to 4 minutes to brown on all sides. Stir in the rice, saffron, and tomato paste. Add the chicken. Pour in wine and 2 cups of hot stock. Bring to a boil over medium heat, stirring constantly. Cover and simmer over medium heat for 10 minutes. Remove the cover and sprinkle in the peas. Sprinkle the shrimp and scallops with the reserved seasoning and arrange over the rice along with the mussels. Cover and simmer over medium heat for 10 minutes more. Add the remaining cup of hot chicken stock, cover, and let stand for 10 minutes on top of the stove. Sprinkle with parsley and serve at once right from the pan. Accompany with crisp greens such as watercress and mushroom salad. If desired, fresh lobster and clams can be included in the paella in addition to, or in place of, the other seafood.

Serves 6–8

OSSO BUCCO

- 6   slices center cut veal shank
  (each 1-1/2" thick with shank bone)
- 1/2   cup flour
- 1   tablespoon salt
- 1   teaspoon freshly ground white pepper
- 2   tablespoons olive oil (extra virgin, preferably)
- 2   tablespoons finely minced shallots
- 2   cloves garlic, finely minced
- 1   cup diced carrots
- 1   cup diced celery, or celery root, or both
- 2   cups dry white wine
- 1   cup tomato juice
- 2   cups chopped fresh oregano OR
  1 teaspoon dried oregano
- 2   medium-size ripe tomatoes, peeled and coarsely diced
  Gremolata
- 2   finely minced garlic cloves
- 2   tablespoons chopped fresh parsley
  grated rind of lemon

In a shallow bowl, dredge the veal slices with flour, salt, and pepper. Heat oil in heavy skillet and add the veal slices and brown over medium heat cooking for about 5 minutes on each side. Transfer to a paper towel to drain. Add the minced shallots and garlic to the hot oil and sauté for 2 minutes. Add diced carrots, celery or celery root (or both), and sauté for 5 minutes more. Add the wine and tomato juice and bring to a boil. Add the oregano and shank bone and return to a boil. Cover and simmer over medium heat for 20 minutes. Turn bones over and simmer for 20 minutes more or until meat is tender and falls away from the bone. Transfer the shank bone to a deep serving platter and surround with the rest of the veal. Add diced tomatoes to the sauce and bring to a boil. Spoon over the meat and sprinkle with the Gremolata and serve at once over steamed rice or with steamed rice or noodles.

ROAST BEEF HASH

2	tablespoons butter
1	cup finely diced onions
3	cloves garlic, finely minced
1	cup finely diced celery
1/2	cup finely diced green bell pepper
4	cups finely diced cooked roast beef (remove all fat)
1	large cooked potato, peeled and finely diced (leftover cooked potatoes are preferable)
1	cup stewed tomatoes
1/4	teaspoon freshly ground black pepper
1/4	teaspoon dried thyme
2	tablespoons chopped fresh parsley

Melt the butter in a large nonstick sauté pan; add onions and sauté for 3 minutes. Add garlic and sauté for 2 minutes more. Add diced celery, green pepper, and roast beef and sauté for 5 minutes, stirring constantly. Stir in diced potato and tomatoes and season with pepper, thyme, and parsley. Simmer over medium heat for 10 minutes until hash is golden brown and holds together well. At that point, remove it from the heat. Set a large, nonstick sauté pan over medium high heat. Scoop generous spoonfuls of hash into pan and cook the patties for 5 minutes until nicely browned. Flip to brown other side for 5 minutes more. The patties should be heated through and crisp, but not dry. Serve at once, topping each patty with a fresh poached egg, if desired. The hash would taste best if prepared a day in advance and refrigerated, covered, then made into patties and fried just before serving. Serve with a hot vegetable and crisp green salad and fresh French bread.

APPLE BROWN BETTY

    4   cups dry bread cubes, lightly toasted
    6   tablespoons butter, melted
    4   medium-size tart green apples, peeled and cored
    1   teaspoon cinnamon
1/2   cup plus 1 tablespoon light brown sugar
       juice and grated rind of 1 large lemon
2/3   cup hot water

Preheat the oven to 375° F. Mix the bread cubes with melted butter. Spread 1/3 of the mixture in the bottom of an 8-inch-square casserole dish. Coarsely dice the peeled apples and dredge with cinnamon. Spread half of the diced apples on top of the bread layer in the casserole dish. Top with 1/4 cup of the brown sugar, then cover with another layer of bread crumbs. Sprinkle the remaining diced apples on top of the second layer. Sprinkle with another 1/4 cup of the brown sugar. Sprinkle with the lemon juice and rind. Top with an even layer of the remaining bread cubes. Spoon on the hot water and sprinkle the top with the remaining tablespoon of brown sugar. Bake on lower shelf of a preheated oven for 35 to 40 minutes or until top is golden brown and crusty.

Serves 6 to 8

Author's note: This layered dessert is best served warm with lemon sauce (recipe follows) or a scoop of vanilla ice cream.

LEMON SAUCE

    1/2 cup sugar
      1 tablespoons cornstarch
      1 pinch of salt
      1 pinch of nutmeg
      1 cup boiling water
      1 tablespoon butter
      2 tablespoons lemon juice

In a small saucepan, combine the sugar with cornstarch, salt and nutmeg. Gradually add the water, stirring with a wire whisk to blend thoroughly. Bring to a boil and simmer over low heat for 2 minutes, stirring constantly, until sauce is thick and clear. Add the butter and lemon juice and stir until well mixed. Keep warm until serving time.

Makes 1 cup

OLD FASHIONED FLOATING ISLANDS

10	egg whites, room temperature
1/4	teaspoon cream of tartar
1	pinch of salt
1	cup plus 1 tablespoon confectioners' sugar
4-1/2	cups milk (use only whole milk)
1	cup granulated sugar
10	egg yolks
1	teaspoon vanilla extract

In a clean bowl, beat egg whites with cream of tartar and salt until soft peaks form. Gradually increasing the mixing speed, add one cup of the confectioners' sugar, a few tablespoons at a time, beating until stiff. Continue beating until meringue is very stiff and glossy but not dry. In a large sauté pan, combine 4 cups of the milk with the granulated sugar. Slowly warm over medium heat until hot, but not boiling, stirring constantly. Spoon out meringue by heaping teaspoonfuls and use a second spoon to ease the islands into the warm milk. Poach the meringues for 1 minute or until they puff up. Turn them with a slotted spoon and poach for 1 minute more. Use a slotted spoon to transfer the poached meringue mounds to a baking sheet. Refrigerate the meringues and keep the milk warm. In a mixing bowl, blend egg yolks with the remaining 1/4 cup milk. Stir this mixture into the warm milk. Transfer the milk mixture to the top of double boiler. Cook over simmering water, stirring constantly, until the mixture coats a wooden spoon. Be careful not to overcook or your yolks will scramble. Stir in vanilla. Set pan in a bowl of ice to cool, stirring often with a wooden spoon. Pour the cold custard into a large glass serving bowl. Remove the meringues from the refrigerator and dust lightly with the remaining confectioners' sugar. Quickly glaze under a hot broiler for 2–3 seconds, just enough to lightly brown. Use a metal spatula to carefully set the meringues on top of the custard. Cover tightly and refrigerate for several hours or overnight. Serve very cold topped with Creme Anglaise au Kirsch or raspberry sauce (recipes follow) and fresh fruit such as strawberries, kiwi, or raspberries, if desired.

This recipe serves 10 people.

Author's note: One of President Reagan's favorite desserts. The Reagans sometimes served it with a colorful fruit topping such as raspberry sauce with sliced kiwi, Creme Anglaise or fresh red raspberries.

RASPBERRY SAUCE

> 1   10-ounce package frozen raspberries, defrosted

Puree the raspberries in a blender and strain. Pour over puddings, ice cream, or frozen fruit soufflés. This recipe is wonderful if you want to add a raspberry liqueur (optional); and if so, you only need about 1 ounce.

Makes 1-1/2 cups

CREME ANGLAISE AU KIRSCH

    5   egg yolks
    1   cup cold milk
  1/2   teaspoon vanilla extract
  1/2   cup sugar
    1   cup hot milk
    1   tablespoon kirsch

In the top of a double boiler, mix the egg yolks with sugar, using a wire whisk. Add cold milk and blend with a wire whisk until smooth. Stir in hot milk; cook slowly over medium heat, stirring with a plastic or wooden spoon for about 7 minutes or until almost at the boiling point. Custard should be smooth and coat a spoon. Remove double boiler from heat and stir over bowl of ice until cool. Stir in vanilla and kirsch and strain before serving.

Makes 2 Cups

FRESH PEACH MOUSSE CARDINAL

This is one of the premiere White House dessert recipes

2	pounds ripe peaches
	juice of 2 lemons
1-1/4	cups granulated sugar
2	packages (1/2 ounce) unflavored gelatin
1/4	cup peach brandy, warmed
2	cups heavy cream
1	10-ounce package frozen strawberries
2	tablespoons confectioners' sugar
2	cups whipped cream

In a large saucepan, cover peaches with water and bring to a boil. Add the lemon juice, cover, and simmer over medium heat for 5–10 minutes or until peaches are tender (a sharp fork should pierce them easily, then you'll know they're done). Remove from the heat and let them cool. Peel the peaches and cut each in half, removing the pits and discard them. Puree the peaches in a blender. Transfer 2 cups of puree to a 3-quart mixing bowl. Mix in granulated sugar until well blended. In the top of a double boiler, set over hot water, and dissolve the gelatin in the warm brandy. Stir into peach puree and let cool.

In a cold mixing bowl, whip the heavy cream until stiff peaks form. Fold this into the peach puree. Transfer peach mixture into 1-1/2 quart mold, filling to 1/2" from the top. Smooth the surface. Refrigerate for 3–4 hours, or overnight, or until mousse is set.

In a blender, combine strawberries with confectioners' sugar and puree until very smooth. Refrigerate the sauce until serving time.

Just before serving, dip the mold briefly in hot water and turn mousse out onto a serving platter. Top with the chilled fruit sauce and garnish with whipped cream. (Use a pastry bag fitted with a small star tip to create a decorative effect with the whipped cream, if desired.)

Serve at once, with almond cookies.

George Herbert Walker Bush
Barbara Pierce Bush

"I have spoken of a thousand points of light, of all the community organizations that are spread like stars throughout the Nation, doing good. We will work hand in hand, encouraging, sometimes leading, sometimes being led, rewarding. We will work on this in the White House, in the Cabinet agencies. I will go to the people and the programs that are the brighter points of light, and I will ask every member of my government to become involved. The old ideas are new again because they are not old, they are timeless: duty, sacrifice, commitment, and a patriotism that finds its expression in taking part and pitching in."

GEORGE H. W. BUSH INAUGURAL ADDRESS, FRIDAY, JANUARY 20, 1989

GEORGE H. W. BUSH BY ABRAMS © WHHA (WHITE HOUSE COLLECTION)

What can I say about George Herbert Walker Bush, the ultimate preppie President who, when someone is in trouble says, "Oh, he's in deep tapioca!" Just once, I'd like to hear him say it correctly. But anyway, the man is from a well-named, well-to-do family, a real blue blood related to Benedict Arnold, President Franklin Pierce, Teddy Roosevelt, FDR, Abraham Lincoln and Winston Churchill. Not forgetting Dan Quayle, Gerald Ford and, of all people, Marilyn Monroe. George Bush, even with his family background, is a self-made man who raised four sons and a daughter, who all turned out well.

Among other things, George Bush was a congressman, a businessman, director of the CIA, U.S. ambassador to the United Nations, chief United States liaison in China, chairman of the Republican National Committee, and vice president of the United States before he ascended to the presidency on January 20, 1990. He was the first sitting vice president since Martin Van Buren to be elected President.

During his four years, President Bush masterminded the fall of the Sandinistas in Nicaragua, invaded Panama and captured General Manuel Noriega. His most notable effort came in the Persian Gulf as commander in chief of Desert Storm.

The collapse of communism was the hallmark of his foreign policy and the most important foreign relations event since World War II. Presidents from Truman to Reagan were preoccupied with anticipating the Soviet threat. The Bush administration maneuvered brilliantly, which left the respective governments to fall of their own weight. This end of the Cold War yielded the new world order. At a summit meeting in Washington in the spring of 1990, Presidents Bush and Gorbachev agreed on the framework of a reduction in strategic arms and chemical stockpiles and to cooperate on atomic energy research. At another summit in Paris, Bush and Gorbachev and twenty other leaders of the nations that made up NATO and the Warsaw Pact signed a mutual nonaggression pledge proclaiming the end of the Cold War. Bush signed the treaty and declared we are "a new world order." After all the negotiations, the reunification of Germany and the democratization of Eastern Europe, missile sites were dismantled and the American and Russian leaders signed the pact with pens made from the metal of the destroyed missiles.

George and Barbara Bush came to the White House with great experience on the international scene. The rigorous schedule of entertaining required at the White House was almost second nature to the President and First Lady. They both enjoyed the special state dinners held for Mikhail Gorbachev, the diplomatic corps, and the Emir of Kuwait.

George Bush was the kind of guy who would rather talk than fight, but was very capable of taking care of himself. After eight years as vice president, Bush developed a reputation as reserved and deferential. When he became President, he emerged as a tough administrator and earned the grudging respect of his long-time critics for his leadership in the Gulf War. During the crisis, Bush clung to a normal work and recreation schedule to avoid appearing to be under siege. He even went fishing with his national security advisor at Kennebunkport, Maine, his summer residence, during the emergency. This was done in the hopes it would show Saddam Hussein that he wasn't important enough to be a concern. I liked the approach—a nice touch on the President's part.

An emotional man, President Bush had to skip talking about the casualties of Desert Storm in a major speech because he choked up with emotion during the rehearsals and did not want to appear weak to the people of Iraq. He developed an informal diplomatic style during his tenure, building personal relationships with heads of state and world leaders, and becoming personal friends with most of them. He kept frequent telephone contact and wrote personal notes and letters to most of the world's leaders. Being in the public spotlight for as many years as he was, President and Mrs. Bush had garnered these friendships long before entering the White House.

George Bush has often been described as warm, generous, witty, engaging, considerate, unpretentious, and unerringly polite. His friends also said he could be flighty at times. John White, an old friend and former Democratic national chairman said, "George has always been like popcorn on a hot griddle."

In praising George Bush, President Ronald Reagan said, "George Bush is a man of action, a man accustomed to command. The vice presidency doesn't fit easily on such a man, but George is a patriot, and so he made it fit and served with distinction like no one has ever done before."

Sheik Jaber Al-Ahmed Al Sabah, Emir of Kuwait, said, "His principled, courageous, and decisive position in the face of Iraq's aggression on Kuwait is a true expression of the unabated faith and commitment of the American people to the humanitarian morals for which the United States of America was founded."

Some people, such as Robert Strauss said, "George is a damn good guy, but he doesn't come through well. It's a case of choking. It takes eleven hours to get George ready for an off-the-cuff remark."

Jim Hightower, the agriculture commissioner of Texas, once said, "If oil ever reaches $40 a barrel, I want the drilling rights on George Bush's head."

But Ross Perot said, "All you can hear from Bush is Lawrence Welk music, wonnerful, wonnerful, wonnerful, and we're spending $400 billion of your children's money this year to try to get you to vote for us again."

Bush said of himself, "I am a Conservative, but I am not a nut about it." He said, "I don't feel the compulsion to be the glamorous one-shot, smart comment kind of guy and I think experience, steadiness, and knowing how to interact with people is a way to get things done."

During a meeting of world leaders in London in 1991, President Bush tried hard not to let it bother him that Mikhail Gorbachev was getting the lion's share of attention. One night, however, his ego got the best of him.

At the queen's dinner for all the world leaders who attended the London summit, the wife of one of the foreign ministers came up to the president and greeted him warmly, "Oh, Geoffrey," she cooed, "It's so nice to see you."

Bush stiffly responded, "Madam, I'm George Bush, President of the United States."

The woman, without batting an eye, sniffed, "Well, you look a lot like Geoffrey."

Once, according to former President Gerald Ford, George Bush was in the Middle East and during a sight-seeing tour asked his guide, "How dead is the Dead Sea?"

The guide answered, "Very!"

Bush was amused and not offended by Dana Carvey, the comedian on Saturday Night Live who did satirical imitations of him. President Bush often invited Carvey to the White House and the two became good friends. On one such visit, the two of them stood in front of the fireplace in the Oval Office and talked at the same time with Carvey doing Bush and Bush doing himself. The President doubled over in laughter as Carvey suddenly began chopping the air with one hand and imitating the way the President defended vice president Dan Quayle against criticism.

"Daaaan Quaaaayle is getting stronger, learning ev-er-y daaaay."

George Bush was a created Texan. But that's okay, because most of the men who died at the Alamo were from somewhere else. Bush learned very early on, though, that Texans do not use "summer" as a verb or wear blue ties with little green whales on them nor do they call trouble "do-do".

"We are not setting the standards here," remarked Molly Ivans of the Dallas Times Herald, "but here they are."

Amused by George Bush, Russell Baker of The New York Times said, "Bush's efforts to present himself as old-shoe George made him look like an Ivy League hayseed. Who is he really?

"He is George Bush, Yankee son of rich and elegant investment banker,

Prescott Bush, who became a senator from Connecticut. He is George Bush of Andover and Yale. He is George Bush who knows what a debutante ball is and doesn't know that Iowa farmers don't. He is the top drawer, upper crust, one of the snobs. He summers in Maine and knows about sailing. He says 'golly' and 'gee' and 'gosh' and maybe even 'damn' and 'heck', mostly 'darn' and 'heck' and says them naturally because he was brought up that way to believe that gentlemen don't use vile language. That's George Bush!"

Barbara Bush is probably the best match for this man. She is a wonderful lady who never let any grass grow under her feet. A mother, grandmother, and wife, Barbara Bush is the true power of the Bush family. She never tried to be an equal to the President or to advise her husband unless asked. She was her family's main support system who took on the responsibilities of First Lady with grace and charm that has not been in the White House since Edith Roosevelt. Barbara Bush, however, truly had a wicked wit and once in New Hampshire, during a primary campaign, her husband was asked about his stand on abortion. The woman who asked the question also added her own two cents.

Mrs. Bush turned to a friend and whispered, "There's a B.S. question."

On the podium, George Bush struggled with the answer and tried very hard not to offend anyone.

Barbara Bush leaned over to her friend again and said, "And that's a B.S. answer."

Like Edith Roosevelt, Mrs. Bush has always been an impeccable hostess who enjoyed her job. She especially liked her husband's tour as UN ambassador, where entertaining and diplomacy were closely intertwined. "I'd pay to have this job," she once told a reporter.

She even learned Chinese at the age of 50 so she could communicate with her hosts when she lived in Beijing.

All the diplomacy and entertaining was just a warm-up for the White House years. As the vice president's wife, she hosted 1,192 events at the vice presidential mansion and attended 1,132 events as a guest. She traveled 1,330,000 miles with her husband to 68 countries and 4 territories, which is an equivalent of 54 times around the world. Before she even moved into the White House, she had met every political leader in the world.

After the president's defeat to Bill Clinton, Mrs. Bush said, "I didn't like it, but having said that, I think I'll put it behind me. It's not my style to brood over the past, especially when the future is full of good things."

Mrs. Bush moved back to Houston with her husband and immediately picked up with her old friends after 20 years, without missing a beat. Both she and Mr. Bush have yet to say no to volunteerism and to boards and charities. It's part of their continuing commitment to the One Thousand Points of Light, Bush's famous call for the help necessary to improve life in America.

I have never met Barbara Bush, but I must say it would indeed be a privilege. She seems to be the type of person everyone would want as a personal friend.

President Bush is not known for his epicurean prowess. He fishes, but does not particularly like seafood (he often releases his catch or gives it to his Secret Service detail). He prefers Mexican and Chinese food and likes to snack on pork rinds doused with Tabasco® sauce.

He barred broccoli from Air Force One menus saying, "I haven't liked it since I was a little kid and my mother made me eat it. Now I'm President of the United States and I'm not going to eat any more damn broccoli!"

His favorite way to spend an evening is a long lingering dinner with friends at a restaurant. He likes to sip an occasional beer or vodka martini. Some of the Bush family's favorite recipes follow.

EAST ROOM OF THE WHITE HOUSE - WHGB, 20TH ED., P.34-35 ©WHHA

LOBSTER THERMIDOR A LA WHITE HOUSE

       3 2-pound Maine lobsters
     1/4 cup olive oil
     3/4 cup butter
     1/4 cup prepared mustard
          salt to taste
       2 cups heavy cream
       3 tablespoons flour
       1 cup milk
     1/2 cup grated Parmesan cheese
          freshly ground black pepper

Split the lobsters. Brush with oil and sprinkle with salt and pepper. Broil under medium heat for 5 minutes. Remove from the broiler and dot with 6 tablespoons butter. Bake in a hot oven (400° F) for 10 minutes. Remove lobster meat from shells and slice it. Save the coral. Brush inside of each shell lightly with mustard.

Meanwhile, simmer cream over low heat for 30 minutes, stirring occasionally. Melt 4 tablespoons butter, stir in flour and 1/2 teaspoon salt. Add milk slowly; cook until sauce thickens, stirring constantly. Mix in cream and lobster coral. Return lobster meat to shells and cover with sauce. Sprinkle the top with Parmesan cheese and dot with remaining 2 tablespoons butter. Bake in hot oven (400° F) for 10 minutes.

Serves 6

Author's note: You may also mix paprika with the Parmesan cheese when putting on top of lobsters—it adds a nicer color.

SALMON WHITE HOUSE

     6   salmon steaks
     1   tablespoon vinegar
     1   teaspoon salt
   1/2   cup butter, melted

Combine vinegar, salt, and 2 quarts water in a skillet. Bring to a boil; add the salmon. Reduce the heat and simmer for 12 minutes. Drain the salmon and serve with the melted butter.

Serves 6

OYSTER POULETTE

- 2 dozen oysters, shucked
- 3 tablespoons butter
- 2 tablespoons flour
- 2 egg yolks
- 1/2 teaspoon salt
  freshly ground black pepper to taste
- 2 tablespoons minced parsley
- 1/4 pound mushrooms
- 1 tablespoon lemon juice
  dash of nutmeg
- 1/2 cup heavy cream
- 6 slices toast

Remove mushroom caps. Slice and save them. Cook mushroom stems in 3/4 cup water for 20 minutes. Drain and save the mushroom liquor. Discard the stems. Meanwhile, drain oysters and save the liquor. Simmer oysters in 1 tablespoon butter, lemon juice, salt, and pepper until the edges are curled. Remove from heat and set aside. Melt remaining 2 tablespoons of butter in top part of double boiler. Add the flour and stir until smooth. Add 1/2 cup of the mushroom liquor and 1/2 cup of the oyster liquor and cook, stirring constantly, until thickened. Add oysters and their sauce, mushrooms, and nutmeg. Simmer for 5 minutes, stirring occasionally. Place over hot, but NOT boiling, water and stir in egg yolks, beaten with the cream. Cook over hot water for 10 minutes, stirring occasionally.

Serve over toast and sprinkle with parsley.

Serves 6

Author's note: One of the best appetizers ever.

SZECHUAN NOODLES

1	pound narrow egg noodles, boiled and drained
1/4	pound cooked shrimp, cut up
2	tablespoons finely chopped cooked ham
2	tablespoons finely chopped cooked pork
2	tablespoons finely chopped cooked chicken
2	tablespoons dry sherry
1	tablespoon finely chopped green pepper
2	tablespoons finely chopped parsley
2	teaspoons ground ginger
1/2	teaspoon Tabasco® sauce
1	tablespoon soy sauce
2	tablespoons corn starch
1/4	cup chicken bouillon
2	tablespoons peanut oil

Combine the shrimp, ham, pork, chicken, sherry, vegetables, and seasonings. Mix cornstarch and bouillon together. Add to the shrimp and meat mixture. Cook in oil in a large skillet or wok over high heat for 5 minutes, stirring constantly. Serve with the noodles.

Serves 6

CODFISH CAKES

- 1 pound salt codfish
- 6 medium potatoes, boiled
- 1 large onion
- 2 eggs, lightly beaten
- 1/2 teaspoon curry powder
  cayenne pepper to taste
- 1 cup dry bread crumbs
- 1/2 cup butter
  tomato sauce

Wash cod in warm running water for 5 minutes. Soak in 4 cups water, overnight, to remove the salt. Drain and discard the water. Put cod, potatoes, and raw onion through a food grinder. Stir in eggs, curry powder, and a few grains of cayenne pepper. Shape into 12 cakes. Dip cakes in crumbs and sauté in butter until brown. Heat tomato sauce and serve with the codfish cakes.

Author's note: I recommend using Italian dry seasoned bread crumbs. The First Family enjoyed these crab cakes at their Summer Home in Kennebunkport, Maine.

GREEN PEPPERS WITH CRAB MEAT

6 green peppers
1 cup light cream
1/4 teaspoon ground nutmeg
1/4 cup dry white wine
1 cup cooked rice
1 teaspoon salt
2 cups crab meat
4 tablespoons butter
2 tablespoons cornstarch
1 teaspoon lemon juice
   paprika

Cut tops off peppers and remove the seeds. Parboil peppers for 5 minutes and drain. Scald the cream and add the butter and nutmeg. Mix the cornstarch, wine, lemon juice and salt. Add those ingredients to the cream.
Cook until thickened, stirring constantly. Combine with crab meat and rice, and spoon into the peppers. Sprinkle the top with paprika. Bake in a greased baking dish in moderate oven (350° F) for 20 minutes.

Serves 6

Author's note: Perfect for Friday night dinner.

ROAST PHEASANT WITH BRANDY AND CREAM

3	whole pheasants
2	cups heavy cream
1/4	cup butter
6	slices bacon
1	teaspoon salt
1/2	cup brandy
8	shallots, thinly sliced
2	cups chicken bouillon
1/4	cup horseradish
	freshly ground black pepper to taste

Sauté the shallots in butter in a roasting pan for 5 minutes. Add pheasants and sauté over high heat for 15 minutes or until brown on all sides. Pour some brandy into a ladle and the rest over the pheasants. Warm the ladle over a match, light the brandy and flame the pheasants. When flames die, add the bouillon, salt and pepper. Put bacon over the pheasants' breasts and roast uncovered in a moderate oven (375° F) for 45 minutes, basting frequently. Stir the cream and horseradish into the pan juices and continue roasting for an additional 15 minutes, basting frequently. Serve pheasants and sauce with popped wild rice.

Serves 6

Author's note: I would highly recommend using just the pheasant thighs and breasts, skinless.

SHERRIED QUAIL CASSEROLE

6	quail, quartered
2	tablespoons dry sherry
1/4	cup butter
1/2	cup chopped onions
1/2	cup chopped parsley
1	tablespoon cornstarch
1	cup chicken bouillon
2	tablespoons chopped parsley

Sauté the quail in butter for 10 minutes. Remove the birds and sauté onions and celery in butter remaining in skillet for 5 minutes, stirring constantly. Add the cornstarch dissolved in bouillon and cook, stirring constantly until thickened. Stir in sherry and parsley. Arrange quail in shallow casserole and pour sauce over them. Bake in moderate oven (350° F) for 15 minutes.

Serves 6

OPPOSITE: CHINA FROM AUTHOR'S PERSONAL COLLECTION

CHICKEN CHOW MEIN

3	cups finely shredded cooked chicken
1-1/2	cups diced canned water chestnuts
1-1/2	cups diced canned bamboo shoots
3/4	cup diced mushrooms
1/2	cup oil
2	cups sliced Chinese cabbage
3/4	cup thinly sliced green beans
2	cloves garlic, minced
3	cups chicken bouillon
1/4	cup soy sauce
	freshly ground black pepper to taste
3/4	cup toasted almonds
3	cups diced celery
1	large green pepper, diced
9	scallions, finely chopped
1	tablespoon sugar
3	tablespoons cornstarch
1	tablespoon salt to taste
	chow mein noodles

Fry vegetables, sugar, salt, and pepper in oil for 1 minute, stirring briskly. Add the bouillon; bring to a boil, reduce heat, cover and simmer for 10 minutes. Combine cornstarch, soy sauce and 4 tablespoons water. Add to vegetable mixture and cook until thickened, stirring constantly. Add chicken and cook for 5 minutes. Serve with noodles and garnish with almonds.

Serves 6

CHINESE STYLE BOILED RICE

Boiled in the Chinese manner, rice is very light and fluffy. Allow 3 cups of long-grained rice for 6 servings. Rinse rice in cold water until water runs clear. Put rice in a deep, heavy saucepan. Add water, measuring proper amount by placing hand slightly on rice and adding enough to cover the back of the hand. Add salt to taste. Fit lid tightly on top of pot. Bring to a boil over a high heat. Cook for 3 minutes after steam shows around the lid. Then cook over a medium heat for 5 minutes. Turn to lowest heat and cook for 12 minutes more. Remove from the heat and let stand at least 10 minutes before serving.

Author's note: Do not wash rice and reheat. Serve as is.

CREOLE PORK SKILLET

4	cups diced pork
3	cups canned tomatoes
2	large onions, sliced
1/2	cup chopped green peppers
1/2	cup chopped celery
1/4	cup oil
1	teaspoon chili powder
1	teaspoon sugar
2	tablespoons flour
1-1/2	teaspoons salt
1/2	teaspoon cayenne pepper

Sauté the onions, green pepper, and celery in oil for 10 minutes. Add pork, tomatoes, chili powder, sugar, cayenne pepper and salt. Bring to a boil. Reduce heat, cover and simmer for 45 minutes. Combine flour and 1/4 cup water and stir into mixture. Cook, stirring until slightly thickened.

Serves 6

Author's note: Spicy and fun to eat. Also great over rice. President Bush loved this dish.

ROASTED FRESH HAM

1	12-pound fresh ham, skinned and scored
2	large onions, sliced
1	stalk celery, cut up
2	cloves garlic, sliced
3	cloves
2	cups dry white wine
1/4	cup flour
3	cups chicken bouillon
	orange sections

Roast ham with onions, celery, garlic, cloves and wine in a slow oven (325° F) for 5 hours, or until meat thermometer registers 185° F. Baste the meat frequently. Remove ham from pan and pour off all but 2 tablespoons of fat. Add flour and stir until smooth. Add bouillon and cook, stirring constantly until thickened. Serve sauce with the ham. Garnish ham with orange sections.

Serves 12

BEEF VINAIGRETTE WITH PEPPER AND HERBS

2	cups julienne strips of roast beef
2	onions, sliced
1/4	cup wine vinegar
1/2	cup olive oil
4	tablespoons capers
2	tablespoons chopped parsley
2	tablespoons chopped chervil
2	teaspoons chopped chives
1/4	teaspoon dry mustard (use Coleman's, if possible)
	Tabasco® sauce to taste
	freshly ground black pepper to taste

Separate onion slices into rings. Combine with beef, vinegar, oil, capers, herbs, mustard, a few drops of Tabasco®, and pepper. Let stand at room temperature for at least 3 hours, stirring occasionally. Chill thoroughly.

Serves 6

Author's note: It is preferable to use leftover roast beef, such as top round or prime rib.

ONION AND CHEESE PIE

1/2	pound Swiss cheese, grated
1/2	recipe pie crust
4	eggs, lightly beaten
1	cup milk
1/4	teaspoon ground nutmeg (preferably fresh)
	Tabasco® sauce to taste
	freshly ground black pepper to taste
1	large onion, sliced
2	tablespoons flour
1	cup heavy cream
1/2	teaspoon curry powder
1	teaspoon salt

Roll pie crust 1/8-inch thick and line 10-inch pie plate with it. Flute edges of the crust. Mix cheese thoroughly with flour and spread in bottom of pie shell. Separate onion slices into rings and arrange rings on cheese mixture. Beat eggs lightly. Beat in cream, milk, curry powder, nutmeg, 2 drops Tabasco® sauce (or more if desired), salt, and pepper. Pour egg mixture over cheese and onion rings. Bake in moderate oven (350° F) for 45 minutes.

Serves 6

SOUR CREAM DRESSING

1-1/2	cups sour cream
1/2	cup cider vinegar
3/4	cup oil
2	tablespoons grated onion
2	tablespoons horseradish
2	tablespoons chopped capers
1	teaspoon dill seeds
1	teaspoon paprika
1	teaspoon salt
	freshly ground black pepper

Combine all the ingredients in jar and cover. Shake well before using.

Makes about 3 cups

Author's note: I prefer to use fresh dill rather than dill seeds, but this can be your option.

SWEET AND SOUR DRESSING
(OIL & VINEGAR)

- 1 cup oil
- 1 cup red wine vinegar
- 1/2 cup sugar
- 1/4 cup minced chives
- 1/4 cup minced celery
- 2 tablespoons minced green pepper
- 2 tablespoons minced watercress
- 2 teaspoon dry mustard (use Coleman's, if possible)
- 1 tablespoon Worcestershire sauce
- 2 teaspoons salt
  freshly ground black pepper to taste
- 1 clove garlic, minced

Combine all ingredients in a jar or cruet. Cover. Shake well before using.

Makes about 3 cups

CLASSIC FRENCH DRESSING

    3   parts olive oil
    1   part wine vinegar
        salt
        freshly ground black pepper to taste

When making the dressing at the dinner table, pour olive oil over greens and toss until greens are coated lightly. Add the vinegar, salt, and pepper and toss well. When making the dressing in advance, simply combine all the ingredients in a jar or cruet. Cover. Shake well before using.

Author's note: For a slight change, you may add some grated Parmesan cheese or Pecorino cheese for additional flavor.

VARIATIONS OF CLASSIC FRENCH DRESSING

Capers
Add chopped capers, crushed garlic, or garlic salt and a few drops of Tabasco® sauce.

Chili
Add chili sauce and a dash of paprika.

Chutney
Add finely chopped chutney.

Curry and Onion
Add curry powder and finely minced grated onion.

Egg and Olive
Add chopped or sieved hard-cooked egg and minced ripe olives.

Garlic
Sprinkle salt in salad bowl and rub salt around bowl with a cut garlic clove until the clove is crushed.

VARIATIONS OF CLASSIC FRENCH DRESSING (CONTINUED)

Herb
Add some dried herbs or finely chopped fresh herbs. Try dill, basil, chervil, marjoram, parsley, oregano, tarragon, or watercress, separately or in a combination.

Horseradish
Add prepared horseradish and a few drops of Tabasco®.

Lemon
Substitute lemon juice for the vinegar or use half lemon juice and half vinegar and add grated lemon rind.

Mustard
Add a pinch of dry mustard, preferably Coleman's, and a few grains of cayenne pepper.

Onion
Add onion juice and a few drops of Tabasco® sauce or substitute onion salt for plain salt.

Roquefort or Bleu Cheese
Add softened, crumbled Roquefort or bleu cheese.

Tarragon
Use tarragon vinegar and add some finely chopped, fresh tarragon.

Wine
Substitute dry white or red wine for the vinegar.

BASTING SAUCE

3/4	cup olive oil
3/4	cup dry red wine
1	tablespoon lime juice
1	clove garlic, mashed
1/3	cup finely chopped onion
1	teaspoon oregano
1/2	teaspoon thyme
1	teaspoon sugar
1	teaspoon salt
	freshly ground black pepper to taste

Combine all ingredients and beat or shake until well blended. Spread liberally over steak while cooking, both before and after turning.

WESTERN HERB SAUCE

2	tablespoons chopped scallions
1/2	pound mushrooms, sliced
1/4	cup olive oil
1/4	cup butter
2	tablespoons chopped chives
2	tablespoons chopped tarragon
3	tablespoons chopped parsley
1/2	cup chopped pickled walnuts
1/2	teaspoon salt
3	tablespoons bottled Escafia sauce diabla
	freshly ground black pepper to taste

Sauté scallions and mushrooms in combined olive oil and butter for 5 minutes. Add remaining ingredients and simmer for 5 minutes.

This makes a thick sauce that can be thinned by adding 1/2 cup beef bouillon and simmering the sauce an additional 5 minutes.

Makes about 3 cups sauce. Serve hot with broiled steak.

WHITE HOUSE MUFFINS

1/3	cup soft butter
1/3	cup sugar
1	egg
1-1/2	cups sifted flour
1	tablespoon double-acting baking powder
2/3	cup milk

Combine the butter, sugar, and egg and beat until light and fluffy. Combine the flour and baking powder and sift together. Add to butter mixture, alternately with milk. Fill twelve greased muffin pans, 2/3 full of the batter. Bake in a hot oven (400° F) for 20 minutes.

Yields 1 dozen

RUM CUSTARD CREAM

    2 tablespoons dark rum
1/2 cup sugar
    2 tablespoons flour
    1 egg, beaten
2/3 cup light cream
    1 cup heavy cream, whipped

In top part of double boiler, combine sugar, flour, egg, and light cream. Cook over the boiling water, stirring constantly for 5 minutes. Add rum and cook for 5 minutes. Remove from heat and cool. Chill for 1 hour in the refrigerator. At the last minute, fold in whipped cream.

SUGAR YARN

    2   cups sugar
  1/4   teaspoon cream of tartar
    1   teaspoon white corn syrup

Combine the sugar, cream of tartar, and corn syrup with 2/3 cup of water in saucepan. Cover and bring to a quick boil over a high heat. Remove the cover. Warm a candy thermometer in hot water and lower it carefully into the boiling syrup. Continue boiling until thermometer reaches 312° F. Remove immediately from heat and set pan into cold water for 2 to 3 minutes to stop the cooking. Remove from the cold water and set the pan in a bowl of hot water.

Butter the handles of 2 long wooden spoons (or use 2 clean, thin sticks). Place spoons on table about 24 inches apart and let the handles extend 10 inches out from the table. Place weights on the bowls of the spoons so that they will not fall. Cover the table and floor under the spoons with paper. Dip a wire whisk or rotary beater into the syrup and quickly move it back and forth so that the syrup threads are spun over and between the handles. Remove the spun sugar yarn from the handles. Trim the ends and form into any desired shape.

CRYSTAL BOWL

    1-1/2   cups diced fresh fruit
            kirsch liqueur
            ice cream
            sweetened whipped cream

Put fruit into individual crystal bowls. Pour in some kirsch. Add a ball of ice cream and top it with whipped cream. Garnish with creme chantilly in the shape of a little horn. Put a teaspoonful of melba sauce in the horn. Cover everything with a skein of sugar yarn shaped like a dome and sprinkle with tiny pieces of candied cherry.

Serves 6

Creme chantilly

            melba sauce
            sugar yarn (see previous page)
            candied cherries

Whip ice-cold heavy cream until it becomes very stiff—much stiffer than regular whipped cream.

PINEAPPLE CUP

 1 large pineapple
 1 cup whole strawberries
 1 cup honeydew balls
 1 cup cantaloupe balls
 1 cup cherry liqueur

Cut the pineapple in half lengthwise. Scoop out the center leaving a 1-inch shell. Remove the core and cut the rest into cubes. Chill the pineapple shell. Combine pineapple cubes with strawberries, melon balls, and liqueur and let stand at room temperature for 1 hour. Chill for at least 4 hours.

To serve, spoon fruit and marinade into the pineapple shells.

Serves 6

COFFEE WHIPPED WITH ALMONDS

1	ounce unflavored gelatin
1	cup cold water
1	pint hot water
1	pound granulated sugar
1	quart milk, hot
1/4	cup fresh coffee powder
1	quart heavy cream or evaporated milk, whipped
1	teaspoon vanilla
1/4	pound sliced almonds, toasted

Soak the gelatin in cold water for 5 minutes. Add hot water and stir until gelatin is dissolved. Melt the sugar in heavy iron skillet over low heat. When it is medium brown, remove from the heat and add hot milk. Stir over low heat until sugar is all dissolved. Add this mixture and the instant coffee to the gelatin. Cool until the gelatin begins to congeal. Then whip it until frothy and fold in the whipped cream, vanilla, and toasted almonds. Spoon into serving dishes and chill thoroughly before serving.

Yields 32 servings

William Jefferson Clinton
Hillary Rodham Clinton

"And so today, we pledge an end to the era of deadlock and drift—a new season of American renewal has begun.

To renew America, we must be bold.

We must do what no generation has had to do before. We must invest more in our own people, in their jobs, in their future, and at the same time cut our massive debt. And we must do so in a world in which we must compete for every opportunity.

It will not be easy; it will require sacrifice. But it can be done, and done fairly, not choosing sacrifice for its own sake, but for our own sake. We must provide for our nation the way a family provides for its children."

BILL CLINTON FIRST INAUGURAL ADDRESS, WEDNESDAY, JANUARY 21, 1993

PRESIDENT CLINTON BY SIMMIE KNOX © WHHA (WHITE HOUSE COLLECTION)

When George Bush joined Jimmy Carter at the Clinton White House in 1994 to push for the North American Free Trade Agreement, he listened to his successor's pitch for the trade pact and remarked, "I thought that was a very eloquent statement by President Clinton, and now I understand why he's inside looking out and I'm outside looking in."

A Rhodes scholar, and a Yale Law School graduate, Bill Clinton became the youngest governor in America, representing Arkansas.

A Georgetown University friend recalled, "Bill exhibited all the signs of someone who was on the way to somewhere else, and in a hurry to get there. If he had not been so totally amiable, genuinely kind, open, and friendly, he would have been intensely disliked by one and all. But he has no pretense about himself and that, of course, makes him irresistible."

Bill Clinton met Hillary Rodham at Yale Law School in the library. Hillary, annoyed at the furtive glances from Bill Clinton, finally came over to introduce herself by saying, "If you're going to keep looking at me, and I'm going to keep looking at you, and we're going to be looking back and forth, we ought to get to know each other." They began dating soon after.

Bill and Hillary Clinton became the most political couple ever to occupy the White House. At the beginning of the Administration, Mrs. Clinton's office was located in the West Wing of the White House where senior staff members work. Later, she moved it to the old Executive Office Building. She is also the first lawyer to become First Lady.

Hillary Clinton is probably the most valuable asset the President has ever had. Voted one of the 100 best lawyers in the United States, Mrs. Clinton takes a very active role in children's rights and her husband's career.

After Clinton became President, he remarked after criticism for trying to give his wife a government job, "Heck, if I weren't married to Hillary, she'd be first in line for any of the appointments."

An old friend replied, "If you weren't married to Hillary, you wouldn't be making any of the appointments anyway."

President Clinton clearly enjoys being President. He enjoys the responsibility and all the trappings. He firmly believes in having fun at his work and when he no longer enjoys the work, he believes he should move on to something else.

When Clinton entered law school, there was a table in the cafeteria where black students ate. This was self-segregation and accepted by one and all with one notable exception—Bill Clinton. He violated the unspoken taboo by sitting at the table one night to eat and chat. At first, his presence caused discomfort, but soon Clinton engaged the blacks in good conversation and he became a regular at their table.

Bill Clinton hates bigotry. He hates the thought of someone in America feeling unequal. He reaches out to people and when he hugs you, it's genuine. He is really concerned about people and their problems, and takes the problems to heart. His mother used to say that even as a young boy, Bill would bring people home for dinner. He couldn't stand the thought of someone missing out on a Thanksgiving dinner. A very sensitive man who appears incredibly loyal to friends, he demands the same loyalty in return.

The President does have a temper, though, and this is usually displayed every morning—as was evidenced during his campaign for a second term. Mr. Clinton stopped in my hometown, Buffalo, New York, on his way to the Chautauqua Institute, to prepare for the upcoming debate with Bob Dole. When Air Force One landed in Buffalo, he was scheduled to transfer to Marine One, the helicopter that was to take him on the last leg of the trip to the institute.

The White House hired me to cater a buffet luncheon out of my restaurant for the White House press corps. My orders were to have plenty of "Buffalo food" plus lots of regular fare. The President wanted to try some of it and came to the shelter where we were serving. The Secret Service prevailed and said they didn't recommend it because the area was not secure for his visit. Well, he blew his top because the area was supposed to be secure and he wanted to try the food and mingle with the press corps on an informal basis.

We fixed a nice plate for him and under the watchful eye of the Secret Service, he ate it alone on Air Force One. I felt sorry for him. The Secret Service uniformed division was really doing its job well. As a matter of fact, they even made CNN's Wolf Blitzer, a native Buffalonian and senior White House correspondent, go through the metal detector twice because it beeped the first time through.

George Bush once said, "There is a pattern of inconsistencies that go along with Bill Clinton." He was referring to how Clinton avoided the draft, his ambivalence on the Persian Gulf, his artfully crafted position on the NAFTA that sought to support free trade in principle without alienating organized labor, and offered it as evidence of a pattern of deception. He coined a new disease called "Clintonesia" with the symptoms of weak knees, sweaty palms, and an incredible desire to say anything on all sides of any issue depending on who you're trying to please.

The Clintons loved the elegance of the White House and entertained personally in the family quarters, preferring small, intimate gatherings rather than the large soiree events that plagued many first families. The privacy factor is held sacred by both the President and Mrs. Clinton.

When the Clintons had dinner, Mrs. Clinton tried very hard to make sure the President ate well. He is known for his love of comfort food.

Mr. Clinton received more mail than any President in history. Americans were very enthusiastic about their new President and they even included gift coupons for McDonald's Big Macs, prescriptions for losing weight, jogging caps, and homemade remedies to clear his sinuses. Most Presidents receive letters written in a formal tone, befitting the office. But the letters written to Clinton were friendly and informal. There was no awe in the way the letters were written. People felt they could relate to him.

As I said before, Mrs. Clinton tried to serve healthy foods. I believe this was a sure sign that Mrs. Clinton was trying to get up to speed with the decision many other First Ladies dreaded and therefore hesitated to make: the decision to fire the White House chef. She replaced the great French chef, Pierre Chambertin, with a modern American chef who specialized in "light cuisine." Some people speculated that getting rid of Chambertin and his rich food was an attack on her husband's waistline. But most likely, it was an attempt to streamline the type of foods her generation purports to enjoy.

The President's first state dinner was the team effort of Mrs. Clinton and her new chef, Walter Scheib III, for the Emperor and Empress of Japan in June 1994. Mrs. Clinton decided to hold the dinner on the White House lawn, partly because the Emperor's father, Hirohito, had been entertained there in 1976. It was risky, but brilliant, because Washington, D.C., is usually very hot and humid in June. The First Lady equipped the huge white tent with air conditioners, but it worked out perfectly. By 9:00 p.m., when the guests sat down for dinner, a cool breeze blew in from the Potomac and there was no need to turn on the air conditioners. Since that big event, President and Mrs. Clinton have hosted state dinners for Russia's Boris Yeltsin, South African leader Nelson Mandela, and many others.

"I like working with the staff on these dinners," said Mrs. Clinton, "I worry about the flowers, the menus, and about everything you have to do to make it look beautiful." This is a side of Mrs. Clinton that few people saw and it's a shame.

The zone of privacy in the lives of President and Mrs. Clinton was very important. Most chief executives before Mr. Clinton had given up on the zone because of the relentless pursuit of the media. Bill Clinton loved being President, but at times he couldn't help feeling confined by the exact regimen that goes with the job. This exalted position puts these people in a glass house that covers 18 acres.

Once, soon after his inauguration, President Clinton invited political consultant, Paul Begala, to the White House and gave him the "official presidential tour." When it was over, he and Clinton adjourned to the Oval Office for coffee. Begala was overwhelmed by the grandeur of the room and started to buckle at the knees when he thought of all the momentous and historical decisions that were made there.

"Don't let it get to you," said the President as he observed his friend's reaction. Then he added, "This is the crown jewel of the federal penal system."

Beset by scandal, President Clinton, the only elected President ever to be impeached, remained unbothered by stress. Instead, he felt bolstered by a good economy, world peace, and a huge surplus at home.

Senator Harris Wolford once said, "Bill Clinton has been through the hottest fire American politics has ever had to test somebody, and has come out like fine-tempered Pennsylvania steel."

Newsweek said, "Mr. Clinton may not have an agenda, but he does have a vision. Bill Clinton is the best politician of his generation. Bill believes in the value of public service. He refuses to be part of the belief that the American dream is lost. He believes there is a bridge to build and he is ready to build it."

DEVILED CRAB A LA WHITE HOUSE

1	pound lump crab meat
1/4	cup minced celery, with leaves
1	clove garlic, minced
1/2	cup butter
2	cups soft bread crumbs (Italian bread crumbs)
1/2	cup heavy cream
2	eggs, beaten
1	hard-cooked egg, chopped
1	tablespoon white wine vinegar
1/2	cup minced onion
1/4	cup minced green pepper
1	tablespoon chopped parsley
1	teaspoon Worcestershire sauce
1/4	teaspoon thyme
	Tabasco® sauce
1	teaspoon salt

Sauté onion, celery, green pepper, garlic, and parsley in 6 tablespoons butter for 10 minutes. Cool down. Combine 1 cup bread crumbs, cream, raw and cooked eggs, vinegar, Worcestershire, thyme, a few drops of Tabasco®, and salt with sautéed vegetables. Add the crab meat and toss lightly to mix. Spoon mixture into 12 scallop dishes or individual baking dishes. Melt remaining 2 tablespoons butter and toss with remaining 1 cup bread crumbs. Top the crab mixture with butter and crumbs.

Place shells in shallow baking pan. Put 1/4 inch water in bottom of pan. Bake in hot oven (450° F) for 10 minutes or until browned and hot.

Serves 6

Author's note: One really easy and popular "Clinton" dish.

SHRIMP A LA WHITE HOUSE

1	pound cooked bay shrimp, shelled
6	tablespoons cognac
1-1/2	teaspoon dry mustard (use Coleman's, if possible)
2	tablespoons finely chopped celery
2	tablespoons horseradish
1	tablespoon chopped parsley
1	cup olive oil
2	tablespoons lemon juice
	freshly ground black pepper
3	avocados
1/4	cup white vinegar
3	egg yolks
1	tablespoon chopped chives
2	tablespoons chopped shallots
6	tablespoons chili sauce
	salt

With a melon baller, make small balls of avocados. In six supreme dishes, put a layer of avocado balls then a layer of bay shrimp. Combine the remaining ingredients; mix thoroughly and spoon over the shrimp. Serve well chilled.

Serves 6

SHRIMP FRIED RICE

    2 cups chopped cooked shrimp
    4 cups boiled white rice
1/4 cup oil
    2 eggs, lightly beaten
    2 tablespoons soy sauce
    1 teaspoon salt
       freshly ground black pepper
    3 scallions, chopped

Fry the shrimp in oil in a deep frying pan or wok for 1 minute, stirring constantly. Add eggs, salt, and pepper and fry over medium heat for 5 minutes, stirring constantly. Add the rice and soy sauce and fry for 5 more minutes, stirring frequently. Garnish with the chopped scallions.

Serves 6

Author's note: Diced cooked chicken, pork, or ham may be used instead of shrimp.

LOBSTER FIGARO

1 tablespoon chopped (fresh) tarragon
3 2-pound lobsters, boiled and split
2 cups cooked crab meat
1 cup mayonnaise
1 tablespoon tomato paste
1 tablespoon lemon juice

Remove the lobster meat and chop in chunks. Save the shells. Combine the lobster and crab meat together. Mix mayonnaise, tarragon, tomato paste, and lemon juice. Add to seafood and fill the shells with this mixture served chilled.

Serves 6

Author's note: A show stopper. Wonderful on a buffet or just on a hot summer evening. The Clintons love lobster but President Bush Sr. doesn't.

OYSTERS FLORENTINE

2	dozen oysters, shucked
1/2	cup finely chopped cooked spinach
2	tablespoons finely chopped onion
1	clove garlic, mashed
2	tablespoons heavy cream
1	egg yolk
6	tablespoons dry bread crumbs (Italian bread crumbs preferred)
1	teaspoon salt
	freshly ground black pepper
3	tablespoons butter
1	egg

Drain the oysters and save the liquor. Chop 12 of the oysters. Set all oysters aside. Sauté onion and garlic in 1 tablespoon of butter for 5 minutes. Add chopped oysters, spinach, cream, salt, and pepper. Cook over low heat for 5 minutes, stirring constantly. Remove from heat and add combined egg and egg yolk, stirring briskly. Simmer the whole oysters in 1 cup of oyster liquor until the edges are curled. Drain the oysters and put 2 each in 6 scallop shells. Cover with oyster/spinach mixture. Sprinkle with bread crumbs and dot with remaining 2 tablespoons of butter. Bake in hot oven (450° F) for 15 minutes.

Serves 6

CHICKEN KIEV IMPERIAL A LA WHITE HOUSE

	breasts of three 1-pound chickens, skinned
9	tablespoons chilled, sweet butter
1	cup flour
4	eggs, beaten
1/2	cup milk
3	cups sifted fresh bread crumbs (Italian style bread crumbs, seasoned, if desired)
	vegetable shortening

Bone the chicken breasts leaving a joint of wing attached. Flatten the breasts with a cleaver, then stuff each one with 3 tablespoons butter. Carefully seal the edges with toothpicks. Dip the stuffed breasts in flour then into the eggs beat with milk, and roll in bread crumbs. Then re-dip the breasts in flour, egg and milk mixture, then bread crumbs again.

Fry in 3 inches hot vegetable shortening (375° F) for 8–10 minutes, or until golden brown. Remove the toothpicks and serve immediately.

Serves 6

CHICKEN ROLL SANDWICH

2 cups diced, cooked chicken
1 green pepper, chopped
1 cup sour cream
 lettuce or other salad greens
1 teaspoon salt
 freshly ground black pepper to taste
 pink pickled eggs
2 cups diced celery
1 cup mayonnaise
1 teaspoon curry powder
 white grapes
 large hard rolls

Combine the chicken, celery, green pepper, mayonnaise, sour cream, curry powder, salt, and pepper. Line in a salad bowl with lettuce leaves and put this chicken salad in the center. Arrange the grapes around the chicken. Cut 1/2 slice from the top of each roll and scoop out the soft center.

To serve, fill the hollow rolls with the chicken salad. Serve with grapes and pink pickled eggs.

Serves 6

PINK PICKLED EGGS

          6 eggs
          1 cup canned beet juice
          1 cup cider vinegar
          1 clove garlic, crushed
        1/2 bay leaf
        1/4 teaspoon ground allspice
          1 teaspoon salt
             freshly ground black pepper to taste

Hard cook the eggs and plunge them into cold water and shell immediately. Put eggs in a quart jar. Combine remaining ingredients and pour over eggs. Cover, cool, and refrigerate overnight, or for at least 8 hours.

RISOTTO WITH PORK

1-1/2 cups white rice
    2 cups cooked pork, in julienne strips
    3 cloves garlic, minced
    2 tablespoons oil
    3 cups beef bouillon
    1 cup dry white wine
  3/4 cup thinly sliced scallions

Sauté the rice and garlic in oil until rice is lightly browned. Add the bouillon, pork, wine, and scallions. Cover and simmer for 30 minutes.

Serves 6

CORNED BEEF HASH

    1/2 cup canned corned beef hash or
           chopped leftover corned beef brisket
              or corned beef round
      1 tablespoon catsup
    1/2 teaspoon dried onion flakes
      2 tablespoons bacon fat

Combine the hash, catsup, and dried onion flakes thoroughly. Sauté in bacon fat in covered skillet over low heat for 10 minutes.

Makes 1 serving

Author's note: Very good served with a poached egg on top.

JAMBALAYA

2	cups diced leftover ham
1	green pepper, diced
1/4	cup butter
3-1/2	cups canned tomatoes
1/4	teaspoon basil
1/4	teaspoon Tabasco® sauce
3	onions, sliced
1	clove garlic, minced
1/2	cup dry white wine
1/2	teaspoon thyme
1/4	teaspoon paprika
1	cup white rice

Sauté the onions, green pepper, and garlic in butter for 10 minutes. Add the ham, wine, tomatoes, and seasonings and mix well. Bring to a boil and add rice gradually, stirring constantly. Reduce the heat; cover and simmer for 25 minutes.

Serves 6

Author's note: Great recipe for a quick dinner.

CHEESE AND CHILI BURGERS

     3   pounds ground beef
   1/2   cup dry red wine
     1   teaspoon salt
         freshly ground black pepper to taste
    12   hamburger buns
         butter
         onion rings
         cheese sauce
         chili sauce

Combine ground beef, wine, salt, and pepper and mix well. Divide into 12 burgers and broil. Butter the hamburger buns. Serve the burgers on buns with onion rings and a choice of cheese sauce or chili sauce.

Serves 6

TABASCO HAMBURGERS

    3 pounds round steak, ground
    1 cup chopped onion
  3/4 cup chopped green pepper
    2 cups hot barbecue sauce

Combine round steak, onion, and green pepper with a half cup hot barbecue sauce. Shape into 12 hamburgers. Broil, turning once, basting frequently with hot barbecue sauce.

Serve with remaining barbecue sauce.

Author's note: I believe that this dish is named after the Mexican state of Tabasco rather than the hot sauce.

BEEF BOURGUIGNONNE A LA WHITE HOUSE

```
3   pound beef sirloin, cut into 1-inch cubes
2   cups red Burgundy wine
1/2 cup butter
2   cups quartered mushroom caps
1/4 cup chopped shallots
1   tablespoon flour
```

Melt 6 tablespoons butter in a deep casserole. Add the beef cubes. Cover and braise in hot oven, (400° F) for 20 minutes. Stir occasionally. Meanwhile, sauté mushroom caps and shallots in remaining 2 tablespoons butter. Stir in flour. Add burgundy and mix well. Pour over beef; cover and return to oven for 30 more minutes.

Serves 6

Author's note: I like to add baby red potatoes, baby carrots with 1 tablespoon of minced garlic.

PIZZA SANDWICH

        small loaves of French bread
        olive oil
        canned Italian tomatoes, drained and cut up
        grated Parmesan cheese
        sliced mozzarella cheese
        anchovy filets (optional)
        frozen meatballs
        drained oregano
        thyme

Cut loaves of bread in half lengthwise. Scoop out soft centers, leaving shells about 1/2-inch thick. Brush inside of shells with olive oil. Spread shells with tomatoes and sprinkle with Parmesan cheese. Put mozzarella and anchovies on some shells, mozzarella and slices of meatballs on others. Sprinkle with oregano, thyme and oil. Bake in hot oven (400° F) for 15 minutes.

HUEVOS RANCHEROS

6	eggs
6	canned tortillas
1-1/2	cups chopped onion
1	clove garlic, minced
1/2	cup bacon fat
4	tomatoes, peeled and chopped
3/4	cup finely chopped hot pepper
1/2	teaspoon salt

Sauté onion and garlic in 1/4 cup bacon fat for 5 minutes. Add tomatoes, hot pepper, and salt. Cover and simmer for 10 minutes. Remove cover and simmer for 10 minutes. Meanwhile, sauté the tortillas in remaining 1/4 cup bacon fat for 30 seconds on each side. Remove and keep hot. Fry eggs in fat remaining in skillet. Put one egg on each tortilla and spoon sauce over it.

Serves 6

HOT SPICE DRESSING

3/4	cup tarragon vinegar	
1-3/4	cups oil	
1/4	cup grated onion	
3	bay leaves, crumbled	
1	teaspoon chili powder	
1/2	teaspoon cayenne pepper	
1	teaspoon salt	
	freshly ground black pepper	

Combine all ingredients in a jar or cruet. Cover. Shake well before using.

Makes about 3 cups

SAUCE PARADIS

       1/4   cup butter
       1/4   cup flour
         2   cups double strength veal stock
       1/2   cup Madiera wine
         2   tablespoons red currant jelly
         2   cups seedless white grapes
         2   large truffles, sliced

   Melt the butter; add flour and stir until smooth. Add veal stock and cook, stir-ring constantly, until slightly thickened. Add wine and jelly and stir until jelly is melted. Add the grapes and truffles.

Makes about 4 cups

Author's note: Chicken stock may be substituted for veal stock. You may add this to chicken breasts or veal chops.

HOT BARBECUE SAUCE

2	teaspoons Tabasco® sauce
1	teaspoon chili peppers, minced
1/2	cup lemon juice
2	cups chopped onion
1	tablespoon brown sugar
1	teaspoon dry mustard (use Coleman's, if possible)
2-1/2	cups bottled chili sauce
3/4	cup oil
2	tablespoons tarragon vinegar
2	cloves garlic, minced
1	bay leaf, crumbled
1	teaspoon salt

Combine all ingredients with 1/2 cup water. Bring to a boil; reduce heat and simmer for 15 minutes. Serve with hamburgers, spare ribs, lamb, or chicken. Sauce may be kept covered in refrigerator for at least 1 week.

Makes about 6 cups

Author's note: A nice addition to this barbecue sauce is 3 tablespoons of grape jelly.

APRICOT SAUCE FOR ROAST DUCK

2-1/2	cups canned, peeled apricots (drained)
1	teaspoon grated orange rind
2	cups dry red wine
6	tablespoons butter
3	duck livers, cut up
	duck juices
	freshly ground black pepper

Press apricots through a coarse sieve. Combine apricots, orange rind, wine, butter, and pepper in the top of double boiler. Cook over direct heat for 5 minutes. Press duck livers through a coarse sieve and add to apricot mixture with duck juices. Place over hot water and simmer for 5 minutes, stirring constantly, until smooth and slightly thickened.

Pour over duck and serve immediately.

Makes about 5 cups

BASIL AND TOMATO SALAD

2   tablespoons chopped (fresh) basil
6   ripe tomatoes, quartered
1/2   cup extra virgin olive oil
2   tablespoons wine vinegar
1   teaspoon salt
    freshly ground black pepper
    mixed greens

Marinate tomatoes in mixture of 1 tablespoon basil, the oil, vinegar, salt, and pepper for 4 hours. Stir tomatoes once or twice and baste with marinade. Combine greens with remaining 1 tablespoon basil and arrange in salad bowl. Arrange tomato quarters on greens and pour marinade over them. Before serving, toss well.

Serves 6

BUCKWHEAT PUFFS

1/2	cup buckwheat groats
4	tablespoons butter
1/4	teaspoon Tabasco® sauce
1/2	cup flour
2	eggs
4	tablespoons minced onion
2	teaspoon salt
	oil or vegetable shortening

Bring butter, Tabasco® sauce, salt, and 1/2 cup water to boil. Add flour all at once and cook over low heat, stirring constantly, until mixture leaves sides of pan and forms a ball. Remove from heat and add eggs, one at a time, beating well after each addition. Continue beating until the mixture has a satiny sheen to it. Beat in the groats and onion.

Drop by teaspoonfuls into hot oil (375° F) 2 inches deep. Cook for 5 minutes or until golden brown.

Makes 12 puffs

RICE PUDDING

1	cup rice
5	cups milk
2	eggs, beaten
1/2	cup sugar
1/2	teaspoon ground cinnamon
2	tablespoons butter
1/3	cup slivered blanched almonds
1/3	cup raisins
1	teaspoon salt

Combine the rice and 1 cup boiling water in deep saucepan. Bring to a boil; reduce heat and simmer for 15 minutes. Add milk and simmer for minutes. Add beaten eggs, stir in remaining ingredients, and pour into casserole. Set in pan of hot water and bake in hot oven (400° F) for 45 minutes.

Serves 6

CHOCOLATE ROLLS

    1   package low calorie chocolate cake and frosting mix
    1   teaspoon unflavored gelatin

    Mix cake as directed on package. Pour into two heavily greased and floured 12″ x 18″ pans. Bake in hot oven (400° F) for 8 minutes. Turn out onto lightly floured towels and cover cakes with pans until cool. Cut each cake in half and make 4 strips, about 5″ x 16″. Trim off the crisp edges. Roll cakes with towels into 16-inch-long rolls. When cakes are cool, soften gelatin in 3/4 cup water and bring to a boil, stirring constantly. Add frosting mix. Beat in a warm bowl until fluffy. Unroll the cakes and spread with frosting. Let set for 20 minutes. Reroll the cakes. Wrap loosely in towels and chill for at least 2 hours.

    Cut rolls into 3/4 inch slices with sharp wet knife.

Makes about 88 slices

SALZBURGER NOCKERL A LA WHITE HOUSE

6	egg whites, beaten
	powdered sugar
4	egg yolks
1/2	cup flour
1	teaspoon vanilla sugar
1/2	cup lard

To 1/2 cup of powdered sugar, add beaten egg whites. Beat until stiff but not dry. Add the egg yolks, flour, and vanilla sugar and mix gently. Shape dough into 4 large balls (nockerl). Fry in hot lard, turning frequently until golden brown. Sprinkle with powdered sugar.

Serves 4

Author's note: To make vanilla sugar, split pieces of vanilla bean. Remove the seeds and crush them into 1 teaspoon sugar.

APPLE CONSERVE

1-1/2	pounds apples, peeled and sliced
1	cup raisins
1/2	cup lemons, sliced
1	cup sugar
1/4	teaspoon cinnamon
1/2	teaspoon ground nutmeg (fresh)
	ground cloves
1	cup chopped nuts
1/2	teaspoon salt

Combine apples, raisins, lemons, sugar, cinnamon, nutmeg, salt, pinch of cloves, and 1 cup water in large saucepan. Bring to boil; reduce heat and simmer for 2 hours, stirring occasionally. Remove from heat and stir in nuts.

Serve warm or cold.

Makes about 3 cups

Author's note: May also add fresh sliced and peeled pears.

CANDIED BAKED APPLES

- 6 baking apples
- 3 figs, chopped
- 3 dates, chopped
- 2 tablespoons chopped, candied ginger
- 3/4 cup granulated sugar
- 1/4 cup butter
- 1/2 cup brown sugar
- 1/4 cup chopped pecans

Core the apples and peel the top half. Combine figs, dates, and ginger and stuff apples. Combine granulated sugar with 1 cup water and boil for 5 minutes. Place apples in shallow baking pan and pour sugar syrup over them. Bake for 45 minutes, basting frequently with the syrup. Combine butter and brown sugar and cook over low heat for 5 minutes, stirring constantly. Stir in nuts. Top apples with this mixture and broil under low heat for 5 minutes.

Serves 6

PETITE FOURS

7	eggs, separated
3	tablespoons liquid sucaryl
1/2	teaspoon almond extract
3/4	teaspoon cream of tartar
	petit four icing
2	tablespoons lemon juice
1/2	teaspoon vanilla extract
1-1/2	cups sifted cake flour
1/4	teaspoon salt

Beat egg yolks for about 5 minutes or until thick and lemon-colored. Combine lemon juice, sucaryl, vanilla extract, almond extract, and 1/2 cup cold water. Add slowly to egg yolks, beating constantly until mixture is thick and fluffy. Beat egg whites until foamy. Add cream of tartar and beat until stiff, but not dry. Fold carefully into the egg yolk mixture. Combine sifted flour and salt. Sift flour, a little at a time, over the egg mixture, and fold it in gently. Pour batter into 2 ungreased 9-inch-square cake pans and bake in moderate oven (350° F) for 30 minutes, or until cake springs back when touched lightly. Invert tin on cooling rack. When cakes are cooled, remove them from the pans and cut into 24 pieces.

Frost with Petit Fours icing

PETITE FOURS ICING

1 egg white
2 cups sifted confectioners' sugar
  food colorings
  flavoring extracts

Stir egg white into sugar. Add about 1/2 cup water, a little at a time, stirring constantly until a thin frosting is formed. Divide frosting into several bowls and tint and flavor each with a few drops of different colorings and extracts. Arrange cake squares 1 inch apart on cooling racks set on waxed paper. Pour frosting over the cakes to coat tops and sides. Decorate with nuts, coconut, or chocolate bits. Let the cakes stand at least 10 minutes before taking them off the racks. The frosting which collects on the waxed paper may be reused by heating it in a small bowl set over warm water for a few minutes, adding a drop or two of warm water if necessary to thin it.

CAKE ST. HONORE

1/2	recipe pie crust
1	cup milk
1/2	cup butter
1-1/4	cups flour
5	eggs
	cream filling

Roll pie crust 1/8-inch thick and with it, cover the bottom of a 10-inch pie pan. Bring milk and butter to a boil in saucepan. Add flour all at once and stir briskly with wooden spoon until dough leaves sides of pan and forms a ball in center of saucepan. Remove from heat and add eggs, one at a time, beating well after each addition. Continue beating until mixture is smooth and satiny. Put it through a pastry bag and form a raised border around the edge of pie crust dough and against sides of pan.

Bake in hot oven (400° F) for 30 minutes. Remove carefully from pan. Cool. Fill with cream filling and chill.

Serves 12

George Walker Bush
Laura Welch Bush

"Today, I also speak anew to my fellow citizens:

From all of you, I have asked patience in the hard task of securing America, which you have granted in good measure. Our country has accepted obligations that are difficult to fulfill, and would be dishonorable to abandon. Yet because we have acted in the great liberating tradition of this nation, tens of millions have achieved their freedom. And as hope kindles hope, millions more will find it. By our efforts, we have lit a fire as well—a fire in the minds of men. It warms those who feel its power, it burns those who fight its progress, and one day this untamed fire of freedom will reach the darkest corners of our world."

GEORGE W. BUSH SECOND INAUGURAL ADDRESS, THURSDAY, JANUARY 20, 2005

GEORGE W. BUSH
COURTESY OF THE STATE PRESERVATION BOARD, AUSTIN, TX
ACCESSION ID: CHA 2001.9; PHOTOGRAPHER: ERIC BEGGS 12/14/2001

*L*et us all set aside recounts and hanging chads. Let us not refer to the thirty-six days from hell we all shared with Mr. Bush and Mr. Gore after election day.

Allow me to talk first about Laura Bush, our nation's First Lady. Now where would you start? Before or after the ascension to America's Royal House? I think I'll start after the rocky road to the White House.

Julia Reed wrote an article this summer for Vogue Magazine. In it she said, "Laura Bush is so thoroughly unself-conscious it seemed as though I had plopped down on a friend's couch instead of the Mark Hampton sofa recently moved upstairs from the oval office."

Ms. Reed continued, "The President may have Dick Cheney by his side, but his greatest strength comes from the First Lady." She is first in command when it comes to her family.

I will add, this isn't faux camaraderie—she is a real down-to-earth person who cares about what she's doing and about people. I think we all lucked out having Laura Bush for our First Lady. She stands at the President's side ready to keep him zoned.

One of Mrs. Bush's gifts is the ability to stay focused. She keeps her daily life as uncluttered as she can—no matter what the role, be it wife, mother, First Lady or friend.

As the First Lady of Texas, she was spotted standing in line at the Post Office. When asked what she was doing there, she replied very matter of factly, "I'm mailing a letter."

I like people who do not forget where they come from.

Also, this is a warning—if you're ever invited to visit the ranch—don't worry about what to wear. The Bushes have had the same clothes for the past 30 years. "Just broken in and comfortable," they say. You will be told "relax, we don't update down here." They are very unpretentious, regular people. Rack suits and dresses and drugstore makeup suit them well.

I hope this down-to-earth attitude will filter through the White House, because when I decided to update my book, I called and was given the brush off. I had no response for two months. But then I realized the gestation period is nine months. When the First Lady's office found out about my dilemma, they were right there to help. Maybe because everyone there is so new or the mail got lost or whatever. The main thing is they sent their apologies and four recipes I can include in this chapter. It's a start.

Now a few words about George W. Bush. All new Presidents, no matter what their prior experience, must go through on the job training. Even LBJ, who brought a vast amount of knowledge to the table, had to learn the job hands-on.

Number 43, as he is known or ("Trailblazer" by the Secret Service), has had a rough time. And his gestation period is not over.

He has been called "Toxic Texan," "Presidential Thief" and much more.

Still fresh in our minds is the 56% of the popular vote for Mr. Gore and 44% for Mr. Bush. The hang-up was Florida with its ten electoral votes.

The race to count and re-count the ballots over and over again was well underway. Low and behold, America learned a new word—-"CHAD." (I always thought "CHAD" was some yuppie at The Club saying, "Tennis Anyone?")

At the very end of this mess, when there was no clear cut winner, the decision was thrown into the hands of the United States Supreme Court. And guess what? We had a winner—George W. Bush, by one vote. This was the first time since Rutherford B. Hayes took office that the winner had fewer votes than the loser.

This is a very tough way to start. Forty four percent think he's great and 56 percent want his head on a plate.

Our constitution has a unique way of cleansing itself. Four years from now, if we don't like the job he's doing, we can vote him out. If you approve of the "Trailblazer," give him four more years or another way of putting it, a stay of execution.

The reputation of George W. Bush so far is "he is not the sharpest knife in the drawer." Whatever people may think you must admit he makes us laugh. There is a new coined word, "Bushisms".

Let me share with you some of my favorites.
When asked whether the violent protests in Genoa had influenced his views, our believer-in chief replied: "I know what I believe. I will continue to articulate what I believe and what I believe, what I believe is right."

ON THE KYOTO ACCORD

"First, we would not accept a treaty that would not have been ratified, nor a treaty that I thought made sense for the country."

IN QUEBEC CITY

"It's very important for folks to understand that when there's more trade, there's more commerce."

ON HIS TRAVELS

"I think there is some methodology in my travels."

ON EDUCATION

"You teach a child to read and he or she will be able to pass a literacy test."

ON AIDS

"We're concerned about AIDS inside our White House—make no mistake about it."

ON PRIME MINISTER JEAN CHRETIEN OF CANADA

"I confirmed to the Prime Minister that we appreciate our friendship."

ON EXECUTIVE POWER

"I am mindful of not only preserving executive power for myself, but for predecessors as well."

HE HAD THIS TO SAY ABOUT SECRETARY OF LABOR DESIGNATE
LINDA CHAVEZ

"I do remain confident in Linda. She'll make a fine Labor Secretary. From what I've read in the press accounts, she's perfectly qualified."

ALSO

"I know how hard it is to put food on your family."

"I understand small businesses. I was one."

"The most important job is not to be Governor, or first lady in my case."

"I know that the human being and the fish can coexist peacefully."

AND, LAST BUT NOT LEAST, MY FAVORITE

"They want the Federal Government controlling Social Security like it's some kind of Federal program."

I'm sure someday you will see a book on the shelves titled "Bushisms and other Brain-Droppings." Not since Dan Quayle have the press and political satirists had so much fun.

Personally, I love all this buffoonery. But on a serious note—George Bush has had high ideals and values. He has brought a calm to the nation and the White House. We all need that.

The one thing I've learned in my research on Mr. Bush is that he is his own man. I've also learned he is his Protocol Chief's worst nightmare.

On a recent trip to Europe, the press asked him about drugs and he replied with this statement, "I was young and irresponsible when I was young and irresponsible." OOOKAY!

We all learned a geography lesson on this day as well when the President said, "Africa is a nation that suffers from incredible disease."

In Sweden, number 43 declared, "Europe should have more countries."

President Bush looked many of his peers in the eyes, declared them good honest men, and then called them by the wrong names.

In spite of all this silly stuff that we can laugh at in America, our President and First Lady are decent people, who are committed to doing a good job. I wish them both good health and good luck.

Enjoy the Bush family recipes.

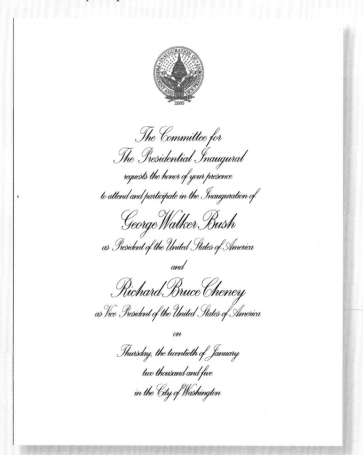

The Committee for
The Presidential Inaugural
requests the honor of your presence
to attend and participate in the Inauguration of

George Walker Bush
as President of the United States of America

and

Richard Bruce Cheney
as Vice President of the United States of America

on

Thursday, the twentieth of January
two thousand and five
in the City of Washington

BAKED POTATO SOUP

    6 cups leftover mashed potatoes
    2 tbsp. butter or margarine
    1 medium onion: diced
  1/2 lb. bacon: diced, cooked, and drained well (freeze
         bacon for easier cutting)
    1 large red pepper: diced to taste
    2 cups sharp cheddar cheese: grated
  1/2 cup chives: minced
    4 tbsp. sour cream
       approx. 2 to3 cups of whipping cream, half and half, or milk
       Kosher salt and fresh ground pepper to taste

In a large soup pot, sauté onions and red peppers over medium heat in 2 tablespoons butter until onions are clear. Add bacon, potatoes, and whipping cream to desired consistency. Skim milk or chicken stock may be used to reduce calories. Salt and pepper to taste. Serve with a garnish of a dollop of sour cream, grated cheese, and chives.

BOSTON CODFISH BALLS: WHITE HOUSE

      1-1/2 cups fibered salt codfish
         3 cups diced potatoes
       1/3 cup milk
         2 eggs, well beaten
            freshly ground black pepper
            oil or vegetable shortening

   Soak codfish in cold water for 10 minutes. Drain. Repeat twice. Add cod to potatoes with 1 cup of water. Boil for 15 minutes or until potatoes are soft. Drain and mash. Add milk, eggs, and pepper. Drop mixture by teaspoonfuls into 1 inch of hot oil (375° F). Fry for 5 to 8 minutes or until golden brown. Drain. Serve hot.

Serves 6

BASS LIVORNESE:
WHITE HOUSE

1	4-pound striped bass or black bass (large or small mouth)
1	onion, thinly sliced
1	clove garlic, minced
1/4	cup olive oil
1/4	cup chopped parsley
1/2	cup dry white wine
1/2	cup peas
1/2	cup canned tomatoes
	Italian bread slices, toasted

Cut bass into 1-1/2-inch slices. Sauté onion and garlic in olive oil for 10 minutes. Add bass and remaining ingredients, cover and simmer for 20 minutes. Serve on toasted bread.

Serves 6

PRESSED DUCK: WHITE HOUSE

    3   4-pound oven-ready ducks
1/2   cup duck consommé
1-1/2 cups port wine
1-1/2 cups cognac
       juice of 3 lemons
       salt to taste
       freshly ground black pepper to taste

First prepare a consommé from the duck wings, necks, gizzards, and hearts. Put them in a saucepan with 2 cups water, 1 onion, 1 tablespoon chopped parsley, and 1 teaspoon salt. Bring to a boil and reduce the heat and simmer for 20–30 minutes. Strain and save the stock.

Roast the ducks in a hot oven (425° F) for 30 minutes. Crush the duck livers and put them into a chafing dish with port and cognac. Cut the duck breasts into thin slices and put them in the chafing dish. Cut off the legs and set them aside. Crush the carcasses in a duck press to extract the juices. Pour duck consommé through the press. Pour the juices and consommé over the duck slices, livers, and the wine and cognac. Add the lemon juice.

Cook in the chafing dish over a high flame for 20–25 minutes, stirring briskly until the sauce becomes thick and chocolate colored. Salt and pepper the pressed duck to taste. Serve hot.

Broil the legs under medium heat for 10 minutes. Serve them separately as a second course.

Serves 6

MEAT PIE A LA WHITE HOUSE

3	pounds beef tenderloin
1/2	cup flour
1/2	cup oil
1-1/2	cups sliced onion
1	clove garlic, minced
2	cups condensed consommé
1	bay leaf, crumbled
1	tablespoon dry mustard
1	teaspoon Kitchen Bouquet®
2	teaspoons soy sauce
2	teaspoons Worcestershire sauce
1-1/2	cups peas (preferably fresh, frozen are okay)
1/2	recipe pie crust
1	teaspoon Ac'cent® (optional)
1	teaspoon salt to taste
	freshly ground black pepper to taste

Cut beef into cubes. Place flour, Ac'cent®, salt, and pepper in a paper bag. Put beef cubes in bag with flour mixture and shake well to coat meat thoroughly. Brown meat in oil in a large saucepan. Remove the meat; add onion and garlic to oil remaining in the pan and fry for 10 minutes, stirring constantly. Add the meat back into the pan with consommé, 1 can water, and seasoning. Bring to a boil; reduce heat, cover and simmer for 1-1/2 hours. Add peas and pour into casserole or individual baking dishes. Top with pie crust, rolled 1/8 inch thick and bake in hot oven (425° F) for 30 minutes or until crust is brown.

Serves 6

FARMER'S MARKET

1-1/4 cups pinto beans: soaked overnight and drained
1 tsp. salt
1 bay leaf
1 tsp. dried oregano
1 lb. tomatoes (fresh or canned): peeled, seeded and chopped (juice reserved)
2 ancho chilies
1 lb. mixed summer squash
4 ears corn (about 2 cups kernals)
1 tsp. ground cumin
1/2 tsp. ground coriander
2 tbsp. corn or vegetable oil
2 yellow onions: cut into 1/4-inch squares
2 cloves garlic: finely chopped
2 tbsp. red chili powder (or more to taste)
8 ounces green beans: cut into 1-inch lengths
4 ounces jack or muenster cheese: grated
1/2 bunch cilantro leaves: roughly chopped
Whole cilantro leaves for garnish

Cook the pre-soaked beans for about 1-1/2 to 2 hours in plenty of water with the salt, bay leaf, and oregano. Remove them from the heat when they are soft but not mushy, as they will continue to cook in the stew. Drain the beans, and save the broth. Prepare the tomatoes. Open the chili pods, and remove the seeds and veins; then cut the chilies into narrow strips. Cut the squash into large pieces. Shave the kernels from the corn.

Heat the oil in a large skillet, and sauté the onions over high heat for 1 to 2 minutes. Lower the heat and add garlic, chili powder, cumin and coriander. Stir everything together. Add a little bean broth, so the chili doesn't scorch or burn.

Cook until the onions begin to soften (about 4 minutes); then add the tomatoes and stew for 5 minutes. Stir in the squash, corn, green beans, and chili strips along with the cooked beans and enough broth to make a fairly wet stew.

FARMER'S MARKET (CONTINUED)

Cook slowly until the vegetables are done (about 15 or 20 minutes). Taste the stew, and adjust the seasoning. Stir in the cheese and chopped cilantro, and garnish with whole leaves of cilantro. Serve with cornbread or tortillas. A great one-dish meal if you have a garden or have just visited the Farmer's Market.

6 servings

RUM PUDDING

2	egg yolks
2	egg whites
1/3	cup sugar
1/2	pint heavy cream
1	tbsp. gelatin, unflavored
1/2	cup hot water
1	wine glass rum or sherry

Beat egg yolks with sugar; beat egg whites; beat cream. Mix together carefully and add rum. Soften gelatin with a little water 5 minutes. Add enough boiling water to make 1/2 cup. Be sure gelatin is all dissolved. Cool for about 10 minutes but do not allow to stiffen. Mix gelatin and rum mixture together. Pour into mold which has been rinsed in cold water. Place in refrigerator to stiffen. Decorate with whipped cream or drained marchino cherries, red or green.

COWBOY COOKIES

3	sticks of butter
1-1/2	cups of sugar
1-1/2	cups of brown sugar
3	eggs
1	tbsp. vanilla
2	cups coconut
2	cups pecans
3	cups of flour
1	tbsp. baking powder
1	tbsp. baking soda
1	tsp. salt
1	tbsp. cinnamon
3	cups chocolate chips
3	cups oats

Cream butter and sugars. Add eggs and vanilla. Beat. Add dry ingredients until blended. Stir in remaining ingredients. Bake at 350 degrees for 10-12 minutes.

Barack Hussein Obama
Michelle LaVaughn Robinson Obama

"Let it be told to the future world ... that in the depth of winter, when nothing but hope and virtue could survive ... that the city and the country, alarmed at one common danger, came forth to meet [it].

America, in the face of our common dangers, in this winter of our hardship, let us remember these timeless words. With hope and virtue, let us brave once more the icy currents, and endure what storms may come. Let it be said by our children's children that when we were tested, we refused to let this journey end, that we did not turn back nor did we falter; and with eyes fixed on the horizon and God's grace upon us, we carried forth that great gift of freedom and delivered it safely to future generations."

PRESIDENT BARACK OBAMA INAUGURAL ADDRESS, TUESDAY, JANUARY 20, 2009

BARACK OBAMA © WHHA (WHITE HOUSE COLLECTION)

*T*he election of President George W. Bush to his first term in office can be defined by the word CHAD— those flimsy little pieces of paper that hung off the voting cards in Florida. The election of President Obama can be defined by the word CHANGE. His message during his campaign was loud and clear—"In this campaign, you have already shown what history teaches us—that at defining moments like this one, the change we need doesn't come from Washington. Change comes to Washington." *Yes We Can!* became his much-repeated slogan.

In a speech given the night before he was chosen the Democratic Party's nominee for President he said "Sixteen months have passed since we first stood together on the steps of the Old State Capitol in Springfield, Illinois... Millions of voices have been heard. And because of what you said - because you decided that change must come to Washington; because you believed that this year must be different than all the rest; because you chose to listen not to your doubts or your fears but to your greatest hopes and highest aspirations, tonight we mark the end of one historic journey with the beginning of another - a journey that will bring a new and better day to America...."

Barack Hussein Obama promised change so we elected him. The majority of Americans were willing to change with him and handed him the keys to the Oval Office. As reported by ABC News reporter Jennifer Parker on August 28, 2008, Barack Obama "strode on stage and into the history books becoming the first black American to be nominated by a major political party as the nation's commander-in-chief. " A crowd of 84,000 supporters were dancing and cheering in Chicago's Invesco Field as he accepted their presidential nomination.

The world embraced him. After being in office for only eight months he was awarded the Nobel Peace Prize. Critics wondered what he had done to deserve this prestigious prize. My feeling, shared by millions, is that this recognition adds to his stature worldwide (already impressive), and that hopefully, together with other accomplishments, this will help to achieve a better life for all concerned.

The jury is still out as to whether the promise has become reality. The American people are divided, we know we need change but are afraid to see it happen. Well our new President is not afraid, and he's doing his best to change things from "business as usual." I say let's give him enough faith and let him lead. He has made some mistakes, and will make more, because that's what happens when you try to make changes in Washington. Some things work and others don't. His challenge is that he inherited, among other things, a disastrous economic crisis, two wars and constant threats of terrorism.

In his column reporting the award of the 2008 Teddy Award for The Courageous Political Performances of '08 to Barack Obama, Joe Klein dedicates his column to the words of Teddy Roosevelt: "It is not the critic who counts: not the man who points out how the strong man stumbles or where the doer of deeds could have done them better. The credit belongs to the man who is actually in the arena, whose face is marred by dust and sweat and blood, who strives valiantly, who errs and comes up short again and again ... who spends himself in a worthy cause; who, at the best, knows, in the end, the triumph of high achievement, and who at the worst, if he fails, at least he fails while daring greatly." Joe Klein goes on to say that TR would probably not have liked Obama, "But our President-elect certainly merits this year's lead Teddy Award, distributed to mark honorable behavior in the political arena. He deserves it for displaying a trait memorialized by Roosevelt's contemporary and fellow imperialist Rudyard Kipling: "If you can keep your head when all about you/ Are losing theirs .../ you'll be a Man, my son!"

There is another side to President Obama and that's food. I have heard our President is a "foodie" but have not been able to confirm this. I do know he likes to cook but have no idea how good he is at it. Obama likes chili and I have heard his chili is one of the best. He also likes pizza, especially Chicago pizza. He has been in office for such a short time he has hosted only one State Dinner which was made famous by the couple who arrived and gained entry without an invitation.

President Obama is very much a family man. He is a frequent visitor to DC restaurants, and enjoys "date nights" with his wife. This is a great way to relax. I can just imagine what a logistical and security nightmare it is when he takes the First Lady out for an intimate dinner.

The First Lady has taken on a great cause. The first year, other than planting a Victory Garden and some personal appearances, she was smart and got used to the notoriety first. A somewhat shy First Lady she is perfect for the President, for what he lacks she indeed makes up for. It took the President to announce to a joint session of Congress that she had started working on child obesity and HIV/AIDS. It's a commendable effort to get Americans as a whole to eat healthy. When I was working as a Chef way back in the day the word was "Thin may be in but fat's where it's at." Not so anymore. The new Chefs are now trained more to the desires of their patrons and healthy foods. Mrs. Obama's efforts are a commendable start.

Please enjoy the recipes on the following pages. Some I know are to the liking of the First Family, while others are White House recipes served to guests.

Please enjoy them as much as I have, and do try his chili.

PRESIDENT BARACK OBAMA AND FIRST LADY MICHELLE OBAMA STAND AT THE NORTH PORTICO OF THE WHITE HOUSE AS THEY AWAIT THE ARRIVAL OF INDIAN PRIME MINISTER MANMOHAN SINGH AND MRS. GURSHARAN KAUR FOR THE STATE DINNER. NOVEMBER 24, 2009. (OFFICIAL WHITE HOUSE PHOTO BY PETE SOUZA)

CHEESE PUFFS

      1 lb. feta cheese
     12 oz. package pot cheese
      5 eggs
    1/2 lb. butter
      1 lb. phyllo pastry sheets

Crumble feta cheese into small pieces. Add pot cheese and blend well. Add eggs and beat thoroughly. Melt butter. Carefully cut phyllo pastry into 3 equal portions. Refrigerate two-thirds until needed and cover the remaining third with slightly dampened towel. Remove one sheet of phyllo pastry and place on a flat surface, and butter well. Fold in the long sides towards the middle making a strip about 2 inches wide; butter again. Place one tablespoon of cheese mixture in the bottom right-hand corner of strip and fold over into triangle shape. Continue folding, making sure, with each fold, that the bottom edge is parallel with the alternate side edge. Lightly butter finished triangle. Continue in this manner until all the cheese and/or phyllo sheets are used. Bake triangle puffs in a 425 degree oven for 20 minutes or until golden brown, turning once. Allow to cook about 5 minutes before serving. Serve warm.

Yield 75 pieces.

Note: Phyllo (pronounced 'pheelo') pastry sheets are available fresh at Greek bakeries and also frozen in the frozen food compartments of other specialty food outlets. The fresh ones freeze well and keep for a long time if well wrapped in moisture- and vapor-proof paper or aluminum foil. Phyllo pastry sheets are usually sold by the pound and there are many, many sheets per pound, for each is as thin as tissue paper. They are 12 inch x 18 inch rectangles and actually look like tissue paper. They dry out quickly so must be kept constantly covered with a slightly dampened towel when not being used.

GUACAMOLE

4	ripe avocados (preferably Haas)
1	lime, juiced
1	clove of garlic: finely minced
2	medium vine-ripened tomatoes: seeded and diced
1	medium yellow onion: diced
2	jalapenos: seeded and diced
	(wear rubber gloves)
1/4	cup of cilantro leaves: washed, dried and finely chopped
	Kosher salt and fresh ground pepper to taste

Halve and pit avocados and scoop out flesh into a bowl. Mash avocado to desired consistency and mix in remaining ingredients. Cover with plastic wrap and refrigerate for about an hour before serving. Serve with tortilla chips.

CHICKEN SOUP WITH AVGOLEMONO SAUCE

    1   4-5 lb. stewing hen, ready to cook
        few peppercorns
    1   small carrot
    1   onion
    1   stalk celery
        salt
    1   cup rice

Wash hen and place in heavy kettle. Cover with boiling water and add peppercorns, carrot, onion, and celery stalk. Cover and simmer over low heat for 2 to 4 hours, or until hen is tender, adding salt to taste during last hour of cooking. Strain and remove extra fat. Add rice and continue to cook until rice is tender. Remove broth from heat and wait for boiling a stop. Add either of the avgolemono sauces below according to directions.

8 to 10 servings

AVGOLEMONO SAUCE

Method 1

    4   eggs
    2   lemons, juice of

Beat eggs well and gradually beat in lemon juice. Add hot broth slowly to egg sauce, beating constantly. Return soup to heat and stir vigorously until thickened.

Method 2

    4   eggs, separated
    2   lemons, juice of

Beat egg whites until they form soft points. Add yolks one at a time and continue beating. Gradually beat in lemon juice. Add broth slowly to egg sauce, return soup to heat, and stir furiously until thickened.

SPINACH SOUP

1	pkg. frozen chopped spinach
1/3	cup canned beef consommé
2	tsp. salt
1/2	tsp. pepper
1-1/2	cups milk
4	egg yolks, well beaten

Cook the spinach in the consommé until tender. Season with salt and pepper. Add milk to the spinach and stir until well blended. Now pour a little of the hot soup into the beaten egg yolks stirring constantly, then stir egg mixture into the soup. Simmer all together for a minute or so and serve hot. Sprinkle a little grated nutmeg over each serving.

Serves 6

YELLOW PEA SOUP, SMOKED HAM

1 smoked butt plus ham bone or 1 smoked picnic
1 lb. whole yellow peas
1 bunch leeks or 1 large anion
   salt
   small potatoes
   small rutabagas, kohlrabis, or yellow turnips

Soak peas in water at least 3 hours or overnight. Put butt and hambone (or picnic) in large pot, enough water to cover. Add sliced leeks (or onion) and the peas. Cook slowly until peas are tender (2 - 3 hours). If the butt is small, do not put it in until the last hour or so. It might get over-cooked. Salt to taste. (The size of the ham and amount of water decides the strength of the soup. If too thin, cook uncovered until strong enough. Should be good and strong.) After serving the soup, serve the ham sliced, with mild type mustard (French or Swedish), boiled potatoes and sliced, cooked (but not over-cooked) rutabagas.

FISH FILLETS IN CREAM SAUCE

        8   fish filets
        2   small lobsters
    1/2   lb. mushrooms
        4   egg yolks
        2   cups light cream
        4   tbsp. butter
        2   tbsp. flour
            sherry
            salt

Roll 8 fish filets and tie with string. Cook 8 minutes in fish stock, remove from stock but keep hot. Sauté mushrooms in butter. Stir in flour, add a little fish stock and a little veal stock, let boil slowly 5 minutes. Beat cream and egg yolks and add it to the stock gradually under constant stirring. Add diced meat from the boiled lobsters. Salt to taste. Let simmer till piping hot, but do not boil. Just before serving add a little sherry to taste. Pour sauce over fish filets and serve. (Remove string from filets before serving.)

ROAST LAMB WITH ARTICHOKES

6	artichokes
	cold water, salted
6	lemons, juice of
2	tbsp. flour
4	lb. lamb roast
	salt and pepper
1	tbsp. oregano
1/2	cup butter
2	cups water
	parsley sprigs

Remove tough outer leaves of the artichokes and cut of part of the stems. Cut 1/2 to 1 inch off tips of remaining leaves. Rub cut stems of artichokes with a cut lemon and cut in half lengthwise. Rub cut surfaces with lemon. Cut and scrape the fuzz or choke from the artichoke hearts. Place the artichoke in a bowl of cold salted water to cover, into which the juice of 2 lemons and the flour have been stirred. This solution helps keep the artichokes green. Soak at least 1 hour. Preheat oven to 450 degrees. Rub meat with salt and pepper, oregano, and the juice of 1 lemon. Roast 20 minutes and reduce heat to 350 degrees. Spread half the butter over the meat. Add 1 cup of water to the roasting pan and cook 15 minutes longer. Add remaining butter and water to the pan and continue cooking for 30 minutes or until meat is done to taste. Baste occasionally with pan drippings. If necessary, add more water. There should be 2 cups of liquid drippings in the pan when the meat is done. Transfer the lamb to a warm platter and keep warm. Add the artichokes to the roasting pan. Bake them, cut side down 1 hour or until tender but not overcooked. Baste occasionally while cooking. Arrange the artichokes around the lamb and garnish with parsley.

Serves 6

Note: To reduce cooking time, the artichokes may be parboiled before baking. Or, if roasting pan is large enough, artichokes may be added to the pan with the lamb after the temperature has been reduced to 350 degrees.

ROAST PORK WITH DUMPLINGS AND SOUR CABBAGE

        2   lbs. roasting pork
            salt
            caraway seed
        1   head of cabbage
        1   onion
        2   tbsp. lard
            vinegar

Dust pork with salt and caraway seed. Place in pan with a little water and roast at 350° - 400° F until done (about 90 minutes). Baste frequently and turn roast during cooking time.

Sour Cabbage (sauerkraut may be substituted)

Shred cabbage. Place in pot and add cup of boiling water. Boil until water evaporates. Add salt and 2 tbsp. of vinegar and finely chopped onion which has been browned in lard. Cook slowly, stirring frequently, until tender. Add sugar and vinegar to taste.

Dumplings

        2   cups sifted flour
        1   tbsp. Farina
      1/2   tbsp. salt
        2   egg yolks
      1/2   cup milk
      1/2   tsp. baking powder
        1   cup dry French bread cubed

Sift flour with baking powder and Farina into a bowl. Mix milk, salt and egg yolks into cup and pour into bowl. Whip mixture with a wooden ladle until paste flows freely and air bubbles form. Mix in the cubes of French bread and form a dumpling by hand (which should be moist) about 7 inches long and 3 inches thick. Boil for 15 - 20 minutes in 2 - 3 quarts of boiling water. Turn the dumpling during boiling. Cut the dumpling with a strong cotton string and coat with melted butter.

Serves 4

THE PRESIDENT'S FAMOUS CHILI RECIPE

President Obama likes Planter's Trail Mix, roasted almonds, pistachios, Dentyne Ice and, last but not least, Nicorette. He also likes broccoli and spinach. He dislikes mayonnaise, salt & vinegar potato chips, along with asparagus. He drinks water not soft drinks.

1	large chopped onion
1	chopped green pepper
	several cloves of garlic, chopped
1	tsp. olive oil
1	lb. ground turkey or beef
1	tsp. cumin
1	tsp. ground oregano
1	tsp. turmeric
1	tsp. ground basil
1	tbsp. chili powder
3	tbsps. red wine vinegar
	several tomatoes, chopped
1	can red kidney beans

Sauté onion, green pepper and garlic in olive oil till soft. Add turkey or beef and stir till brown. Combine spices, then add to ground meat. Add red wine vinegar. Add tomatoes and let simmer till they're cooked down. Add kidney beans and cook for a few more minutes. Serve over white or brown rice. Sprinkle shredded cheddar cheese, more chopped onions or scallions and sour cream over as garnish.

Serves six

BEEF ROLLS

4	slices beef rump
3	ozs. lard
1-1/2	ozs. bacon
2	pickles or cucumbers
4	ozs. salami or smoked pork
1	onion
1	tsp. flour
	butter
	salt
	pepper
	mustard

Pound the meat. Sprinkle with salt, pepper and spread with mustard. Place on each piece of meat sliced onion, pickle, salami, bacon. Roll meat. Fasten with thread or toothpick and dip in flour. Heat butter in saucepan and add sliced onion. Turn rolls while frying. Pour water under the rolls and stew until tender. Take out thread or toothpick and serve with rice or boiled potatoes.

SLICED BEEF EN GELEE: WHITE HOUSE

    6 slices cold cooked roast beef or pot roast
  1/2 teaspoon thyme
       carrot slices
    2 cans condensed consommé
    1 teaspoon Worcestershire sauce
  1/2 teaspoon salt
  1/2 teaspoon basil
       green pepper slices
    2 envelopes unflavored gelatin
       cayenne pepper
       freshly ground black pepper

Arrange overlapping slices of beef in a shallow serving dish. Sprinkle with thyme, basil, salt, and black pepper. Garnish with carrot and green peppers. Soften gelatin in 1/2 cup of cold water. Bring 1 can consommé to a boil and add it to the gelatin, stirring until gelatin is dissolved. Add the remaining 1 can of cold consommé, 1 cup of cold water, Worcestershire sauce, and a few grains of cayenne pepper. Cool for 30 minutes or until gelatin mixture is syrupy. Pour the mixture over the beef slices and chill in the refrigerator for at least 2 hours or until gelatin is set.

Serves 6

CHATEAUBRIAND EN PAPILLOTE (IN PAPER BAG): WHITE HOUSE

2 double filets of beef
3 cups Bordelaise sauce

Broil filets under medium heat for 30 minutes or until medium rare. Cut each filet in half horizontally. Spread the bottom half of each filet with cooled Bordelaise sauce, then sew the filets together. Place each filet on a piece of parchment paper brushed with oil. Bring the paper covers up over the filets in a shallow pan and roast them in a hot oven (450° F) for 3 minutes or until the paper puffs out. Serve filets immediately in their paper bags. Rip the paper open and slice the filets.

Serves 6

Notes to Research

My task in researching this book and compiling the recipes started forty-five years ago. I have collected over 6,000 recipes from all the First Families and embassies in the United States, enough for several books.

The project was shelved for many years while I raised my family, did my stint as a legislator, and started a business. Little did I know at the time of the great interest that Americans had in their past Presidents. Nor did the first ladies know of the interest that future generations would show in their families' food preferences. No doubt they would have been more careful to record for posterity the smallest details having to do with the presidential household and kitchen.

Unfortunately, this was not the case. Indeed, not even the periodicals of the time offered much help. These newspapers, magazines, etc., showed scant interest in recording such things as the eating habits of Presidents. Remember, the new America was very basic. The population was made up of farmers. Life was tough. The newspapers made political hay when the President was an epicurean, such as Thomas Jefferson, who brought the first French chef into the White House when he became President, or Martin Van Buren, for his fondness of lavishly prepared foods. As a matter of fact, Van Buren's opposition made much ado about his aristocratic tastes, then went on to defeat him for re-election.

There was a light at the end of the tunnel when I discovered a wonderful cookbook written by Mrs. John Custis, mother-in-law to Martha Washington, by her first husband. Mrs. Washington used this book and passed it on to her granddaughter, Eleanor Park Custis.

I researched the National Archives' Presidential Libraries, interviewed Presidential families and friends, discovered living descendants and searched through their family papers in old trunks in their attics. It was a lot of work, but great fun. Old recipes had to be reworked and tried, which I did at my farm, with my friends to see if they were acceptable to the modern palate. As time went on and I was researching the contemporary presidents, the work became easier and provided an opportunity to experience and experiment with recipes and elegant dinners.

Some of these recipes are included in this book, with the remainder to be published later.

My thanks to all the people at these libraries, foundations, societies and organizations for their interest and invaluable support of this project:

The Society for the Preservation of New England Antiquities, Inc., for John Quincy Adams.
The Harding Memorial Association, for Warren G. Harding.
The Thomas Jefferson Memorial Foundation, for Thomas Jefferson.
The James Monroe Memorial Foundation, for James Monroe.
The Woodrow Wilson House, Washington, D.C., for Woodrow Wilson.
Ladies Hermitage Association, for Andrew Jackson.
The Lockwood Memorial Library, The State University of New York at Buffalo, for Millard Fillmore.
The Buffalo and Erie County New York Historical Society, for Millard Fillmore.
The Rutherford B. Hayes Library, for Rutherford B. Hayes.
The Manuscript Division of the Library of Congress.
The Ulysses S. Grant Association, for Ulysses S. Grant.
The Curator of Manuscripts at the University of Virginia Library, for Thomas Jefferson.
The Sagamore Hill National Historic Site, for Teddy Roosevelt.
The National Society of Colonial Dames in the State of New York, for Millard Fillmore.
The Tea Council of the United States of America, Inc.
The Historical Society of Pennsylvania, for George Washington.

Also valuable in my reasearch were the following books:
First Ladies, by Margaret Truman.
Presidential Anecdotes, by Paul F. Boller Jr.
The Complete Book of U.S. Presidents by William A. Degregorio.

Recipes

Notes

Notes

Notes

Notes

Notes